# The Psychological Treatment of

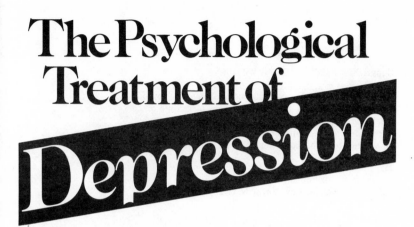

# Depression

## A Guide to the Theory and Practice of Cognitive-Behaviour Therapy

# J. Mark G. Williams

M.R.C. Applied Psychology Unit
Cambridge

THE FREE PRESS
A Division of Macmillan, Inc
New York

The Free Press
a division of Macmillan, Inc
866 Third Avenue, New York, N.Y. 10022

Library of Congress Cataloging in Publication Data

Williams, J. Mark G.
    The Psychological treatment of depression.

    Includes bibliographical references.
    1. Depression, mental.  2. Cognitive therapy.
3. Behavior therapy. I. Title. [DNLM 1. Depression  −
Therapy.  2. Behavior therapy.  WM 171 W724P]
RC537.W55   1984        616.85'27        83-20674
ISBN 0-02-934660-6


Printed and bound in Great Britain

# CONTENTS

*Contents*

# PREFACE

It was not until the late 1960s and early 1970s that behavioural and cognitive approaches began to be applied in the treatment of clinical depression. Like the earlier applications of behavioural techniques for anxiety-based disorders, researchers have since used a variety of strategies to investigate efficacy and elucidate the factors affecting successful treatment outcome. Single case studies in the early writings have given way to treatment analogue studies and subsequently to larger scale outcome studies with clinical groups. There now exist several careful reviews of these studies. Although each of these points to areas in the outcome literature where there are problems in interpretation, the reviewers converge on the same conclusion:

'Generally, behavioural and cognitive strategies can have a significant effect on depression' (Rehm and Kornblith, 1979)

'From these studies, there appears adequate evidence that depressives can respond to psychological intervention' (Whitehead, 1979)

'Several of the specific behavioural and cognitive-behavioural interventions appear to have survived initial tests of efficacy' (Hollon, 1981)

These reviewers also agree that combinations of cognitive and behavioural techniques seem to be more effective in ameliorating depression than either alone and their conclusions suggest that clinicians may be optimistic in using such techniques or combinations of techniques in their therapeutic practice, but how to proceed? The problem is that, although some techniques have rationales and procedures which have been clearly documented by their proponents (e.g. the excellent *Cognitive Therapy Manual* by Beck *et. al.*, 1979), this is by no means true for all the techniques which the reviewers of outcome studies cite as being effective therapeutic strategies. Some techniques which hold out clear promise as effective practices are to be found only in partial descriptions, scattered throughout the behavioural literature. When such studies are reviewed, the reviewer rarely has sufficient space to give more than one or two sentences to describe the technique under consideration. We end up knowing something of what might be most therapeutic for our clients, but little or nothing about how to go about it. It is to help fill this gap that this book has been written.

The techniques I have chosen to describe represent a range of those currently practised by cognitive-behavioural therapists. Some are suitable for in-patient management, others more suitable for out-patient or primary care work. Some are suitable long-term strategies, others more suitable for brief therapy interventions. The therapy chapters form the central portion of the book. Their aim is to describe the techniques in sufficient detail to be useful for clinicians who want to apply such methods in their work with depressed patients, and as such, they are not written as a justification of these methods over and above alternative treatment approaches. Had space permitted it may have been possible to give details of more broad-based psychothera-peutic approaches, or of the new and challenging field of clinical ecology. (Readers interested in introductions to these fields might refer to Malan (1979) and Rippere and Adams (1982) respectively.) Unlike the arguments surrounding the growth of behaviour therapy for anxiety-based disorders, there is now a more constructive debate be-tween proponents of different therapeutic schools. Each is more prepared to believe that patients differ in the extent to which they benefit from the techniques of the different therapeutic schools. The responsibility of practitioners of each orientation is to make plain what methods are used in their particular therapy so that individual clinicians may choose rationally which approach is appropriate for which patient. Such a description of cognitive-behavioural techniques is what is attempted as the central aspect of this book.

Preceding the core therapy chapters is a chapter on assessment which gives a representative range of techniques (e.g. Beck, Hamilton) in full. The therapy chapters are followed by a section on Training Exercises which aims to give clinicians ideas to use in development of their own skills.

The book begins and ends on a theoretical note: the first two chapters set the context for psychological approaches to depression; the last two raise some basic theoretical and research issues. I hope these more theoretical sections will be of interest to students of psychology, clinical psychology and psychiatry in their 'abnormal psychology' or 'experimental psychopathology' courses. However, the book will have fulfilled its purpose if it provides for the clinician an introduction to and encouragement to try out techniques, the utility of which can only ultimately be judged in the clinical situation itself.

# ACKNOWLEDGEMENTS

This book grew out of a series of teaching seminars and workshops I gave while at the Department of Psychiatry, University of Newcastle-upon-Tyne between 1979 and 1982. I am grateful to many people for their support, encouragement and ideas during this period, but especially to some colleagues with whom a great deal of this work was discussed: Will Barker, Anne Goodwin, Veronica Gore, Charles Lund, Angus McGregor, Ian McKeith, Jan Scott, Lindsay Shrubsole, Debbie Spaull, Stephen Tyrer and Ian Wilkinson. Since moving to Cambridge, I have been grateful for discussions with Fraser Watts, and throughout the period I have been helped by talks I have had with Chris Brewin.

Secretarial assistance has been a great asset in the drafting and redrafting of the text, and thanks are due to Sue Lowe and Gerry Mulholland in Newcastle, and to Sharon Basham in Cambridge.

For permission to use their scales and questionnaires, I am grateful to Professor A. T. Beck, Professor Max Hamilton, Dr. Ivy Blackburn and Ian Wilkinson.

Less direct, but no less important support came at the inception of the project at work and home: at work, from Peter Britton and Donald Eccleston, colleagues whose encouragement was highly valued; at home, from my wife Phyllis, and from Robert, Jennifer, and Anne-Marie whose love and support has been a source of strength throughout.

Finally, there are two people who deserve special mention; two clinical psychologists who died within a few weeks of each other at about the time this book was started; May Davidson and Roger Garside. One started me in my career as a clinical psychologist; the other was a source of valued support as a colleague when I joined the Department of Psychiatry in Newcastle. To the memory of May Davidson and Roger Garside, I should like to dedicate this book.

Mark Williams

# 1 PSYCHOLOGICAL MODELS OF DEPRESSION: HISTORICAL BACKGROUND AND THEORY

It is perhaps not surprising that of all fields of psychopathology, depression was one of the most recent to capture the attention of psychologists. A great deal of the advances in our thinking about and treatment of other psychological disorders — phobic states, anxiety states, obsessional compulsive neurosis — had originated in the context of a theory of learning which distrusted explanations in terms of 'central states' of the organism — affects, cognitions, etc. It was also clear that in schizophrenia, the one disorder for which attempts had been made to formalise in terms of cognitive processing deficits, no major treatment advance had resulted. It is not hard to see how theorists took the view that such 'internal states' were more epiphenomena of either primary biological processes or behavioural contingencies. In a condition where abnormalities of affect and/or cognitions seem to predominate, behavioural analysis seemed curiously inept.

Take, for example, extinction theory — behavioural repertoire being weakened due to insufficient reinforcement relative to effort expended (response cost). These concepts simply did not seem to do justice to the many and various symptoms of clinical depression: pervasive loss of interest; retardation or agitation; suicidal ideas; dysphoric mood; poor appetite and weight loss or increased appetite and weight gain; sleep difficulty or sleeping too much; loss of energy; fatigability or tiredness; feelings of self-reproach or guilt; and a diminished ability to think or concentrate. Yet it is with such behavioural formulations which this review of the background to cognitive-behaviour therapy must start. Whatever their deficiencies as complete explanations of the phenomena of depression, they were arguably the most significant development in clinical psychological theorising since the interpretations of phobic reactions as conditioned emotional responses earlier in the century. They broke the mould of predominant explanations for depression which were the biogenic amine theory on the other hand and the psychodynamic theory on the other. Having reviewed the behavioural formulations and recent advances I should like to move on to consider recent research on three other psychological models of depression: learned helplessness, cognitive theory and self-control theory. In the case of each theory I shall use as a starting point a key paper written in the mid 1970s, then ask the question: what has become of the theory since then?

## Behavioural Formulations of Depression

I take as my starting point a review article by Clive Eastman published in 1976. None of Eastman's references include research published later than 1975, and it is perhaps surprising that, even then, 29 papers or books had been written on the subject, though four names account for over half the papers (Ferster, Lazarus, Lewinsohn and Seligman). Such was the state of the art in 1975-6. Seligman's theory will be reviewed later, which leaves the other three accounting for four distinct formulations, with Costello accounting for a fifth.

*Reduction of Reinforcement.*    This rather general theory views depression as due to 'inadequate or insufficient reinforcement' (Lazarus 1968). It is not clear whether 'inadequate' implies reduced frequency or quality of reinforcement. It is best seen as a general description for all the more specific formulations which are to follow.

*Reduced Frequency of Social Reinforcement.*    This, by contrast to 'reduction of reinforcement' sounds more specific — 'frequency' is a particular concept and 'social' limits the otherwise wide term 'reinforcement'. It is a theory most often associated with Lewinsohn (e.g. Lewinsohn, Weinstein and Alper, 1970). According to Lewinsohn, a low rate of response contingent positive reinforcement has consequences in terms of the respondent behaviour of the individual (elicits crying, dysphoric mood, etc.) and is itself sufficient explanation for reduced behavioural output in depression. In the early stages of depressive breakdown symptoms may be maintained by reinforcement from others (sympathy), the 'secondary gain' phenomenon, but later on close family and friends are more likely to swing away from rewarding any behaviour and try to avoid the depressed person altogether, thus further reducing frequency of rewards available in the environment.

However the concepts are not so circumscribed as may be supposed. The concept which is important but missing is that of the $S^D$, the 'discriminative stimulus' (Ferster, 1966). This is the stimulus in the environment which signals the availability of reinforcers in rather the same way in which a laboratory animal may learn that food will only be available when a small light is on, and then only when it presses a bar.

If a person were to become less sensitive to stimuli in the environment which normally 'announce' the availability of rewards, then the effect on behaviour would presumably be the same as actual reduced frequency of actual reinforcement. These are very different models, but are almost indistinguishable solely on the basis of their behavioural effects.

Eastman's comments on 'reduced reinforcement' paradigms are mainly concerned with their narrowness. He argues that a truly comprehensive theory would include a greater number of parameters of reinforcement — frequency, duration, magnitude and the amount of behaviour required to obtain the reinforcer (the response cost).

*Loss of Reinforcible Behaviour.* This theory is ascribed to Ferster (1966, 1973) and refers to the reduction of reinforcible behaviour in the repertoire (for any reason). Simply put, if the behaviour is not there to be rewarded, it will not be rewarded. Such reduction in behaviour characteristically follows large and/or sudden environmental changes, which change the stimulus conditions which normally control behaviour, but may also result from reinforcible behaviour being squeezed out of the repertoire by aversively motivated behaviours (escape or avoidance of stress) or by suppressed anger which reduces social reinforcement. Clearly this formulation is very similar to those of 'inadequate or insufficient reinforcement' mentioned above.

*Aversive Control.* This refers to the theory which attributes reduced behavioural output to punishing outcomes, or at least to stimuli signalling the imminence of punishment. This receives little attention by Eastman, reflecting the scant regard for the theory in the literature, perhaps because such concepts are more commonly associated with anxiety. Although several authors have pointed out that depression may result from unusually intense and prolonged anxiety (Lazarus, 1968; Wolpe, 1972) this is different from explaining actual performance deficits in depression in terms of a current expectation of aversive consequences. This is despite the fact that (although anxiety and depression are distinguishable as clinical syndromes), anxiety is very often a component in the depressive state, especially in mild depressions. The significance of 'punishment' or 'stimuli signalling punishment' becomes more clear if Gray's analysis of their equivalence with 'frustrative nonreward' and 'stimuli signalling frustrative nonreward' (respectively) is borne in mind (Gray, 1978). In the circumstances of bereavement, for example, the individual is besieged by stimuli which have normally signalled the presence of their loved one: 'the alarm clock which he always turned off', 'the television programme she always used to watch' and so on. Yet the person is not there when (s)he looks around — surely paradigmatic of 'frustrative nonreward'. Many of the stimuli in the environment must thereby become signals for such nonreward, and reduction in behaviour ensues as certainly as if the behaviour was being systematically punished. This formulation seems inadequate to explain the generalisation of behavioural deficits in depression, yet if one extends the theory to include 'conditioned inhibition' — the reduction in behavioural output owing to the presence of stimuli signalling that no reward is available — it may yet explain a wide range of phenomena.

*Loss of Reinforcer Effectiveness.*   According to this theory (Costello, 1972a) sufficient reinforcers may be available in the environment and the individual might still be capable of procuring them, but for some reason they have lost their *potency* as reinforcers. This is in contrast with those theories which would predict that only techniques which increase total amount of rewarding events or those which teach the necessary skills (e.g. assertion training) to procure such rewards will ultimately be effective in alleviating depression. The formulation seems particularly useful in accounting for depressions which do not seem to follow any loss event (and although many do, a substantial number do not). It also seems to account for the finding of depressives that their discomfort and dysphoria is increased when they attempt to do things which they formerly found pleasurable — an aspect of the syndrome which has been ignored by many theorists. This theory may account for the phenomenon by supposing that when an individual expects from past experience to get pleasure from an activity which, on trying, he finds lacks any rewards, a frustrative nonreward effect will follow, increasing discomfort accordingly.

How does loss of reinforcer effectiveness come about? According to Costello, it may result from endogenous changes in the biochemical mechanisms known to underlie consummatory motivation, or it may result from the disruption of a behavioural chain by the loss of a single reinforcer in that chain. It is this latter behavioural formulation which is potentially of interest to the psychological therapist. It sounds rather as if a single loss may have generalised consequences by its chain disrupting effects, in rather the same way as a house-buying chain of several agreements may be upset by the disruption of one purchase in the chain. The difference here is that all the 'contracts' are being made within the behavioural repertoire of a single individual. Put differently, the stimuli, responses and reinforcers in a person's behaviour are mutually interdependent (Costello, 1972b), and it may be that some people's greater proneness to depression reflects the fact that the mutual interdependence of their behaviour is particularly strong and needs to be weakened. Although it is not clear exactly what constitutes 'mutual dependence' or how it could even be assessed, it perhaps resembles most closely the clinical observation of an individual 'putting all their eggs in one basket'. A patient who says 'If I can't have my lover back, there is nothing for me' is defining all potential reinforcers in terms of a dependence on *one* particular state of affairs — a state of affairs over which they may have little control in any case. A person who, in Eastman's terms, has a 'network' of reinforcers thus dependent on one or two central components (be it love, job, status, children), is thereby rendered vulnerable to disruption in the chain and as a consequence to generalised loss of reinforcer effectiveness. Eastman's analogy is a useful one:

> 'Consider a tightly stretched net, made of some elastic filament. The knots in this net represent behaviours, stimuli and reinforcers, while the filaments between them represent the interdependencies. If a single knot is excised, a large hole appears: the net effectively collapses. This represents the disruption of the relationships between behaviours, stimuli and reinforcers that Costello calls a 'loss of reinforcer effectiveness'. If the net is only loosely stretched in the first place and if there are inbuilt holes (some behaviours, etc. are not interrelated with others), then the removal of one knot will have only a small effect on the total.' (p. 282)

### Evaluation of Behavioural Formulations

The main problem with the behavioural formulations is that they make few unique predictions by which they could be easily distinguished from each other, from biochemical or psychodynamic theories, or from cognitive theories. Very little actual evidence has been cited in support of any of them. Of course, each has some treatment implications, but even if the treatment predicted by the theory to work was effective, demonstrating that the factors mediating treatment outcome were those posited by the theory would be difficult. Table 1.1 shows a summary of the four more specific behavioural formulations, set out according to the factors which render a person vulnerable to, precipitate or maintain the depression.

Table 1.1: Summary of Four Behavioural Formulations

|     | Vulnerability factors | Precipitating factors | Maintaining factors |
| --- | --- | --- | --- |
| (1) | *Reduced frequency of social reinforcement* Lack of social skill (Lack of ability to recognise and use reinforcers) | Loss of reinforcer | Insufficient response contingent positive reinforcement Secondary gain (reinforcement of depressive behaviour) |
| (2) | *Loss of reinforcible behaviour* — | Environmental change or situation that can be altered only by emitting very large amount of behaviour | Reduced frequency of behaviour which others or environment can reinforce. |
| (3) | *Aversive control* Excessive sensitivity to stimuli signalling impending punishment or nonreward | Loss of expected reinforcement (or actual punishment) following behaviour | Same as (1) |
| (4) | *Loss of reinforcer effectiveness* Large mutual interdependence of stimuli, reinforcers and behaviour | Loss of one or more reinforcers in the network | Generalised loss of potency of reinforcement |

Two aspects of behavioural formulations will be considered in evaluating their usefulness, (a) the problem of specifying stimulus-behaviour-reinforcement links and (b) the problem of obtaining evidence for the theories.

*The Generality of the Formulations.*   Part of the difficulty in investigating behavioural formulations is the difficulty of reproducing the effects in the human experimental laboratory. In an experiment where a person has to press a button to obtain reward (in terms of an increase in a number showing on a counter in front of him or her), it may be quite difficult, using a single button, to demonstrate experimental extinction when the counter stops increasing. This is because if there is nothing else to do in the ubiquitous sound-attenuated, light and temperature constant experimental booth, humans will often just carry on pressing the button regardless of the reduced reinforcement contingencies. It is possible to demonstrate experimental control using two buttons and varying the reinforcement schedule between the two, but the outcome has to then be defined in terms of two variables: the probability and intensity of behaviour. This complication need not matter, for it may more nearly represent real-life where all behaviour is multiply determined, and may have both a probability of occurring and an 'intensity factor', once performance has started. But one can see, in the light of these experimental analogues, how simple and even naive the behavioural formulations of depression are. Although many people may object in principle to the reduction of humans to button pressing laboratory organisms, it is hard to argue that the 'real' environment outside the laboratory will be subject to behavioural principles that are more simple and straightforward than the extremely complex behaviours already mapped in the field of applied behaviour analysis in the laboratory.

Where does this leave the behavioural formulations as outlined? It leaves them suffering from being too general in their analysis of human behaviour to enable them to be precise enough to account for the range of depressive phenomena with which the therapist has to deal. This is more than the oft-quoted lack of cognitive and affective emphasis in their theory. Such additions would not help to overcome the lack of precision within the formulation of depressive behaviour itself.

*The Problem of Evidence.* In examining the problem of evidence it is helpful to look at the formulation which has generated most research to date, that of Lewinsohn and co-workers in Oregon. Their theory is broadly as laid out in Table 1.1 (1), and has vulnerability (lack of interpersonal skills), precipitating (loss event), and maintaining (inadequate or insufficient response contingent positive reinforcement) components. Many writers have pointed out the insufficiency of correlational data in establishing this model. The fact that fewer activities are associated with low mood does not imply that the behaviour changed prior to the mood. Indeed, Lewinsohn's own practice in obtaining these correlations would easily allow the opposite to be the case. This is because, in asking subjects in his experiments to rate the number of activities which occurred on any particular day, they are 'always instructed in a daily frequency check to count an activity as having occurred only if it was "at least a little pleasant"'. For example, if watching television is on a subject's activity schedule, then if TV-watching was not experienced as enjoyable (a common occurrence) the subject does not check that particular activity on that day (Lewinsohn, 1975). Small wonder then that Lewinsohn and his colleagues obtain significant correlations between subjects' daily ratings of frequency of activities and daily mood ratings. On a 'good day' (assuming affective state to be prior) a subject will enjoy more activities, so his 'frequency' rating will rise. To suppose from correlations thus obtained that rate of behavioural output is prior to affective change is to look at the results in a very blinkered way indeed.

Two alternatives remain: one is to look for evidence of specific changes in behaviour prior to changes in other variables during behavioural treatment. This strategy has been attempted by Lewinsohn and co-workers (Zeiss *et al.*, 1979) but has not been very illuminating (see p. 39-40). A second is to look for evidence of the deficits in interpersonal skills hypothesised to exist in depressed patients. Youngren and Lewinsohn (1980) have attempted just such a project. They examined the behaviour of 75 neurotically depressed outpatients, comparing them with 69 nondepressed psychiatric controls and with 80 normal controls. The presence of the psychiatric nondepressed group was to control for the possibility that psychiatric morbidity rather than depression *per se* would account for any differences found in interpersonal behaviour. Subjects completed the Interpersonal Events Schedule — a 160 item scale yielding self-ratings divided into eight scales. On five of these (social activity, assertion, cognition, give positive and receive positive) the by now familiar pattern emerged of depressives' self-ratings differing both from normals and nondepressed psychiatric controls. But the authors went beyond the self-rating scales, and took independently observed and coded measures of subjects' behaviour in a dyadic or group situation. Independent ratings were made of activity level, initiation level, actions elicited, positive reactions elicited, negative reactions elicited, speech rate, speech volume, eye contact, smiling, facial expression and gestures (illustrations vs. adaptors). The results showed that *none* of these were uniquely associated with depression. Despite this, when the coders and the depressives' own peers gave a *general* rating of interpersonal style, depressed patients were given lower ratings following their performance in the group situation. Thus depressed patients themselves, their peers, and independent observers rate their behaviour (in general) as maladaptive, but more specific observations fail to reveal the origin of this 'atmosphere of interpersonal inefficiency'. I coin this phrase deliberately to emphasise the genuine ambiguity of what has been shown by this study. The results have at one and the same time damaged and helped Lewinsohn's basic formulation. The damage is that no specific interpersonal deficit has emerged which uniquely characterises the depressed patient, so a major 'predisposing' component of the theory loses credibility. On the other hand, because the theory is concerned with the reactions of others it has been helped, for the reaction of others was unequivocally more negative towards the depressive than towards other patients or controls. The 'atmosphere' of negativity was reflected in the self-ratings, peer ratings and observer ratings — the depressed patient was somehow 'putting people off', discouraging contact in a way too subtle to codify. Since it is the reactions of others in an interpersonal context which will substantially determine the outcome of the situation, it is largely irrelevant that the depressive's interpersonal inefficiency (if that is indeed what it is) seems absent when 'objective' attempts are made to measure it.

It is unlikely that the alternative behavioural formulations would have much more success in demonstrating the necessity of their own postulated processes. Lewinsohn has been more tireless than most in attempting to explicate the aetiology of depression in behavioural terms. This is not to say that the behavioural models have not served a useful heuristic purpose, nor that treatment techniques which have been based upon them have not been effective (see Chapter 2), but the exact impact of reinforcement contingencies on the predisposition and precipitation of depression must remain an open question.

## The Learned Helplessness Model of Depression

As this model started its life in the animal laboratory I take as the starting point a paper in 1976 by Maier and Seligman which reviewed the 'learned helplessness' data up to that time.

In 1967, Overmier and Seligman, in the course of investigating the effects of Pavlovian fear conditioning had found that dogs given inescapable and unavoidable electric shock in one situation (the Pavlovian Hammock) later failed to learn to escape or avoid shock in another situation (the shuttlebox). In a subsequent experiment, Seligman and Maier (1967) used a comparison group of animals for which shock was potentially escapable. By yoking the two groups they were able to ensure that the inescapable shock group received exactly the same pattern and intensity of shock as the escapable shock group. The results showed that animals in the escapable-shock group performed as efficiently in a subsequent shock-escape task as animals which had not undergone shock at all. By contrast, animals which had undergone shock which was not controllable by their own responses showed later deficits in the subsequent task, two-thirds of the animals showing no acquisition of an escape-response at all. This experiment showed that it was not the exposure to the shock *per se* in the first situation which caused the deficient instrumental learning in the second situation, but the *uncontrollability* of the stress. Further research has found similar phenomena in cats, fish, rats, mice, birds, primates as well as man.

Maier and Seligman outlined three outcomes of exposure to uncontrollable aversive events: (a) motivational deficits; (b) cognitive deficits; (c) emotional changes;

(a) *Motivational*. Animals that had been exposed to inescapable shock did not subsequently initiate escape responses in the presence of shock.

(b) *Cognitive*. Animals that had been exposed to inescapable shock were retarded at learning that their responses could control future stresses, i.e. if the animal made a response that produces relief, it had trouble 'catching on' to the response-relief contingency (Seligman, 1974). In man, this effect of uncontrollability had been shown by assessing the number of trials taken for a subject to 'catch on' to the pattern underlying a series of anagrams. Subjects exposed either to inescapable noise pre-treatment or insoluble discrimination problems pre-treatment took longer to perceive the pattern (Hiroto and Seligman, 1975; Miller and Seligman, 1975).

(c) *Emotional*. Maier and Seligman (1976) presented data from a number of sources to support the claim that inescapable trauma had emotional effects: there was evidence that following only one session of inescapable shock with dogs, subsequent helplessness deficits dissipated over 48 hours, which they suggested hinted at a transient emotional (hormonal) effect; rats exposed to inescapable shock had been found to develop more stomach ulcers than another group of rats for whom the shock was escapable (the yoking of the two groups having ensured that the pattern and intensity of actual shock received was the same in the two groups) (Weiss, 1971); human subjects who performed tasks while being shocked but were not allowed to take time-outs when they wished, had been found to show consistently higher blood pressure than subjects who were allowed to specify when they wished to take time-outs (Hockanson, DeGood, Forrest and Brittain, 1971).

The hypothesis proposed by Seligman and co-workers to account for these phenomena was 'learned helplessness' (Seligman, 1974, 1975). It assumed that organisms could learn not only about the contingencies between instrumental responses and the outcomes of those responses but also could weigh up the conditional probability of reinforcement given a response against the conditional probability of reinforcement given the absence of that response. When the probability of reinforcement, given a specific response, does not differ from the probability of reinforcement in the absence of that response, responding and reinforcement are independent, i.e. the organism has no control over outcomes. The learned helplessness hypothesis argued that motivational and cognitive deficits and emotional changes follow when an organism has learned that responding and outcome are independent. The motivational deficits follow inescapable stress because part of the incentive for making such responses is the expectation that they will bring relief. The cognitive deficits follow inescapable stress because, having acquired a cognitive set in which responses are irrelevant to outcomes, it will be harder to learn that responses control outcomes when they actually do. The presence of emotional changes did not follow directly from the helplessness hypothesis, but Seligman had been able to cite evidence that exposure to uncontrollable trauma produced more conditional fear, ulcers, weight loss and defecation in animals, than controllable shock (Seligman, 1974, 1975).

However, it was the suggestion that this learned helplessness phenomenon could be a model of reactive depression in humans which gave the greatest impetus to research, particularly in the attempts to find human analogues of the animal work. Just as animals exposed to inescapable stress showed later motivational, cognitive and emotional changes which undermined effective instrumental responding, so reactive depression may have resulted from stress perceived as uncontrollable which would lead to the expectation that future reinforcements would be out of the person's control. This expectation was hypothesised to lead to the passivity of depression (motivational) the negative expectations of depression (cognitive) and the affective disturbance in depression (emotional).

A great deal has happened in the seven or so years since that paper was published. It has, for example become clear that many of the human laboratory helplessness demonstrations do not require a 'learned helplessness' model to explain them (Coyne *et al.*, 1980; Williams and Teasdale, 1982). Coyne *et al.* referred to the similarity between helplessness phenomena and the large number of studies using similar procedures (to similar effect) in the test anxiety and achievement motivation literature. They surmised that if laboratory helplessness phenomena were anxiety based, they ought to be alleviated with 'pleasant relaxing imagery' inserted between pretreatment and test phases. They indeed found that instructing subjects to imagine a pleasant mountain scene 'in order to relax you' prevented deficits on 20 patterned anagrams following uncontrollable noise pretreatment. Williams and Teasdale (1982) found evidence that behavioural deficits on laboratory tasks used in helplessness research could be reproduced in subjects who had a low expectancy of success on a task thought to be of low importance, and in subjects who had a low expectancy for an important task who then met initial difficulty performing that task. Explanations of these results were proposed in terms of four variables: expectancy of success, motivation to succeed, amount of effort required and the cost of effort. No explanation in terms of perceived or expected noncontingency between action and outcome was necessary.

A more significant development in learned helplessness theory has occurred since Maier and Seligman's 1976 review article. Ironically, even before it was published there was a paper in draft form circulating between London, Pennsylvania and Oxford. A number of doubts about the robustness of the model had occurred simultaneously to Seligman himself (on sabbatical in London in the mid-1970s), to Lyn Abramson in Pennsylvania, and John Teasdale in Oxford. Their important paper in 1978 (Abramson, Seligman and Teasdale) was the result of their extensive deliberations, letters, draftings and redraftings. The paper represented a 'reformulation' of learned helplessness as applied to humans, in attributional theory terms. A summary of their main propositions is given by Seligman in a 1981 paper. The new model has four premises, the co-occurrence of which is hypothesised to be sufficient for depression to occur:

(1)    The individual expects that a highly aversive state of affairs is likely (or a highly desired state of affairs is unlikely).
(2)    The individual expects that he will be able to do nothing about the likelihood of these states of affairs.

(3)   The individual possesses a maladaptive attributional style so that negative events tend to be attributed to internal, stable and global causes, and positive events to external, unstable and specific causes.

(4)   The greater the certainty of the expected aversive state of affairs and the expected uncontrollability, the greater the strength of motivational and cognitive deficits. The greater the importance to the individual of the uncontrollable event, the greater will be the affective and self-esteem disruption.

For a reason which is not entirely clear, most subsequent interest has focused on the third premise, that maladaptive attributional style predisposes the individual to react in a depressive way to the presence of aversive events or nonoccurrence of positive events. This component of the model states that attribution for an uncontrollable event determines the individual's response to that event. For example, if an exam was failed you might say to yourself that it was because you either didn't have the necessary ability or didn't try hard enough (both internal attributions). Note however that ability is a rather more unchanging or 'stable' cause for your failure than effort, which may often be increased the next time the exam comes around. Or you may say that the exams set by that Examination Board are always very stiff (another 'stable', but this time 'external' attribution) or that it was just bad luck and next time may be OK ('unstable' and 'external'). Table 1.2 shows these four possible attributions and their categories.

Table 1.2: Possible Attributions for Failing an Exam

|          | Stable          | Unstable   |
|----------|-----------------|------------|
| Internal | Low ability     | Low effort |
| External | Task difficulty | Bad luck   |

Also: GLOBAL/SPECIFIC (see text)

These attributions may also be either global or specific. You may say you hadn't the ability either specifically, because it was, for example, a statistics exam which for you correlates with no other exam performance, or globally, because you are just no good at taking formal exams and don't understand anything on any of your college courses anyway. Clearly one would expect differences in attributions such as these to make a large difference in the behavioural and affective impact of the original event. The theory proposes that negative events attributed to internal (personal), stable (unchanging) and global (wide ranging) attributions will be more devastating emotionally. In particular, internal attributions for failure (and external ones for success) tend to lower self esteem; stable attributions for failure (and unstable ones for success) tend to produce long-lasting deficits; and global attributions for failure (and specific ones for success) produce depressive deficits which generalise to many situations.

Note that this attributional component of the model is only one of four premises, and that research has neglected the other premises, for example the first and second premises that an event perceived as uncontrollable is deemed a necessary co-occurrence of the other premises for depression to occur on this formulation. That is not to say that depression cannot occur by other means (biological, prolonged anxiety or heavy workload, etc.), but that on this theory, all four premises are necessary. A detailed discussion of these aspects of the model will be found in Chapter 8.

The researchers that have looked at the attributional component of depression have found ambiguous results. Some of these are detailed on p. 177, but it is appropriate here to mention at least one study which has examined these variables in some depth. Hargreaves (1982) examined fifty depressed patients (divided equally between the sexes) who had been referred to psychiatrists or psychologists for management of depression. The sample included inpatients, outpatients, daypatients and General Practitioner patients. All were between the ages of 16 and 65 years, with no psychoticism, mental deficiency or organicity, and no history of alcohol problems or drug addiction. All had a Beck Depression Inventory (BDI) score of at least 15.

Control subjects, matched for age and sex (25 males and 25 females) were recruited from a subject panel. Depressed and control subjects completed the BDI; Seligman *et al's* Attributional Style Questionnaire (which gives a score of an individuals tendency to see positive and negative events as caused by internal, stable or global factors, as well as a rating of the importance of the outcome) (Seligman *et al*., 1979); the Locus of Control Scale (Rotter, 1966); a Self-esteem Questionnaire (Rosenberg, 1965); and the Eysenck Personality Questionnaire (Eysenck and Eysenck, 1975). Thus it was possible not only to see if depressed patients were characterised by any particular attributional style, but also to examine the personality correlates of attributional style.

In answer to the first question, no differences in attributional style were found between the depressed and control groups. Furthermore, when the correlates of attributional style on Seligman's Questionnaire were observed, they were disappointing. For example, there was no significant correlation in the depressed group between Seligman's Internality Scale and the Rotter Locus of Control Internal-External score ($r = -0.252$ and $-0.003$ for internal attribution to success and failure respectively). For nondepressed subjects these correlations were $r = -0.414$ (p $<0.01$) and $0.128$ respectively. This is hardly very good convergent validity evidence for the model. The corresponding correlation between internality and self-esteem is slightly more encouraging: internal attribution for failure vs. self-esteem $r = 0.435$ (p $<$ $0.01$), but the corresponding correlation for success attributions which should be significant in the opposite direction is only $r = -0.190$. (The finding that attributions for failure produce results more consistent with the model than attributions for success has occurred elsewhere, e.g. Metalsky *et al.*, 1982.)

Hargreaves also examined differences between her depressed and control groups in extraversion and neuroticism. She found large and highly significant differences, the depressed group being less extravert and more neurotic. There was no relationship between these personality variables and attributional style.

This study provides virtually no support for the attributional reformulation. Is there an explanation for this? There are two possible explanations of the result which preserve the integrity of the attributional model to some extent. The first is that the definition of depression in this study was a cutoff score on the BDI, rather than a diagnosis of primary depression. Referral to a helping agency for treatment of depression does not guarantee the diagnosis in patients who may have been a mixed group. On the other hand, previous results which have been taken to support the attributional model have used cutoff scores with college students which are a rather more distant group from clinically depressed patients. The lack of diagnostic clarity can therefore hardly be taken as a major criticism relative to these other studies (e.g. Metalsky *et al.*, 1982). The second possible explanation is that many of the patients had perhaps become depressed by an alternative route. Seligman and colleagues do not maintain that their model provides the only way by which individuals become depressed — their premises are sufficient but not necessary for depression to occur. On the other hand, one might have expected some differences to emerge, even if a proportion of the patients had a maladaptive attributional style. It may have been helpful to examine the data to see which patients had suffered a life event which had seemed to precipitate the depression. It is these patients for whom the attributional theory makes the most powerful prediction and failure to find any relationship in this group would be damaging indeed to the model.

It would be misleading to give the impression that no investigation has found the hypothesised relationship between attributional style and depression. Raps *et al*. (1982) found that clinical depressives, but not hospitalised schizophrenics, had a maladaptive attributional style. The authors took this to illustrate that psychopathology by itself was insufficient to account for any differences between depressed and non-depressed individuals in attributional style. Most other findings have used college students (e.g. Seligman *et al*., 1979; Golin *et al*., 1981). These data are examined in detail in Chapter 8.

At this point it is fair to say that the attributional model is 'not proven'. Maladaptive attributional style is a rather elusive feature of depression, though it must be conceded that these are difficult concepts to measure successfully, and paper and pencil tests are a cumbersome way to approach such variables. Nevertheless, the fact that maladaptive attributions *do* occur in *some* patients (Raps *et al*., 1982) indicates that their possible role in all depressed patients must be looked for. Reattribution training as a technique used by itself may only be minimally helpful for the largest proportion of patients, but that is not to say that it will not prove very helpful for some.

## The Cognitive Theory of Depression

Unlike the learned helplessness theory, Beck's cognitive theory of depression arose out of clinical observations rather than the animal or human laboratory. It is therefore to be expected that the observations which form the basis of the theory would have a great deal of validity in themselves. The key work from which our review of this theory may start is *Cognitive Theory and the Emotional Disorders* (Beck, 1976).

In that book three main components of a theory of emotional disorders were outlined. The first component was the presence of *negative automatic thoughts* − 'automatic' by virtue of their coming 'out of the blue', often seemingly unprompted by events and not necessarily the results of 'directed' thinking. They seem 'immediate' and often 'valid' in the sense that they are often accepted unchallenged by the recipient. Their effect is to disrupt mood, and to cause further thoughts to emerge in a downward thought-affect spiral. Depressive thoughts can be characterised in terms of *cognitive triad* − a negative view of the self (e.g. 'I'm a failure'), the world (e.g. this neighbourhood is a terrible place) and the future (e.g. everything will turn out badly).

The second component is the presence of *systematic logical errors* in the thinking of depressed individuals. Several categories (not mutually exclusive) have been distinguished: arbitrary inference (e.g. someone concludes that a friend has fallen out with them because they did not smile at him or her); overgeneralisation (e.g. 'failure on this exam means I'll never pass the other exams'), selective abstraction (e.g. a person only notices the few bad things in a report about himself); magnification and minimisation (e.g. when a person exaggerates the effect of a negative event (catastrophises) or minimises the impact of a positive event); personalisation (when a person attributes bad things to himself despite evidence to the contrary (for example, 'If I'd thought to warn Mr. Jones about the effects of overeating, he'd never have had a heart attack'); dichotomous thinking (all or nothing: black/white thinking, e.g. 'only a miracle can make me well again', or 'if he leaves me, I may as well be dead').

The third component of the cognitive model is the presence of *depressogenic schemata*. These general, long-lasting attitudes or assumptions about the world represent the way in which the individual organises his or her past experience, and is suggested to be the system by which incoming information about the world is classified. This is one of the earliest concepts in Beck's theoretical writings. In 1964 he defined the schema as

'a structure for screening, coding and evaluating impinging stimuli. In terms of the individual's adaptation to external reality, it is regarded as the mode by which the environment is broken down and organised into its many psychologically relevant facets; on the basis of the matrix of schemas, the individual is able to orient himself in relation to time and space and to categorise and interpret his experiences in a meaningful way'.

(This concept is analysed in greater detail in Chapter 9.) According to the theory, depressive schemas develop over many years and, although they may not be evident in later life, remain ready to be activated by a combination of stressful circumstances. Table 1.3 gives the sort of factors in child development which are supposed to cause the depressive schemata to be constructed over time.

The evidence for the cognitive model is almost entirely correlational. It is easy to demonstrate that individuals have more automatic negative

Table 1.3: Factors in childhood history leading to depressive schemata

| | |
|---|---|
| (1) | *Tangible loss*<br>Loss of mother/father<br>Loss of other relative, friend, person close to you<br>(Loss includes death, divorce, separation, desertion, prolonged ill health)<br>Prolonged ill health as a child |
| (2) | *Expectation of loss (reality)*<br>Loss of mother/father/other close person expected for long time before loss actually realised<br>Disappointment by people relied upon<br>Expectation of big reward for something done, which never materialised |
| (3) | *Expectation of loss (fantasy)*<br>Loss (as in 2) expected for long time, but did not actually occur |
| (4) | *Self esteem lowering events*<br>Difficulty in mixing with other children<br>Being bullied over extended period<br>Feeling of being different from peer group<br>Feeling of being unwanted by parents<br>Feeling of being unwanted by everyone ('no one cared')<br>Feeling of being hated by everyone |
| (5) | *Reversal in valuation of object*<br>Sudden change from loving someone very much to hating them<br>Sudden change from self-respect to self-hate — feeling badly about self because of an event |
| (6) | *Background*<br>Depression in close family members<br>Severe punishment by either parent<br>Overprotection by either parent, and/or<br>Isolation from other children<br>Strict rules by either parent<br>History of parents pointing out faults but not good points. |

thoughts when feeling depressed (using thought checklists or less structured diaries on which to record thoughts — see Chapter 7, Section III). It is also possible to classify these thoughts according to the logical error being made at the time. There is little doubt also that depressives are selective in recall of rewards and punishments which favour the schema theory (Gotlib, 1981). There is also a great deal of evidence from laboratory mood induction research that presentation of negative self-statements similar to those which occur naturally to depressed individuals can actually precipitate a downswing in the mood of formerly nondepressed subjects (see Chapter 8). In fact, mood induction studies provide the best evidence that depressive cognitions may act in a causal capacity to effect mood (Goodwin and Williams, 1982). Without this research, one would have to agree with those who have stated that cognitive theory interprets as causal what others claim to be merely symptoms. Since the limitations of cognitive theory are explored in greater depth in Chapter 8, I shall not discuss them further here. Of course, the role of cognitions in the *aetiology* of depression, even if questioned, need not affect their status in the *maintenance* of depression. No matter how precipitated, a depressive reaction characterised by negative expectations about the future, negative estimate of one's own abilities, and a view of the world as being more negative than it really is will tend to be more severe and more prolonged. Even those investigators who find little evidence for the antecedence of cognitions in the aetiology of depressive onset (e.g. Lewinsohn *et al.*, 1981) find that once depressed, the more negative the cognitive style, the longer it takes for the depression to remit. Thus the assessment of, and techniques designed to cope with the cognitive component of depression are likely to be very important. A review of the key treatment outcome studies (Chapter 2) justifies this conclusion.

## Self-control Theory of Depression

This model attempts to combine elements of the behavioural and cognitive formulations described in this chapter. The paper we may take as our starting point is that of Lynn Rehm in 1977 entitled 'A self-control model of depression'. In this, he developed Kanfer's (1970) self-regulation model which divided the control that an individual has over their own behaviour into three stages: self-monitoring, self-evaluation and self-reinforcement. These processes may be illustrated by way of the paradigmatic 'self-control' experiment. In it, an individual performs a task (e.g. attempting to recognise which of three nonsense syllables in an array has occurred in a prior list). Following their choice, subjects can be asked to *monitor* their success or failure rate, to *evaluate* their level of success relative to subjective standards of accuracy, and then to give themselves a *reward* in proportion to how deserving they think they are. Using such techniques, it has been found (Bellack and Schwartz, 1976) that self-evaluation and reinforcement do not necessarily correlate with actual accuracy. It has also been found that if nondepressed subjects are asked to monitor their errors in such a task, they systematically underestimate their true accuracy. This is taken to be analogous to selective biases in depression. Such experiments have made it clear that self-monitoring involves more than the passive registration of stimuli in the environment (Rehm, 1977). Rather it is an active selective scanning which perceives and encodes. Whereas nondepressed individuals perform this function appropriately, depressed individuals are hypothesised to selectively attend to negative aspects of themselves and their world. Self-evaluation is performed on the basis of criteria that are set too high to achieve, so that overt and covert self-rewards are rarely dispersed. Thus the basis for normal rates of behaviour (self regulation) in the relative absence of external control is diminished, and the depressed individual's behavioural repertoire is disrupted. In further statements of the self-regulation model, Kanfer and Hagerman (1981) point out how the depressed person judges his behaviour according to long-term personal criteria rather than short-term situational criteria. If a nondepressed person spills a drink, he may say 'how clumsy, where's the cloth' but a depressed person may recall other similar instances of clumsiness over the past weeks and months and conclude that his brain is weakening. Accessing the wrong criteria for self-evaluation leads to poor or absent self-reinforcement and increased self-punishment.

Evidence consistent with Rehm's 1977 formulation has taken the form of results showing that depressed and nondepressed subjects do indeed differentially reward and punish themselves as predicted by the theory (Rozensky *et al.*, 1977; Lobitz and Post, 1979). The theory has also led to several successful treatment studies (e.g. Fuchs and Rehm, 1977; Rehm *et al.*, 1979), which although not reviewed in Chapter 2 because they used a group rather than individualised approach, represent an integrated version of what is adequately represented in other specific treatment techniques such as self-reinforcement, thought monitoring and evaluation and activity monitoring. The use of the integrated self-control approach to treating depression is illustrated in Rotzer *et al's* 1981 paper (see p. 43). We shall consider the validity of central tenet of both cognitive and self-control theory in the final section.

## Are Depressed People Genuinely Biased, Or Are They Just Realistic?

A central aspect of cognitive and self-control theory is that depressives selectively attend to negative information and thus receive a distorted view of the world. An alternative view is that nondepressed individuals are unduly optimistic and that the apparent pessimism of the depressive is just how the world really is. There seems to be an increasing amount of evidence for this view.

For example, Alloy and Abramson (1979) confronted depressed and nondepressed students with a series of problems varying in actual contingency between performance response and outcome. Nondepressed subjects overestimated the degree of contingency for frequent and/or desired outcomes, but underestimated contingency between response and outcomes for negative outcomes. Depressed subjects were, by contrast more accurate in their judgements. Nelson and Craighead (1977) found a similar result in a study of recall of positive or negative feedback on trials of an experimental task. Depressed or nondepressed students were given an ambiguous task on which they were either rewarded or punished on 30 per cent or 70 per cent of the trials. Depressed subjects recalled receiving less positive feedback than nondepressed (a distortion) but were more accurate in recalling the negative feedback when delivered at low frequency. Nondepressed subjects underestimated the amount of negative feedback (a distortion in the positive direction).

The conclusion that depressed patients may be more accurate in their assessment of themselves, the world and the future than overoptimistic nondepressed individuals is challenging indeed. These results would therefore be of great significance if they could be replicated in a clinical population. Gotlib (1981) examined rates of self-reinforcement and self-punishment on a memory task in 16 depressed and 12 nondepressed psychiatric patients. A patient was classified as depressed if he or she (a) obtained a diagnosis of a 'definite' depressive syndrome according to the criteria of Feighner *et al*. (1972), (b) had a score of more than 11 on the Beck Depression Inventory *and* a minimum of 14 on the Hamilton Rating Scale. Nineteen depressed hospital employees acted as a nonpsychiatric control group. Results showed that whereas both psychiatric groups evidenced less self-reinforcement and greater self-punishment for their trial by trial performance than the nonpsychiatric control group, only the depressed group showed biases in recall of the frequency with which they had rewarded or punished themselves. They recalled giving themselves fewer reinforcements and a greater number of self-punishments. The two nondepressed groups were not biased in their recall in this way. Thus it seems the analogue research was not replicated in this study. There is one way in which the discrepant results could be reconciled, however, because whereas Nelson and Craighead's subjects received rewards and punishments which were administered by the experimenter, Gotlib's patients administered their own reward. Could it be that depressives are more accurate about externally delivered reinforcement, but biased in their judgements about internally generated responses? Only further studies addressed specifically to this issue in a clinical population will answer the question, though Garber and Hollon (1980) did find that depressed college students were more likely to vary the trial by trial expectancy of success on a task as if the test was a matter of luck rather than skill if it was themselves doing the task, but not if others were doing it. This study is not directly comparable to the Nelson and Craighead or Gotlib studies, but it points up the importance of looking at whether the depressed patient is being required to make judgements about the external environment or reflecting his or her 'internal' state of optimism/pessimism.

Another recent paper which claims to address the same issue is that by Lewinsohn *et al.* (1980) entitled 'Social competence and depression: the role of illusory self-perceptions'. They compared observer ratings of depressed and nondepressed patients' interpersonal behaviour, with self-ratings of their behaviour made by the participants. The sample consisted of 71 unipolar neurotically depressed patients, who were compared with 59 psychiatric controls who were not depressed and 73 nonpsychiatric (nondepressed) controls. These individuals participated in four 45-minute sessions during which they were rated for their interpersonal efficiency by independent coders, and after which the self-ratings were made. The important finding was that the discrepancy scores between observer and self-ratings of the depressed group were significantly smaller than those for the control groups at time 1. Over time there was no change in the nondepressed self and observer ratings, but the depressed group changed their self-perception for the better, thus increasing the discrepancy between self- and observer ratings – in short, they became more benign and seemingly less accurate in their self-perceptions. The authors conclude that, since during the study depressed subjects' self-perceptions had become more unrealistic, 'perhaps the key to avoiding depression is to see oneself less stringently and more favourably than others see us'.

In interpreting these results, however, it is important to bear in mind their relativistic nature. What is being suggested is that certain individuals are more 'accurate' by virtue of the fact that they agree with another individual's assessment. But these 'other individuals' (coders) are presumably subject to the same influences as the nondepressed subjects in the experiment who were found to have a positive self-serving bias. (Note that a result that nondepressed subjects are overoptimistic is logically independent from the argument about whether depressed individuals are or are not accurate in *their* assessment of the world.) Just because the 'coders' were designated as 'independent' and not called upon to interact or make judgements about themselves, this does not mean that they themselves are free from bias.

So where is 'reality' located in this? Consider this analogy: Mr Smith meets a person, Mr Brown. Mr Brown believes himself to have a high IQ, and judges Mr Smith to be rather a dullard. Suppose Mr Smith is depressed, and says to Mr Brown 'I'm dumb and stupid'. Mr Brown may concur. Who is being accurate here? Are we going to say that Mr Smith really *is* stupid on the grounds that they agree in their conclusions? By no means. Neither can we assert that depressed patients are being accurate in their self-judgements on the grounds that nondepressed individuals (subject, as we know, to their own misperceptions) say so. Of course, we would trust the independent coders more if, on a reliable coding system, they were able to produce behavioural evidence of the depressed person's interpersonal inefficiency. The same research team in fact examined a sample from the same population of individuals (Youngren and Lewinsohn, 1980; see p. 8, above) and found no actual behavioural evidence for the depressed persons' interpersonal deficits. Taken together with Gotlib's inability to replicate the analogue studies on the 'accuracy' of depressives, and keeping in mind the extensive clinical evidence of the depressed person's excessive pessimism and hopelessness, the validity of the conclusion that depressed persons are in fact seeing the 'real world' must remain in doubt.

## Concluding Remarks

When Blaney came to review the 'contemporary theories of depression' in 1977 he concentrated, rather as I have done, on Lewinsohn's theory implicating low rates of response-contingent reinforcement, on Seligman's helplessness model, and on Beck's cognitive model. He concluded that all of the elements suggested by any one of the three theories (rate of reinforcement, control and perception) are equally implicated in the other two. I have in addition presented Rehm's self-control model as an example of a theory which explicitly links all three variables. The inability to distinguish between the three models need not alarm, since, to some extent, the models use different universes of discourse to describe the same phenomena. Thus Lewinsohn's behaviourally defined insufficiency of reinforcement may lead individuals to believe they are helpless, and be defined by Beck in terms of a cognitive distortion. One's theoretical perspective depends how you choose to look at the evidence rather than on the basic evidence itself. In reviewing the outcome studies in the next chapter it will rarely be possible to distinguish the theoretical perspective on which the study is based.

Distinguishing the models has a major heuristic function however. Separately they can generate and test hypotheses which are more specific than would be possible if all were compared together. In a condition such as depression which is so complex a syndrome, this is no mean feat.

Notice how predominant the theme of *loss* is in every formulation of depression. The loss may be actual or perceived, but seems an almost universal phenomenon. This is consistent also with psychodynamic formulations of depression. There is a general finding of a large discrepancy between the real and ideal self, both because of raising the level of aspiration and lowering the estimate of actual achievement. Since many of these ideas predated the recent flourishing of experimental work in this area, is the experimental approach worth the energy spent on it? I believe the experimental approach indeed can produce novel insights some of which may seem obvious once pointed out, but nevertheless advance our ideas about the clinical syndrome. Let me give just one example. Golin *et al.* (1980) examined the generality of pessimism in mildly depressed (BDI greater than 10) versus nondepressed (BDI less than 6) subjects. All subjects were given ten anagrams, the first six of which were standard, but the last four of which were either difficult, guaranteeing failure or easy, guaranteeing success. Subjects were randomly allocated not only to the failure or success condition, but also to whether they were to receive a free cinema ticket on the basis of their performance on *this* task or whether they were to get a second chance. The dependent variable was how upset subjects became in reaction to the task (Multiple Affective Adjective Check List (MAACL), assessed just after the last anagram). Results showed an expected main effect for whether subjects succeeded or failed, but also an interaction between depression level and whether they were to get only one, or two chances. The depressed subjects were more upset than nondepressed if they failed when they thought they were to get only the one chance, but their mood was equivalent to the low level of the nondepressed subjects if they thought a second chance was available. The authors suggested that these mildly depressed subjects were not characterised by a 'general' pessimism. Rather (and this is the point which might not have been intuited prior to the results) the depressed subjects 'were prone to believe that the important goals they pursue must be attained by means of a single effort and that absence of reward associated with a single failure may be permanent and irreversible'. Of course only a mild manipulation in this analogue experiment − giving a second chance − was required to modify this expectation, but the

authors note how much of the self-talk in clinical depressives is characterised by such phrases as 'the game is over', 'I don't have a second
chance', 'life has passed me by', 'it's too late to do anything about it'
(Beck, 1976, p. 118). This dichotomous 'now or never' thinking fits
with Beck's cognitive formulations very well. The Golin *et al.* study is
a good example of how clinical and analogue research may converge
onto a single phenomenon by different routes, each complementing the
analysis of the other, but neither would have been helpful if research
had remained at the purely descriptive level. The next chapter will overview some of the research which has applied these concepts in actual
clinical treatment.

# 2 PSYCHOLOGICAL TREATMENT OF DEPRESSION

Although theories about the aetiology, precipitation and maintenance of depression differ from each other (Chapter 1), the treatment techniques predicted to be effective by the various models tend to converge. That is not to say that there are only a few methods used. On the contrary, I shall list over 20 techniques which have been applied, usually grouped in some multifaceted procedure, to clinically depressed patients. But each of these techniques could be argued to be effecting a subsystem of several of the psychological models outlined in Chapter 1. In this chapter I should like to overview these procedures and the evidence for their effectiveness. In addition, I wish to discuss three other issues. First, the supposed commonality in procedures and in the factors mediating recovery. Second, the evidence for whether there exist any indications and contraindications for the use of cognitive-behaviour therapy with depressed patients, or any evidence on which technique to use with which patient. Finally, the relationship of cognitive-behaviour therapy to pharmacotherapy will be discussed.

Whitehead (1979) outlines four general, though distinct, rationales from which cognitive-behavioural strategies may be derived:

(1)    That the depressive behaviour *per se* constitutes the disorder and can be modified by suitable manipulation of reinforcers;

(2)    That depressive behaviour is a result of (or is maintained by) a reduced rate of positive reinforcement and that this reinforcement should be reinstated by a suitable manipulation;

(3)    That the depressed individual fails to respond because he believes himself to lack any control over his environment. Treatment should be directed towards demonstrating his capability for such control;

(4)    That depression results from the person's negative view of himself and his circumstances and treatment is directed towards correcting this misconception.

Table 2.1 lists some clinical techniques used by cognitive-behaviour therapists, and corresponding rationales. Of course, there may be a difference between the supposed rationale and the actual therapeutic component of these techniques, but that is an issue which can be left until after the outcome research has been reviewed.

Table 2.1: Treatment components in cognitive-behaviour therapies[*]

(1) Teaching self-monitoring of activities (2,3,4)

(2) Teaching self-monitoring of mood (2,3,4)

(3) Teaching self-monitoring of thoughts (3,4)

(4) (Graded) task assignment (2,3,4) — teaching how to set appropriate goals

(5) Teaching self-evaluation of behavioural achievement; Mastery and Pleasure techniques (2,3,4)

(6) Teaching self-reinforcement for behavioural achievement (2,3,4)

(7) Instructions in geographical control for negative thinking (2,3,4)

(8) Instructions in temporal control for negative thinking (2,3,4)

(9) Teaching thought-catching and how to identify themes in thought content (4)

(10) Teaching 'distancing' of thoughts by labelling as 'hypotheses' (4)

(11) Teaching how to evaluate evidence for 'hypotheses' (reality testing) (4)

(12) Teaching how to deal with implications of thought evaluation (3,4)

(13) Teaching how to find alternative rational responses to negative thoughts (4)

(14) Listing positive self-descriptions (3,4)

(15) Using Premack principle to increase low frequency thoughts/activities (coverant conditioning) (1,4)

(16) Contingency management (1)

(17) Social skills/assertion training exercises (modelling, rehearsal, etc.) (1,2,3,4)

(18) Reattribution training (3,4)

(19) Anticipation training (3,4)

(20) Systematic resensitisation (1,2)

(21) Relaxation and desensitisation (for anxiety component and initial insomnia) (2)

(22) 'Alternative therapy' (3,4) ('Decision Analysis')

(23) Role playing (2,3,4)

(24) Cognitive rehearsal (3,4)

(25) Stress Inoculation (2,3,4)

(26) Teaching how to set up 'reciprocal contracts' within relationships (1,2,3)

(27) Thought stopping and/or Distraction (4)

(28) Instructions to increase formerly or potentially pleasant activities (2,3,4)

[*]Note: The numbers in brackets refer to the supposed rationales outlined on p. 26

## Research on the Efficacy of Cognitive-behavioural Techniques

There have been several recent reviews of the outcome literature (Rehm and Kornblith, 1979; Weissman, 1979; Whitehead, 1979; Blaney, 1981;

Hollon, 1981). These vary in their scope, particularly in the extent to which they include one-off uncontrolled case studies, analogue studies using student volunteers, or controlled single case or group design studies. Out of some fifty studies reviewed by Rehm and Kornblith, only 36 involved in- or outpatients, and of these, only 16 used single case or group controlled designs. This sounds a small number, but considering the short history of cognitive-behaviour therapy for depression and that the first group design studies did not appear until 1973, it actually represents quite a large body of data, collected in many different locations over that first six year period (1973-9). In the review which follows, I shall consider only controlled studies which have used either clinically depressed patients or individuals who have come forward in response to advertisements offering treatment for depression. That is, I shall not consider those studies which use college students recruited for experimental purposes for course credit, etc. Second, because this book is concerned with individual therapy rather than group approaches, I shall consider only those studies using individualised treatment strategies. Third, because the reviews mentioned above are easily available for those who wish to follow up the more diverse methods, I shall confine my review to those studies mentioned by at least three of the five reviewers, together with studies which have been completed since some of these reviews were compiled. The aim in applying these constraints is to confine attention to the 'core studies' — those which most clearly represent the accepted body of opinion amongst cognitive-behaviour therapists on the efficacy of their treatment techniques. There are eleven such studies, and they are listed in Table 2.2 (see also notes 2 and 5).

Also in Table 2.2 I have attempted to list the specific techniques used by these investigators, the numbers referring back to Table 2.1. This itemising of techniques is not always easy to do since the studies vary in how detailed the description of therapeutic techniques are, but this analysis allows a gross comparison of one study with another in terms of overall number of techniques espoused. As can be seen, the number of techniques varies from 19 to 1. The techniques listed vary in how specific they are. Thus 'thought monitoring' is specific but 'social skills/assertion training' is very general and itself involves many specific techniques. Despite this, the overall picture emerges of therapeutic strategies which are enormously complex which makes it rather difficult to find out exactly what a therapist has done with any client! Nevertheless, we shall proceed on the assumption that we are evaluating 'families' of techniques which do hold together to make a a coherent strategy. I shall examine the studies in chronological order, since they overlap so much in terms of the particular combinations of behavioural and cognitive strategies used.

Table 2.2: Core studies in cognitive behavioural research

| | Study | Techniques* |
|---|---|---|
| (1) | Hersen *et al*. (1973) | Contingency management (16) |
| (2) | McLean *et al*. (1973) | Marital contracting (4,6,17,23,26) |
| (3) | Padfield (1976) | Activity scheduling (1,4,28) |
| (4) | Taylor and Marshall (1977) | Cognitive (2,3,9,10,11,12,13,14,15) Behavioural (1,4,17,22,23,28) |
| (5) | Rush *et al*. (1977) | Drugs vs. CBT (1,2,3,4,5,6,9,10,11, 12,13,17,18,22,23,24,25,27,28) |
| (6) | McLean and Hakstian (1979) | Relaxation vs. psychotherapy vs. drugs vs. CBT (1,2,3,4,6,7,10,13,14, 16,17,24,25,27,28) |
| (7) | Zeiss *et al*. (1979) | Social skills (4,7,23) Pleasant activities (1,2,4,21,28) Cognitive (3,9,10,11,12,13,14,15,27) |
| (8) | Blackburn *et al*. (1981) | Drugs vs. CBT (see Rush *et al*.) |
| (9) | Weissman *et al*. (1981) | Drugs vs. interpersonal therapy (5,6, 16,22,23,26) |
| (10) | Rotzer *et al*. (1981) | Activity scheduling (1,2,4,17,28) vs. AS + self regulation (1,2,4,17,28 + 5,6) vs. AS + coverant control (1,2,3,17,28) + 14,15,24) |
| (11) | Kovacs *et al*. (1981) | See Rush *et al*. |

*Note: The numbers in brackets refer to the techniques listed in Table 2.1

*Hersen, Eisler, Alford and Agras (1973).* This study is a convenient place to start a review because it represents one extreme of theory about the nature of depression. This theory is that depression *is* the observable 'depressed' behaviour of the individual — increased frequency of crying, etc., and decreased frequency of constructive behaviours. Ayllon and Azrin had previously suggested that such behaviour could be modified by selective reinforcement of 'positive' behaviours incompatible with symptomatic manifestation (Ayllon and Azrin, 1968). Hersen *et al.* used an ABA design in which blue tokens (index cards) were issued noncontingently (A), contingent upon occurrence of 'positive' behaviours (B), and again noncontingently (A). During the B phase, the target behaviours reinforced related to four areas: work, occupational therapy, responsibility and personal hygiene. Patients were expected to plan each day every morning during 'banking hours' during all phases of the study. Tokens could be exchanged for privileges according to a predetermined points system.

Three neurotically depressed inpatients were included in Hersen's study. Assessment during the study consisted of the Williams *et al.* (1972) Rating Scale (see p. 69) which assesses amount of talking, smiling and activity on a time sampling basis. Results showed a marked diminution of observable depression during the contingency management phase. The impressions of the staff confirmed this result. They reported that the patients were less depressed in the B phase and more irritable in the A phases.

The significance of these results is weakened by the fact that the assessments were done by staff who, though blind to the experimental hypothesis, were not blind to the procedures used in the study, and therefore presumably knew what the investigators' intentions were. To some extent this problem is mitigated by the fact that the behaviour which was assessed was not that which was being reinforced in the study and was chosen to be as objectively assessable as possible. A more damaging criticism however is that all three were on psychotropic medication during the study. The fact that this remained unchanged for all three phases implies that the specific improvements noted could not be attributed to the drugs, however it is not known to what extent the drugs may have made the patients more amenable to the behavioural intervention. I shall discuss this question in a later section on the interaction of cognitive-behavioural therapies with pharmacological procedures.

Why does this investigation qualify as a 'core study'? Perhaps because it was one of the earliest controlled demonstrations of the potency of behavioural methods in this clinical population. One must bear in mind that until the late 1960s the predominant formulations of depression were either psychodynamic or biological. Neither of these theories would have predicted that contingency management would be effective. The fact that experimenter/therapist control was demonstrated was therefore an important result.

*McLean, Ogston and Grauer (1973).* Three theoretical approaches provided the source-material for the rationale of this study of conjoint therapy. First, Ferster's analysis of depression as a response to a 'diminished reinforcement field' (Ferster, 1966); second, Costello's analysis of depression as a loss of reinforcer effectiveness (Costello, 1972a); and third, Stuart's analysis of depression as an adaptation to maladaptive interpersonal encounters (Stuart, 1967). McLean *et al.* build upon these models, as well as work on social skill deficits in depression (e.g. Lewinsohn and Shaw, 1969) and derive a model of dysfunctional marital communication, in which 'the relationship between the patient and the spouse is characterised by a coercive communication pattern which precludes effective problem solving'. Their therapy was therefore aimed at modifying the couple's verbal interaction styles. Three categories of therapeutic strategy were used: (a) training in social learning principles; (b) immediate feedback as to the perception of verbal interactions between patient and spouse using cue boxes; and (c) training in the construction and use of reciprocal behavioural contracts. The 'cue box' was a box on which pressing one of two buttons operated red and green lights. Each box also had an electric counter for each light to record frequency of use of that button.

Couples were instructed to conduct short (20-minute) conversations at home on a topic which normally caused some friction (finance, child rearing, etc.), and to push the red or green button as follows. They were to operate the red light if they perceived the other's comments to be negative (e.g. sarcastic, indifferent). They were to operate the green light if they perceived the other's comments to be in any way positive (e.g. complimentary, constructive). The aim was to 'provide immediate feedback as to how their verbal interactions were being perceived'. The idea was that, no matter how a comment is *meant*, it is how it is *received* which would determine the other's reaction. For example, one individual genuinely felt he was being constructive when he said 'you'd feel better if you didn't weep so much'. His partner (perhaps not surprisingly) perceived it as critical. Couples were told to hold these 20-minute conversations 5 days a week for the first 4 weeks of treatment. Couples apparently found the cue boxes 'contrived but educational'. Details of reciprocal contracting methods are given in Chapter 4.[1]

Twenty couples (one member of each having been referred for treatment of a neurotic depression) were randomly allocated to this three-component treatment or to a control condition (in which case they were referred back to the referring agent and treated by routine methods which varied from antidepressant medication alone or in combination with social case work to irregular physician consultations). Experimental treatment took place in 8 weekly sessions, 1 hour per week. Detailed assessment was made of verbal interaction style before and after treatment by careful analysis of tape recording made by the couple of conversations between them. Outcome was additionally assessed by self-rating on the Depressive Adjective Check List (DACL) and by self- and spouse-rating of certain problem behaviours (social withdrawal, sleep disturbance, domestic or job incompetence impaired concentration, poor motivation, inability to make decisions, suicidal preoccupation, decreased interest in hobbies, sports, etc. and decreased sexual satisfaction).

Results showed the experimental treatment to be superior to the control treatment on all outcome measures. These improvements were maintained at follow-up 3 months later. McLean *et al.* conclude that the result justifies the assumption that depressive states are associated with a failure to control one's interpersonal environment. They suggest that the efficacy of the experimental treatment 'appears to reside in its pragmatism and the ease with which patients and their spouse can be involved in monitoring and altering daily behaviours – patients . . . responded positively to the application of feedback techniques and to the specificity involved in reciprocal behavioural contracts'.

The main problem with the study is its lack of adequate control procedures. Not only was there an unequal amount of time spent with the experimental and control groups, the control group's treatment was unsystematic and uncontrolled. Some may even have been inappropriate. Nevertheless, the investigation is justifiably included in this list of core studies since it further demonstrated the usefulness of some quite specific behavioural procedures.

As such, it was the main precursor of a major study 6 years later, based on the same principles, by McLean and Hakstian (reviewed below).

*Padfield (1976).*   This early study examined the comparative effects of behavioural and nondirective counselling on intensity of depression in 'rural women of low socioeconomic status'. Subjects for the study were recruited through physician referral and newspaper advertisement. Twelve weekly individual sessions were held in both treatments (thus controlling for therapy contact). The behavioural treatment was derived from Lewinsohn's writings, and consisted of teaching clients first to monitor then to increase the frequency of formerly or potentially pleasant activities (Chapter 4 for further details of this approach). Outcome was assessed using the Zung Self Rating Scale, Lubin DACL, Pleasant Events Schedule, and the Grinker Feelings and Concerns Checklist. Results showed superiority of the behavioural treatment on this latter measure, but not the other three.

The fact that the behavioural group was marginally superior on one measure must be set against the lack of significant difference on the Pleasant Events Schedule – the measure which purported to assess the factors which were supposed to mediate the therapy's anti-depressive effectiveness. It seems that, ironically, what little effect this specific behavioural therapy had was not mediated by an increase in frequency of pleasant activities.

*Taylor and Marshall (1977).* This study is important despite the fact it used solicited patients rather than true outpatient depressives. Forty-five subjects with BDI scores greater than 13 and whose self-reported depressed mood had lasted at least 2 weeks were recruited through advertisement. Although the mean BDI was 21.2 ('moderately severely depressed'), the possible difficulties in generalising to clinically diagnosed cases must be borne in mind. Nevertheless, the study gains its importance from its careful control, and tight specification of the treatment packages used. Subjects were randomly assigned to one of four groups: cognitive only, behavioural only, cognitive and behavioural combined, and waiting list control. The rationale for the cognitive therapy given was that 'depressed mood is rooted in self-evaluation'. Subjects were taught how to become aware of thoughts which occurred between an event and consequent affective disturbance, and instructed to use alternative self-statements to cope with such situations when they occurred. With therapist's help, a list of positive self-statements was constructed, and subjects were instructed to read through the list before engaging in a high probability behaviour ('coverant control' using the Premack principle of making a high probability behaviour contingent upon a low probability behaviour). The rationale for the behavioural treatment was that 'depression results from insufficient positive reinforcement'. Subjects were given help in identifying situations which produced depressed mood, and in learning new alternative patterns of behaviour. Role play, modelling and homework assignments to rehearse new techniques were used, often with the aim of promoting more assertive, socially skilled behaviour. The combined treatment would have made it impossible to spend more than half the time (on average) on each component. Despite this, the results of the six 40-minute sessions over 4 weeks showed a clear superiority for the combined treatment over each one alone, which in turn were superior to no treatment (assessed by BDI, MMPI (D) and visual analogue mood scales). The trend of these results was still clearly visible on follow-up assessment 5 weeks later.

This study is important because it was the first to address directly the issue of which elements in a cognitive-behavioural package are responsible for therapeutic progress. Padfield's earlier study had suggested that behavioural treatment by itself was not very powerful, and that even the gains that were noted were not due to changes in the supposed mediating variable (pleasant activities). The finding that integrating behavioural into a cognitive context (and *vice versa*) works better than spending the full time engaging in one or the other model has direct therapeutic implications if work with depressed patients bears it out. Surprisingly, there has been little work of this kind done using a clinical sample.[2] The nearest is that of Rotzer *et al*. (1981) which will be reviewed later on. Without going into detail, it is relevant at this stage to point out that Rotzer *et al's* findings are consistent with Taylor and Marshall's conclusion.

*Rush, Beck, Kovacs and Hollon (1977)*. During the 1970s the interest in cognitive-behaviour therapy grew very fast. Yet there was no satisfactory comprehensive outcome study to confirm what seemed to have been evident from single case work for some time. As late as 1976, McLean, in reviewing the evidence for the cognitive theory of depression wrote 'Currently there are several factors which limit the clinical utility of this model. . .' of which the first was '. . .controlled clinical research is necessary to establish clinical efficacy. At the moment only several case studies are available'. The study by Rush *et al*. was a breakthrough then, not only for the practice, but also the theory of depression on which it was based. Despite criticisms that have been made of it, which I will mention later, it was possibly one of the most important contributions to clinical practice of that decade. The study itself was quite simple. Forty-one outpatients with a clear and unmixed diagnosis of depression, and scores of 17+ on the BDI and 14+ on the Hamilton Rating Scale, were randomly allocated to 12 weeks of either cognitive-behaviour therapy (up to 20 sessions – the mean number of sessions was 15, over an average of 11 weeks) or imipramine pharmacotherapy (up to 250 mg per day) and weekly supportive visits of 20 minutes each. Assessment was made by BDI, MMPI, Hamilton and the Raskin Rating Scale.

The results showed that both groups improved, but cognitive-behaviour therapy produced greater improvement than drugs. At the end of the twelve weeks therapy, the mean of the CBT group was within 1 s.d. of the mean for a nondepressed normative group and within 2 s.d. of the equivalent value for the MMPI (D scale). The mean of the drug group remained several s.d. above the nondepressed mean level on both assessments. Perhaps more significant clinically was the differential drop-out rates for the two groups — 32 per cent for pharmacotherapy and only 5 per cent for the CBT. Most of these drop-outs occurred in weeks 1-4 of the respective therapies. Retrospective analysis showed that those who dropped out were not distinguishable on demographic characteristics, history of illness factors, or pretreatment severity on clinical or self-rating scales.

Three main problems with the study have been raised. First, the drug group did not have equivalent therapist contact, so perhaps the effects were attributable to the additional support available in the CBT group. This complaint is reminiscent of that against McLean *et al's* (1973) control group, however they are not comparable. McLean's control group received a range of nonspecific treatments unsystematically, but by contrast, Rush *et al's* control involved regular contact, systematic treatment with a plausible rationale. Second, the drug dosage was not as high as some pharmacotherapists might have set it, thus favouring the CBT group treatment. Furthermore, the design of the study necessitated drug withdrawal beginning at week 10 so that patients were drug-free at final assessment. It has been argued that a psychopharmacotherapist would normally keep patients on a maintenance dose of tricyclics. On the grounds, then, of dosage level and method of drug examination, the suggestion has been made that Rush *et al's* drug therapy was suboptimal. The response to these criticisms is as simple as it is obvious. There is no reason to suppose that the cognitive-behaviour therapy was not also suboptimal both in its method of delivery, and its termination at 12 weeks. Many behavioural psychotherapists would argue that 'maintenance' or 'tailing off' sessions are necessary in any psychological therapy to prevent quick relapse. (Actually, only one of the drop-outs in the drug group occurred between weeks 10 and 12 of the trial, suggesting that it was not as upsetting as might be supposed.) In any event, the suboptimality argument fails because it applies equally to both treatments. Furthermore, no patient was admitted to the trial if they had a history of nonresponse to pharmacotherapy, with no such constraint applied to patients with a history of psychotherapy 'failure'. Thus any bias in the sample would have favoured the drug regime's effectiveness. In the light of these considerations, Rush *et al's* results are all the more surprising, and important.

*McLean and Hakstian (1979)* studied the effectiveness of three active treatments: behaviour therapy (which actually included some cognitive components – see Table 2.2); short-term psychotherapy and pharmacological therapy (amitriptyline, 150 mg/day). A plausible control treatment – relaxation training – was also used. Clients who were married or living as married encouraged their partners to attend to 'work together on the programme'. All treatments involved 10 weekly outpatient visits (minimum of 8 and maximum of 12 visits). Therapists had pretraining to maximise agreement about treatment procedures, as well as regular peer-monitoring sessions throughout the investigation. In addition, all sessions were audiotaped and sampled to monitor the use of techniques. The therapists in the *psychotherapy treatment* were using their preferred methods of therapeutic practice, and focused on the restoration of pre-episode level of functioning through the 'development of insight into the psychodynamic forces that initiated the current depression, and through the recognition of personality problems'. The *cognitive-behaviour therapy* was based on the rationale that 'depression is the result of ineffective coping techniques used to remedy situational life problems'. Patients were discouraged from ruminating upon negative experiences and encouraged to interact more with their environment. Therapy components included hierarchies of treatment goals, activity monitoring, and contingency plans for coping with stress. The *drug therapy* group were on medication throughout the trial and attended four weekly visits for a 'physiological review' of 15 minutes each. Blood samples were drawn on two occasions (randomly specified) within the 11 week period. Blood serum levels were checked to monitor compliance with self-medication as prescribed. Patients in *relaxation therapy* were given a rationale of depression as tension-induced. Clients received ten 1 hour sessions of training together with homework assignments for relaxation practice and log-sheets to monitor relaxation effectiveness.

The study used 178 outpatient depressives between the ages of 20 and 60 years. Their depression had to be of at least 2 months duration prior to the study. Patients also had to be of sufficient severity to be functionally impaired (unable to work, socially withdrawn, suicidally preoccupied), and to be diagnosable as 'primary depressives' on Feighner *et al's* (1972) criteria. The minimum Beck Depression Score was 23. Thus this large study took as subjects a group of patients whose neurotic depression was really quite severe. The controls against which cognitive-behaviour therapy was compared were excellent which adds to the robustness of the study. But what makes the study even more interesting is the comprehensiveness of its assessment procedures. These are detailed in Table 2.3. As can be seen, in addition to socio-demographic, life events and personality variables a large number of self-descriptive scales covered a large range of issues.

Table 2.3: List of variables assessed in McLean and Hakstian (1979)

| Cognitive | Social |
|---|---|
| Memory | Arranging activity with others |
| Decision-making ability | Time/day with friends |
| Negative thoughts | Had friends over |
| | Went out with friends |
| *Coping* | Phoned a friend |
| Coping ability | Verbally praised someone |
| No. productive hours | People spoken to (excluding work) |
| No. wasted hours | |
| Procrastination | *Somatic* |
| | Hours of sleep |
| *Personal activity* | Fatigue rating |
| Working on hobby | Relaxation rating |
| Writing letters | |
| Watching TV | *Mood* |
| Doing paperwork | DACL |
| Home or car improvement | Laughing out loud |
| | Crying |
| Beck Depression Inventory | |
| Depression history (since age 16) | *Average Satisfaction* |
| Depression history (this episode) | Satisfaction with job |
| Employment status | Satisfaction with housekeeping abilities |
| No. life events | Marital satisfaction |
| EPQ — Neuroticism | Average complaint rating |
| — Extraversion | Average goal attainment |
| Age | Negative thoughts re self |
| | Sex |

Ten categories are derived: cognitive, coping, personal activity, social, BDI, satisfaction, somatic indicators, mood, average goal attainment, and average complaint rating. In addition to their usefulness as outcome variables, some of these derived categories (pretreatment scores) could be combined with the demographic variables for cluster analysis. The results of this analysis will be mentioned later in connection with the question of 'what works best for whom?' Meanwhile, the main results on the efficacy of the treatment procedures can be reported. The first thing to note is that all groups improved markedly from pre- to post-treatment. It is impossible to say to what extent this was due to the efficacy of the individual treatments since depression tends to remit spontaneously after 6-9 months, and the inclusion of criteria of at least 2 months duration implies that some individuals would be tending to recover anyway towards the end of a 10/12 week therapy programme. Superimposed on this general improvement was a clear-cut tendency for behaviour therapy to be superior to the other three treatments. On the BDI, complaints, goals, social adjustment, average satisfaction and mood, behaviour therapy was superior to psychotherapy, and on all but BDI and social adjustment, was superior to relaxation and drug therapy as well. On six of the 10 measures, psychotherapy scored most poorly. Pharmacological therapy did no better nor worse than the relaxation control treatment. This pattern of results was maintained at follow-up 3 months later. Although the scale of the differences was diminished, the behaviour therapy group was still superior to the others on seven out of ten outcome variables, and significantly so on social adjustment. On the mood variable, both behaviour therapy and drugs were superior to psychotherapy with relaxation differing from neither. Interestingly, the drop-out rate differed markedly for the different treatments, average 5 per cent for cognitive-behaviour therapy, with the other three varying between 26 and 36 per cent.

The results showing unequivocal superiority of cognitive-behaviour therapy in this study gain a great deal of robustness from the careful way in which the study is constructed. Hollon's (1981) review applauds this aspect, but comments that the low dosage of drug used makes it difficult to draw firm conclusions. In fact, Hollon's conclusion is based on false evidence. He says (p. 55) that McLean and Hakstian used 125 mg/day of imipramine, whereas in fact they used 150 mg/day of amitriptyline. The first would have been an inadequate dose, the second is not. It is a pity that Hollon not only made the initial factual error but then chose to comment upon it. (It is the only mistake in an otherwise excellent and thoughtful review.)

McLean and Hakstian's study is useful not only because of the care taken to ensure that the drug group really was taking the medication, but also because they included the psychological treatment groups to compare with the cognitive-behaviour therapy group. These other treatments were forcefully presented with a plausible rationale and one (relaxation) also involved homework assignments. Yet they did not produce as much improvement as the CBT. Thus these authors can not be accused of producing results which can easily be explained in terms of therapist attention and other nonspecific effects. Of course, some nonspecific treatment effects are inevitable, perhaps reflected in the fact that even the relaxation group improved to some extent. But they cannot provide the complete answer and thus this study makes an important point about the validity of the claims of cognitive-behaviour therapists to have collected together a set of techniques with active and incisive therapeutic potential.

*Zeiss, Lewinsohn and Munoz (1979)*. These investigators used recruited subjects for an interesting study which combined research on outcome with a study of process. Media advertisement of 'therapy for depression as part of a research project' elicited replies from a large range of individuals, of whom 44 (aged 19-68 years, mean 34) were admitted to the project on the basis of an MMPI(D) score greater than 80 and a structured interview. Subjects were allocated to one of four groups: cognitive therapy, interpersonal skills training, pleasant activity scheduling, or waiting list. In addition to using MMPI(D) scores as a general outcome measure, seven hours of comprehensive assessment procedures were implemented every month (four occasions in all) to assess the specific subcomponents purported to mediate the efficacy of the various therapies. Thus three ratings (including one observer rating) of interpersonal behaviour were taken; four ratings (including an observer rating) of cognitive style were taken; and the Pleasant Events Schedule was used to assess frequency and subjective pleasantness of activities performed. Results showed no differences between the three active therapy groups, though they all produced more improvement than the waiting list controls. More significantly, however, all assessments improved equally in the three different types of treatments. It was not the case that each therapy had its effect by modifying the particular mediating variable purported to underlie its particular set of therapeutic strategies. Rather, the authors suggest 'the label of therapy does not ensure that the behaviours labelled will be those most directly affected', and conclude that psychological treatment may be producing 'nonspecific' improvement no matter what treatment model is being tested.

There is little doubt that nonspecific treatment effects are present in studies of the effects of cognitive-behaviour therapy but does this study constitute strong evidence for their involvement? I think not. Even accepting that the results may be generalised to clinically depressed individuals whose motivation is not perhaps as consistently positive as these recruited volunteers, there is evidence that none of the individual procedures used in the study are by themselves, very effective treatments (e.g. Taylor and Marshall, 1977; Rotzer *et al.* 1981). Under such conditions, a floor effect of noticeable though minimal therapeutic improvement might be expected which would not differentiate the treatments. However, it is not the outcome data which are damaging to those who wish to claim specificity for their treatments, but the process data. The lack of discriminable difference between treatments in the processes they affected seems conclusive; however the assessments of these variables were only made once a month, hardly frequent enough to justify such a general conclusion. The time scale over which cognitive changes, if present, would be expected to affect mood and behaviour would be hours and days, rather than days and weeks, and this could be said to be true of the effect of interpersonal skills training and activity scheduling on the other process variables. This makes the once-a-month monitoring seem very inadequate. Admittedly, the seven hours of assessment used each month in the study could not realistically have been programmed each day or even each week, but investigators might in future content themselves with less assessment of each variable at any one time, with more frequent assessments being scheduled. Furthermore, it is naive to expect that wholesale changes in one variable will occur prior to wholesale changes in the next. It is more likely that change will be interactive, with small changes in one variable predicting small changes in the next, and so on. There is a danger that we will find such a complex sequence of interactions impossible to map. This may be so, although the more experimentally based tasks outlined in Chapter 9 may help. In any event, we are a long way from having done sufficient process research to justify giving up yet. Zeiss *et al's* study represents a first step on that road, but it is not the last.

*Blackburn, Bishop, Glen, Whalley and Christie (1981).* It may not have escaped the notice of readers that virtually all of the outcome studies on the efficacy of cognitive-behavioural methods have been from North America. For some time, there was the suspicion that crosscultural differences between continents would make generalisation to Europe difficult. Furthermore, cognitive therapy in particular had been subject to criticism on the grounds that, as a 'logical' therapy, it would not be suitable for the less-verbally intelligent, less psychologically-minded patient. Blackburn *et al's* (1981) study was therefore very significant. First, it was the first outcome study to use a British population, and second, many of the sample were from a down-town end of the city.

Sixty-four primary major depressives[3] (Research Diagnostic Criteria, Spitzer *et al.*, 1978), all of whom had a BDI score of 14 or more, were randomly allocated to receive maximum 20 weeks of cognitive-behaviour therapy, pharmacotherapy (mainly amitriptyline and clomipramine up to 150 mg/day, but at the doctor's discretion) or a combination of CBT and drugs. Assessment was made using the BDI, HRS(D), Snaith's IDA (Irritability, Depression and Anxiety) Scale (Snaith *et al.*, 1978). Twenty-four of the sample were patients attending their family doctor, and forty were hospital outpatients. The hospital sample had significantly more education, a higher socioeconomic level, longer duration of illness, greater number of previous episodes, a higher total psychopathology score on the Present State Examination (Wing *et al.*, 1974), and were less outwardly irritable than the General Practitioner sample. (Where necessary these variables were partialled out for analysis of the main effects of therapy.) Importantly, there were no differences between hospital and GP samples in age, sex ratio, initial severity of depression (BDI, HRS(D), presence of suicidal ideas and attempts (PSE: Item 24) or presence of endogenous features in the psychopathology.

Results showed that the GP sample required less of the combination treatment (approximately twelve sessions) than the hospital sample (approximately seventeen sessions). For the outcome results, Snaith's scale showed few overall changes, but the BDI and HRS(D) both revealed clear-cut effects. In the hospital sample, the combination of drugs and CBT produced greater proportionate changes in BDI and HRS(D) than either CBT or drugs alone, which did not differ significantly from each other except on Anxiety where CBT produced more improvement than drugs. In the GP sample, on the other hand, the combination treatment and the CBT alone were both equally effective and considerably better than drugs alone. Both samples contained a large proportion of endogenomorphic as well as nonendogenomorphic patients (for the total sample, 27 and 37 respectively). Analysis of outcome as a function of endogenomorphicity revealed no differences in response for any of the three treatments.

Commenting on the difference btCCween this result, and that of Rush *et al.* (1977) who found CBT to be superior to drugs in mood and attrition rate, Blackburn points out that in their study, the drug regimen was tailored to the individual patient, thus presumably enhancing effectiveness. Patients were also still on drugs when assessed at the end of treatment, unlike those of Rush *et al.* Blackburn *et al.* do not consider another plausible alternative, that Rush *et al's* outpatient population may have been more comparable to Blackburn's GP sample, in whom the results were very similar. On the other hand, the important characteristic of Blackburn's GP sample was that it was drawn from a family practice serving a population of 6633 in a largely working-class area of a large city. That drugs are ineffective for a group of people who may have major social problems is hardly surprising, but for many it will be no less surprising that individualised cognitive-behaviour therapy works so well in this context. Perhaps the emphasis in CBT on not minimising real problems is an important component of its success.

*Weissman, Klerman, Prusoff, Sholomskas and Padian (1981).* Although this study did not use cognitive behaviour therapy as such, the psychotherapy (Interpersonal Psychotherapy – IPT) shares many characteristics in common with CBT (see Table 2.2) and offers a similarly structured approach in a 'here-and-now' therapy. Its premise is that the social and interpersonal *context* in which depression occurs is important to its maintenance, and consequently to its recovery. Weissman *et al.* studied its effectiveness over sixteen weekly 50-minute sessions either alone or in combination with amitriptyline (100-200 mg/day). The study also included a drugs alone group and nonscheduled treatment group (in which patients were assigned to a psychiatrist whom they were told to contact whenever they felt a need for treatment). Ninety-six patients – all nonbipolar nonpsychotic acute primary major depressives (Research Diagnostic Criteria) who scored greater than 7 on the Raskin Depression Scale – were included. Psychotherapy failures and drug nonresponders were excluded. Assessment was by Raskin, HRS(D) symptom checklists, Global Illness rating and a Social Adjustment Scale.

In the initial trial, results showed the combination treatment to be better than both alone which were equally effective as each other. There was evidence that amitriptyline mainly affected vegetative symptoms (sleep, appetite, etc.) and the IPT affected mood, apathy, suicidal ideation, work and interests, these changes occurring slightly later than vegetative changes at 4-8 weeks. There was no differential change during the 16-week trial on measures of social functioning. The 1981 study followed up 60 patients after one year and found no difference on outcome measures of general depression between the three groups. The proportions of patients evidencing various degrees of improvement are shown in Table 2.4.

Despite the lack of difference between groups on the general measures of depression, the IPT groups were superior at follow-up in social adjustment (social and leisure activities, functioning as parent, functioning as member of family unit, an interviewer's global rating of social and leisure activities, and overall adjustment). This difference is all the more interesting since this was the one assessment which did not distinguish the groups at the end of the 16-week trial. The finding is

Table 2.4: Treatment outcome one year after IPT, drugs or combination
(N = 60; no difference between treatments)

| | | |
|---|---|---|
| 28% | (17) | asymptomatic |
| 35% | (21) | depressed at first — gradual improvement |
| 15% | (9) | periods of depression and periods without symptoms (mostly well) |
| 10% | (6) | periods of depression and periods without symptoms (mostly depressed |
| 3% | (2) | gradually more depressed |
| 8% | (5) | chronically depressed |

[Total of 7 patients from above list (12%) were readmitted at 1 year's follow-up]

reminiscent of a much earlier finding by the same research group
(Weissman *et al.*, 1974). In that study of maintenance therapy (along
the same lines as IPT) differential effects of psychotherapy on social
functioning took 6-8 months to develop. The important additional
information added by the 1981 study is that improvement in social
adjustment following IPT took place whether or not the patient had
received a tricyclic in addition to the psychotherapy.

*Rotzer, Koch and Pflug (1981).* In a paper presented at the European
Conference for Psychotherapy Research in Trier (1981), these authors
reported preliminary results from an ongoing trial of cognitive-behaviour therapy. The data are worth reporting here despite the small
number of subjects that had gone through the trial at that time, because
the study was so carefully controlled. The study randomly allocated
primary unipolar depressives (with BDI scores greater than 20) to one
of 3 groups each receiving different psychological treatments. Within
each group, half were to receive additional medication, and half no
additional drugs. The three groups were: (a) *activity training*, based on
Lewinsohn's work, and including the attempted increase in activities
which were potentially or formerly rewarding, graded task assignment,
and assertion training where necessary. The two other groups included
all aspects of this activity training, but each included an additional
cognitive component: (b) *activity training plus self-regulation training*,
based on Rehm's work; training was given in self-monitoring, self-
evaluation and self-reinforcement. Daily activities and mood ratings
were noted in a diary. Patients were taught to differentiate short-
term from long-term consequences (positive and negative), and to set

realistic, attainable goals expressed in behavioural terms and subdivided. Patients were trained to evaluate each goal attainment separately and enhance self-reward in material, verbal or covert terms. Therapists reinforced only self-regulatory behaviour. (c) *Activity training plus coverant control*, in which, in addition to treatment (a), patients were taught to build up positive self-evaluation, and no attempts were made to direct therapy towards negative thoughts at all. Specific positive adjectives and abilities relevant to the patient were gathered, facilitated by the use of an adjective list of self-assertive, body image, intellectual and behavioural positive descriptors. Thus derived, the positive statements were typed on index cards and given to the patients for correction. (Note that at each stage the statements were checked so that the patient could accept them as relevant to themselves on present or previous evidence.) The statements were given to patients who were instructed to use the Premack principle of reading and thinking about these self-descriptors (low probability behaviours) before executing a high probability behaviour (drinking). The therapists used modelling, prompting, reinforcement and imaginative rehearsal to help establish the behaviour, and patients were encouraged to move from overt to covert verbalisation. Homework assignments were given of exercising the procedure at least four times a day, and patients were instructed to find a new positive statement every day and add it to the list. All treatments lasted 12 weeks.

By the time of the 1981 progress report, eighteen patients (6 female, 12 males) had gone through the trial, five in the activity training group, six in the activity plus self-regulation; and seven in the activity plus coverant control group. Dependent variables included weekly and daily mood ratings, BDI, a somatic complaints inventory, and blind rating on the HRS(D). Despite the small numbers (which precluded conclusions about drug effects) clear trends for the efficacy of the three treatment conditions emerged with patients who received activity training alone showing little or no improvement over the 12 weeks. The greatest improvement was made by the patients in the covert control and activity combination group. This improvement was also reflected in an 'activity level' outcome measure. In all, twelve dependent measures were used, and the activity training alone group improved on only one (mood) whereas the combination groups improved significantly on 10/12. Note that the emerging differences between self-regulation and covert control if sustained in the final analysis, will contradict Zeiss *et al.* (1979) reported above, who interpreted their results in terms of nonspecific treatment effects. Rotzer *et al's* preliminary conclusions are that building up positive self-statements is a feasible and effective method to improve depression, perhaps because it encompasses a wide range of behaviour and experiences, and refers to noncontingent as well as response contingent positive outcomes. If extended and replicated, these results will prove to be important.[4]

*Kovacs, Rush, Beck and Hollon (1981).* Apart from Weissman's follow-up data on their Interpersonal Therapy, there have been few controlled studies which have followed up their patients over a long period. McLean and Hakstian (1979) observed their group for 3 months, but the main study in which there has been time to follow-up and report comprehensively is that of Rush *et al.*, published as Kovacs *et al.* (1981). Thirty-five of the 46 were followed up (18 CBT and 17 drug). They found no significant difference between dependent measures at the end of one year from those taken at the end of treatment, indicating that treatment gains had been maintained. Despite this, they found considerable variability in the course of both cognitive-behavioural and drug groups' progress, and the difference between the two was not always apparent on the dependent measures. On the other hand, the comparisons always favoured the CBT cell, and reached statistical significance at some points over the year. Defining 'relapse' as a BDI score of over 16 during the year at any time, receiving further psychological treatment (plus either of these or both of these), the drug groups were found to have been twice as likely to relapse as the cognitive therapy group. It is apparent from these data that there is no evidence that any improvement brought about by cognitive-behaviour therapy is merely short-term, and that what differences there are suggest these methods of psychotherapy and behaviour change may be the treatment of choice for these patients.

## Summary of those Studies which use Beck Depression Inventory

Table 2.5 shows those of the studies which have used the BDI, thus enabling some interesting (if crude) comparison from study to study. Where absolute levels only are given, proportionate change has been computed – though Blackburn *et al.* already report their BDI data in this form. Several conclusions emerge from scrutiny of these data. Firstly cognitive-behaviour therapy is efficacious with a variety of populations of depressives – clinical and subclinical, from a fairly wide range of social class, in both the Americas and Europe at least. Secondly, the combination of drugs and CBT is sometimes more efficacious than CBT alone; CBT alone is sometimes more efficacious than drugs alone;

but drugs alone have not so far been found to be superior to CBT. Thirdly, the inclusion by at least one study (McLean and Hakstian) of two alternative psychological techniques each plausible in its theoretical basis, and with one (relaxation) involving homework assignments and the other (psychotherapy) practised by therapists for whom this approach was preferred, strongly suggests that the superiority of CBT is

Table 2.5: Studies using Beck Depression Inventory — changes with treatment

| Study | Treatment | Subjects | BDI Score | | Proportionate change |
| --- | --- | --- | --- | --- | --- |
| | | | Pre | Post | |
| Blackburn | CBT | GP patients | — | — | 0.84 |
| et al. (1981) | CBT + drug[a] | Outpatients | — | — | 0.79 |
| | CBT + drug[a] | GP patients | — | — | 0.72 |
| | Drugs[a] alone | Outpatients | — | — | 0.60 |
| | CBT | Outpatients | — | — | 0.48 |
| | Drugs[a] alone | GP patients | — | — | 0.14 |
| Rush et al. | CBT | Outpatients | 30.3 | 5.9 | 0.81 |
| (1977) | Drug[b] | Outpatients | 30.8 | 13.0 | 0.58 |
| Taylor & | CBT | Nonclinical | 20.0 | 5.6 | 0.72 |
| Marshall | Behav. T. alone | Nonclinical | 22.1 | 10.7 | 0.52 |
| (1977) | Cog. T. alone | Nonclinical | 20.0 | 10.3 | 0.49 |
| Rotzer | Behav. + CC[c] | Outpatients | 31.2 | 9.0 | 0.71 |
| et al. | Behav. + SR[d] | Outpatients | 24.3 | 13.6 | 0.44 |
| (1981) | Behav. alone | Outpatients | 24.8 | 21.4 | 0.14 |
| McLean & | CBT | Outpatients | 26.8 | 9.7 | 0.64 |
| Hakstian | Drug[e] | Outpatients | 27.2 | 14.1 | 0.48 |
| (1979) | Relaxation | Outpatients | 26.8 | 15.0 | 0.44 |
| | Psychotherapy | Outpatients | 27.0 | 16.8 | 0.38 |

a   Amitriptyline and Clomipramine
b   Imipramine
c   Coverant control
d   Self-regulation
e   Amitriptyline

not a function of nonspecifically raised efficacy expectations. Finally, the list indicates that the more techniques that are used, the greater the treatment effects. The poorest outcomes tend to result from the strategy which uses the smallest number of techniques. This suggests that the more techniques over which a therapist is allowed to range, the more likely it is that a combination will be found which is maximally suitable for the particular characteristics of their patient.

## For Whom is CBT most Suitable?

This is a very pressing question to which, at the moment, no definitive answer may be given. Several therapists have invented criteria they believe ought to apply, but these intuitions have not been empirically validated. It is possible to say that research so far has not established its usefulness with bipolar depressives, highly regressed patients, or patients with delusions or hallucinations ('psychotic'), but that is because the research has not been done, rather than because any studies have actually demonstrated its inefficacy. Endogenomorphicity or chronicity seem not to predict outcome (Kovacs *et al.*, 1981; Blackburn *et al.*, 1981). Personality characteristics seem equally irrelevant; neither McLean and Hakstian (1979) nor Kovacs *et al.* (1981) found that Eysenck's scales correlated with outcome; and Prusoff *et al.* (1980) found a diagnosis of 'depressive personality' on the Research Diagnostic Criteria did not predict response either to drugs (100-120 mg/day amitriptyline) or to Interpersonal Psychotherapy or to a combination of the two. McLean and Hakstian's study of 178 primary depressives remains the most comprehensive study of predictive variables. A large number of variables were assessed including sociodemographic variables, number of recent life events, personality (EPI), number of social contacts, cognitive depression – negative thoughts, indecisiveness, poor memory, severity of depression, episode duration, employment status, as well as measures of coping ability. Four distinct groups emerged from a cluster analysis but none did any better with any of their treatment conditions than any other.

Some analyses have been done of response to treatment in general (i.e. including both drug and CBT cells). Blackburn *et al.* (1981) analysed the characteristics of those who did not complete treatment in their study. They were found to be significantly more severely depressed (higher BDI and HRS(D)), more irritable, more negative and less educated than completers, but none of these variables differentiated drug from CBT drop-outs. By contrast, no variables at all could be found by Rush *et al.* which differentiated the patients who dropped out of their trial (demographic characteristics, history of illness factors, pretreatment clinical or self-rating depression scales) from those who completed the trial. When 12 months follow-up assessments of those who did complete treatment were made, depression severity at that time was not predicted by history of illness, sociodemographic variables or pretreatment BDI score. The only predictive variables were patient age (BDI vs. age: $r = 0.29$; $p < 0.66$) and number of previous episodes (BDI vs. no. prev. epis. $= 0.31$; $p < 0.04$). These are small correlations of little clinical significance, and in any case did not distinguish between patients who had received drugs from those who had received the CBT.

Psychologists' responses to this state of affairs have been of two types. On the one hand are those who continue to look for predictive variables so that the clinician may in future be able to make informed decisions on rational criteria. Others, such as Liberman, have scorned 'the happy day when (an) extended data base will permit conclusions about which type of treatment is best for specific diagnostic groups of patients', calling it 'fatuous and unlikely to come to pass'. This is because 'it overlooks the over-reaching importance of individual differences in depression' (Liberman, 1981, p. 231).

The solution to the problem of which techniques to use with which patient is to carefully assess the entire range of problems and to match technique to problem. If behavioural productivity is the main problem, task assignment with graded targets may be used (see pp. 104-105). Decision-making problems will lead to the use of 'decision analysis' or a 'search for alternatives' (pp. 130-133). For problem solving difficulties, cognitive rehearsal as well as alternative therapy may be used (see pp. 127-130). For cognitive self-control, thought monitoring and evaluation (p. 83) and perhaps temporal and geographical self-control of cognitions may be taught (see p. 138). Finally, if the problem is mainly communication, social interaction or assertiveness therapy will be geared to these issues (see pp. 89 and 108). This 'modular' approach depends greatly on the extensive use of reliable and valid assessment procedures. Strictly applied, it demands comprehensive assessment at many stages during treatment as well as at the outset to monitor as 'objectively' as possible the patient's progress towards successful completion of each subgoal. Less strictly, it requires that the therapist constantly keep in mind that any or all subcomponents of a problem may be present at any time during therapy from first to last session, and that the therapist be flexible in his conceptualisation of the problem so that techniques are chosen which are maximally effective.

### Interaction with Drugs

Hollon (1981) gives a good account of the possible ways in which psychological and pharmacological therapy may interact. The outcome may be as good as the most effective of the two treatments, or only as good as the least effective of the two. Alternatively the interaction may be inhibitory (the combination producing a worse outcome than either alone) or facilitatory (the combination producing a better outcome than either treatment alone). Hollon *et al.* (1979) studied treatment outcome when CBT was used alone or in combination with up to 300 mg/day of amitriptyline. Treatment lasted for twelve weeks, and allocation to treatments and exclusion criteria were the same as those used in the Rush *et al.* (1977) study. The results showed significant improvement on the BDI and HRS(D) for both groups and the degree of change was comparable to that of the CBT (alone) group and greater than that shown by the drugs alone group in Rush *et al's* study. But there was no difference between the groups showing that this drug neither potentiated nor inhibited the action of the psychological treatment. This result exactly parallels those found in Blackburn *et al's* general practitioner sample where the combination of drugs and CBT did no better than CBT alone[5]. In this case the drugs were amitriptyline or clomipramine up to 150 mg/day at the clinician's discretion. The picture was different for Blackburn's hospital outpatient group where combined CBT and drugs was more effective than CBT or drugs by themselves, which did not differ from each other. This suggests that the treatments can under some circumstances potentiate the action of each other. Further evidence of such a potentiation effect comes from the studies of Weissman and colleagues. For example, Prusoff *et al.* (1980) found combined drug (amitriptyline 100-200 mg/day) and Interpersonal Therapy superior to either alone. In fact this study is one of the few to find endogenomorphicity interacting with type of technique used. Careful subsampling of their population of 81 acute primary major depressives to find a group of endogenous nonsituational depressives (N = 20) and a group of situational nonendogenous (N = 31) revealed that psychotherapy nor drugs by themselves were particularly effective with endogenous nonsituational depressives, but that the psychotherapy was effective for the situational nonendogenous. For this latter group, combined drugs and psychotherapy added nothing to the effect of psychotherapy alone, but for the endogenous group, the combination had a marked facilitation effect, producing the best outcome of all. The message to be learned from this result seems to be: if 'situational nonendogenous' is the diagnosis, use either IPT alone *or* combined IPT and drugs; if 'endogenous nonsituational' use combined IPT and drugs. Blackburn *et al's* similar facilitation effect with outpatients using combined CBT and drugs also points towards this therapeutic practice being maximal, though no differential effect with the endogenous-nonendogenous dimension was noted. We do not know whether this discrepancy was due to differences between IPT and CBT, or whether due to the fact that Blackburn did not exclude situational depressives from her endogenous group (24 per cent (6) of Prusoff's 'endogenous' group were also 'situational' on the RDC).

In evaluating the usefulness or otherwise of drugs in relation to cognitive-behaviour therapy, it is necessary to bear in mind two factors: the possibility of drop-outs from therapy, and the possible selective effects of drugs and psychotherapy. In the first case, although Black-burn *et al.* found no differential attrition rates for their groups, both Rush *et al.* and McLean and Hakstian, working in different research centres and with different drugs, found a much larger drop-out in their 'drugs' groups. In Rush *et al's* trial, 32 per cent dropped out of the imipramine group, but only 5 per cent left the CBT group. McLean *et al.* found that 36 per cent dropped out of their amitriptyline group, but again only 5 per cent from their behaviour therapy group. In the second case, McLean and Hakstian's comprehensive assessment procedures enabled them to test the 'selective effect' hypothesis of Weissman and co-workers; that drugs affect mainly neurovegetative symptoms and psychological treatment affect mainly mood and social functioning. In fact, no selective effect was found: the CBT generalised to all dependent measures which included cognitive, behavioural and somatic components.

## Concluding Remarks

When Whitehead reviewed the outcome studies in 1979 she rightly complained about the lack of blind assessors, the generally inadequate follow-ups, and the fact that comparison procedures were usually not matched. It would be fair to say that of her complaints, the follow-up issue has now been more adequately addressed in the studies of McLean and Hakstian (1979), Kovacs *et al.* (1981) and Weissman *et al.* (1981). The nonmatching of comparison procedures has also been addressed to some extent by McLean and Hakstian's use of two additional psychological 'treatments'. But the 'blind assessor' complaint has not been addressed sufficiently. This is very surprising given the ease with which videotapes can now be made in most clinical contexts, and could be rated blindly by an independent assessor. A video of a structured interview (e.g. Hamilton) from which such blind ratings could be made would be very useful. How much does the lack of blind assessments prejudice the outcome? Firstly it will be noted from Table 2.5 that the scale of the observed differences between groups are sometimes very large, and unlikely to be due to observer bias — especially on scales with such proven clinical validity as the Beck Inventory. But secondly, the major alternative to the blind observer used in these studies is *not* a nonblind observer but the use of self-rating assessments. This increases our confidence in the results, for unless the individual patients themselves are fully aware of the nature and hypotheses of the study and of the groups with which their own ratings are being compared, then between-group differences cannot be attributed to extraneous bias in judgements. It is far-fetched to assume that in making a rating about their own state of mind, patients make a judgement about the efficacy of the treatment they received relative to that of the (usually unknown) partners in the research trial. Of course there is a problem with self-ratings as with all ratings: the problem of a treatment being geared to a specific target area, and then only that target area being assessed. However the studies here reviewed have frequently used a great many assessments, often including general assessments such as the Hamilton, so the 'non-generalisable' criticism can no longer be levelled against this body of research.

Reviewing the evidence since Whitehead's review, then, and taking account of the advances which have been made in methodology as well as those that have not, it is interesting to be able still to concur with her conclusion (p. 505):

'there appears adequate evidence that depression can respond to psychological intervention; that the extent of this response depends upon the nature of the intervention; and that the most successful therapies are those that involve behavioural manipulation together with consideration of relevant covert processes.'

## Notes

1. Note that the cue-box was only used for first 4 weeks of the experimental treatment after which couples continued to have daily 20 minute conversations to maintain sensitisation to their maladaptive interactive styles and attempt to modify them.
2. A very similar study by Wilson *et al* (1983) used volunteer patients in an 8-week trial comparing behavioural, cognitive and no treatment. They also found no difference between the two active treatments, though both were better than no treatment. They did not employ a 'combination' group, however.

3. Extremely retarded and bipolar patients excluded, as were patients showing delusions and/or hallucinations.

4. Rotzer (personal communication, 1983) has found that initial differences between the groups, reported in 1981, have not been sustained in the larger sample. All groups have improved equally. Further analysis of the data will be needed to reveal whether the psychological treatments differentially interacted with drug treatment.

5. Wilson (1982) has recently also found that amitriptyline (150 mg per day) added nothing to the effect of behavioural therapy, but the use of volunteer depressed subjects makes generalisation to clinical samples difficult.

# 3 THE ASSESSMENT OF DEPRESSION: SOME REPRESENTATIVE PROCEDURES

This section of the book aims to give details of enough aspects of assessment to allow the practitioner to make a comprehensive evaluation of various aspects of the patient's problems. After a brief general introduction, representative scales which include assessment of somatic, behavioural and cognitive variables are individually introduced and printed in full. There are already in the literature, comprehensive reviews of assessment procedures (Kendall and Korgeski, 1979; Rehm, 1981). Because these are easily available, I have not attempted to repeat their work in this section. Rather, it seemed more useful to supply a representative sample of actual tests, chosen to be as comprehensive as possible, covering observational, interview and self-rating methods across the range of somatic, behavioural and cognitive variables. For the behavioural and cognitive components, techniques to assess both general and specific aspects are included.

The extent to which the practitioner wants to make use of this material will depend on whether (s)he is only interested in assessment which will guide treatment strategies and tactics, observing predominant problems and correlations between variables, or whether the interest is mainly in evaluating treatment efficacy by examining general severity before, during and after therapeutic intervention. Two additional and less explicit purposes in assessment may be borne in mind. The first is that a thorough assessment, especially in the context of a structured interview, may communicate hope to the patient that their symptoms are frequent and understandable correlates of the emotional disorder, and that they are not 'dumb', 'lazy' or 'mad', but show discrete behaviours at specific times, at certain frequencies and at certain intensities. The second implicit aim follows from the first: that because assessment techniques can help to objectify and distance some aspects of the problem for the patient, they may be used at any point in therapy as a therapeutic technique, and not just at the predetermined beginning, middle and end of therapy. For example, if the patient reports having had a bad week, detailed assessment of all aspects of the past few days may sometimes be an appropriate strategy, communicating to the patient that the reality of his or her problems is being taken seriously.

Most writers on depression emphasise the triad of somatic, behavioural and cognitive disturbances which are involved in the disorder. McLean (1976) suggests that there is a regularly observed sequence in the onset of depression, with negative and pessimistic thoughts occurring first accompanied by low mood. With increasing severity, these thoughts and feelings generalise to affect behaviour. If the depression becomes even more severe, then neuro-vegetative systems are affected as well.

Evidence supporting this suggestion comes not only from observation at the stage of onset of depression, but also at the stage of remission, where, according to many clinicians, the exact reverse order can be seen — appetite and sleep improving first, behaviour second, and thoughts and feelings last (Weissman *et al.*, 1979). Other evidence of the significance of somatic symptoms as an index of severity comes from the use of different types of depression. Scales which assess somatic aspects of depression (e.g. Hamilton) discriminate better between severely and moderately severely depressed patients (inpatient vs. outpatient depressives) than a self-rating scale (e.g. Zung) which places less emphasis on somatic items (Carroll *et al.*, 1973).

This, then, is the context in which the scales below are reproduced. I am grateful to Professor Max Hamilton, Professor Aaron T. Beck, Dr Ivy Blackburn and Ian Wilkinson for permission to reproduce their scales.

## The Assessment of General Severity, Including Somatic Aspects

### *The Hamilton Rating Scale[1] (1967)*

This is an observer scale in which all known observations about the patient's current mental state are taken into account. These observations can also, however, be supplemented by a clinical interview, and some standard questions for this interview are reproduced below.

The scale includes assessment of cognitive and behavioural components of depression, but is especially thorough in assessing the somatic aspects. Its inter-rater reliability is 0.84 to 0.90, and it has consistently correlated highly with other widely used observer and self-rated scales of depression. (See Rehm (1981) for a more detailed discussion of its psychometric properties.)

Note (a) that the scale cannot be used to establish a diagnosis of depression. The scale is designed to assess severity in patients already diagnosed as having the disorder; and (b) that items are individually scored by a rater during an interview, but that the total score ranges

0-100, representing the sum of two raters' scores or double the score for one rater. Some studies, however, report total scores with 50 as a maximum.

**Hamilton Scale: Assessment of Depression: Summary Sheet**

| Item No. | Score range | Symptom | Score |
|---|---|---|---|
| 1 | 0-4 | Depressed Mood | |
| 2 | 0-4 | Guilt | |
| 3 | 0-4 | Suicide | |
| 4 | 0-2 | Insomnia: initial | |
| 5 | 0-2 | Insomnia: middle | |
| 6 | 0-2 | Insomnia: delayed | |
| 7 | 0-4 | Work and interests | |
| 8 | 0-4 | Retardation | |
| 9 | 0-2 | Agitation | |
| 10 | 0-4 | Anxiety: psychic | |
| 11 | 0-4 | Anxiety: somatic | |
| 12 | 0-2 | Somatic symptoms: gastrointestinal | |
| 13 | 0-2 | Somatic symptoms: general | |
| 14 | 0-2 | Genital symptoms | |
| 15 | 0-4 | Hypochondriasis | |
| 16 | 0-2 | Loss of insight | |
| 17 | 0-2 | Loss of weight | |

Grading

| | |
|---|---|
| 0 | Absent |
| 1 | Mild or trivial |
| 2 3 | Moderate |
| 4 | Severe |
| 0 | Absent |
| 1 | Slight or doubtful |
| 2 | Clearly present |

**(1) Depression (0-4)**

Depressed mood is not easy to assess. One looks for a gloomy attitude, pessimism about the future, feelings of hopelessness and a tendency to weep. As a rule, milder depressive mood is relieved, at least in part, by company or external stimulation. When patients are severely depressed they may 'go beyond weeping'. It is important to remember that patients may interpret the word 'depression' in all sorts of strange ways. A useful common phrase is 'lowering of spirits'.

It is generally believed that women weep more readily than men, but there is little evidence that this is true in the case of depressive illness.

There is no reason to believe, at the moment, that an assessment of the frequency of weeping could be misleading when rating the intensity of depression in women.

> *'Now, I would like to ask you about the way you have been feeling during the last month. Do you keep reasonably cheerful, or have you felt depressed or low spirited recently? How would you describe it? Moody? Downhearted? Dejected? Sad? How often? Does it come and go? Does it get better if you are with someone else? How long does it last? Have you wanted to cry? Does crying relieve it? Do you feel beyond tears? So bad it is excruciating or very painful?'*

0 = *Absent* or very mild or occasional feelings no worse than the patient's normal feelings when well.

1 = *Mild*. Persistent feelings described as moody, downhearted, dejected, or similar ways; more intense, occasional feelings; may be relieved by company, being at work.

2 = *Moderate*. Persistent or frequent feelings of depression, blueness etc.; often feels like crying, may cry occasionally; not easily relieved by company.

3 = *Marked*. More intense feelings; may be frequent tears; more consistent throughout the waking day.

4 = *Severe*. Persistent severe feelings; may be described as usually beyond tears, painful, little relief *or* extremely severe; excruciating, agonising, persistent, unrelieved feelings.

## (2) Guilt (0-4)

This is fairly easy to assess but judgement is needed, for the rating is concerned with pathological guilt. From the patient's point of view, some action of his which precipitated a crisis may appear as a 'rational' basis for self-blame, which persists even after recovery from his illness. For example, he may have accepted a promotion, but the increased responsibility precipitated his breakdown. When he 'blames' himself for this, he is ascribing a cause and not necessarily expressing pathological guilt.

> *'Have you had a low impression of yourself? Have you blamed yourself for things you have done in the past or recently? Have you felt guilty about things? Have you felt you have let your friends and family down? Have you felt you are to blame for your illness? In what way? A little? A lot? Is your condition a punishment?'*

0 = *Absent* or very mild feelings of self-blame on borderline of normality.

1 = *Mild*. Lowered opinion of self with persisting feelings of regret

about past actions which in themselves are not markedly unusual.

2 = *Moderate.* More intense or pervasive feelings of guilt or self-blame which are pathological in the rater's judgement.

3 = *Severe.* Pervasive feelings of self-blame, guilt, or worthlessness regarding many areas of patient's existence. This often leads to a feeling that the illness is a punishment for past misdeeds.

4 = *Delusions of guilt.* Incorrigible beliefs of pathological guilt, with or without hallucinations of voices emphasising guilt.

## (3) Suicide (0-4)

This symptom covers a range of feeling, from life not being worth living to active suicidal behaviour. Note that assessment of intent is nigh impossible, especially afterwards when overlaid by rationalisation. Judgement must be used when the patient is considered to be concealing this symptom, or conversely when he is using suicidal threats as a weapon, to intimidate others, obtain help and so on.

*'Have you felt that life was not worth living? Have you wished you were dead? Have you had any thoughts of taking your life? Have you gone so far as to make any plans to do so? Have you actually made an attempt on your life?'*

0 = *Absent.*

1 = Has felt life not worth living – a persistent thought, which recurs.

2 = Has wished he were out of it, dead, but no suicidal thoughts.

3 = Has thoughts of taking his own life, which may include working out a plan, or has rehearsed plan (e.g. standing on a bridge, holding tablets in hand) or has made minor gesture, e.g. cut on wrists, taken up to 2 tablets.

4 = Suicidal attempt of any but the most minor kind.

## *Insomnia*

Both severity and frequency should be taken into account. Middle insomnia (disturbed sleep during the night) is the most difficult to assess, possibly because it is an artifact of the system of rating. When insomnia is severe, it generally affects all phases. Delayed insomnia (early morning wakening) tends not to be relieved by hypnotic drugs and is often present without other forms of insomnia. If insomnia is not present every night, rate as present if it occurs at least every third night.

*'Have you been taking sleeping pills? Have you had any difficulty sleeping or getting off to sleep? When you do get to sleep do you sleep well? Are you restless, or do you keep waking?'*

(4) Early insomnia (0-2)

0 = *Absent*, or occasional delay in falling asleep, no more than normally experienced.

1 = *Mild*. Delay of half to 1 hour in falling asleep. Recognised to be a change from normal by patient.

2 = *Severe*. Delay of 1-2 hours in falling asleep.

(5) Middle insomnia (0-2)

0 = *Absent* or habitual nocturnal waking to void bladder.

1 = Wakes once or twice during the night but falls asleep again without undue delay.

2 = Wakes frequently, or wakes occasionally but has difficulty falling asleep again.

(6) Delayed insomnia (0-2)

0 = *Absent*. Sleeps with usual time for waking.

1 = *Mild*. Regularly wakes half to 1 hour before usual time.

2 = *Severe*. Awake more than 1 hour before usual time.

(7) Work and Interests (0-4)

It could be argued that the patient's loss of interest in his work and activities should be rated separately from his decreased performance, but it has been found to be difficult to do so in practice. Care should be taken not to include fatigability and lack of energy here; the rating is concerned with loss of efficiency and the extra effort required to do anything. When the patient has to be admitted to hospital because his symptoms render him unable to carry on, this should be rated 4 points, but not if he has been admitted for investigation or observation. When the patient improves he will eventually return to work, but when he does so may depend on the nature of his work; judgement must be used here.

The work of many women who are housewives can be varied, both in quantity and intensity. Women may not complain of work being an effort, but they may say they have to take things easily, or that they neglect some of their work. Other members of the family may have to increase the help they give. It is rare for a housewife to stop looking after her home completely. If she has an additional job outside the home she may have to change it to part-time or reduce her hours of work or even give it up completely. For people who do not engage in hobbies frequently, loss of interest may not be as obvious. Patients may complain of inability to feel affection for their families. This could be rated here, but it could be rated under other symptoms, depending upon its meaning and setting. Care should be taken not to rate it in two places. It is a very valuable and important symptom if the patient mentions it spontaneously but could be very misleading as a reply to a question.

*'Have you been affected at all in your capacity to do your work and other activities? What have you actually been doing in work, housework, hobbies, and interests and in social life? Have you let your appearance go?'*

0 = *Absent*. Full normal activity.

1 = *Mild*. Definite but mild loss of interest or enjoyment in work, hobbies, housework, social activities. Essential tasks continue to be performed.

2 = *Moderate*. The patient reports the beginnings of impairment of performance as well as a more significant loss of interest. Leisure pursuits deserted.

3 = *Marked*. Loss of efficiency becomes impossible to hide, deficiencies occur at work leading to comment, household tasks are not completed, work disorganised, hygiene and self-care start to suffer, withdrawn from friends.

4 = *Severe*. Unable to carry on outside and admitted to hospital for protection (but not for investigation or observation) *or* off work because of illness. Relative or neighbour doing most of housework and shopping. Unable to care for self.

## (8) Retardation (0-4)

Severe forms of this symptom are rare, and the mild forms are difficult to perceive. Although some patients may say that their thinking is slowed or their emotional responsiveness has been diminished, questions about these manifestations usually produce misleading answers. Therefore, rate observed behaviour rather than what the patient claims.

0 = *Absent*.

1 = *Mild*. Distinct flattening of emotional response or fixity of expression.

2 = *Moderate*. Voice is monotonous, delay in answering, tendency to sit motionless.

3 = *Marked*. Slowness of response sufficient for the interview to be difficult and prolonged.

4 = *Severe*. Interview impossible owing to retardation; patient may be stuporose.

(9)  Agitation (0-4)

Severe agitation, when the patient paces up and down, picking at his face and hair, tearing at his clothes, is extremely rare. In milder forms the essential component is motor restlessness, coupled with some impression of tension or distress. Although agitation and retardation may appear to be opposed forms of behaviour, in mild form they can co-exist.

0 = *Absent* or minimal, within normal limits.
1 = *Mild.* Fidgety, moving excessively in chair, tapping fingers, moving feet.
2 = *Moderate.* Pulling at hair, twisting handkerchief or clothes.
3 = *Marked.* Patient has to rise during interview, then may return to seat.
4 = *Severe.* Interview conducted 'on the run'.

(10)  Anxiety (Psychic Symptoms) (0-4)

Many symptoms are included here, such as tension and difficulty in relaxing, irritability, worrying over trivial matters, apprehension and feelings of panic, fears; difficulty in concentration and forgetfulness, 'feeling jumpy'. The rating should be based on pathological changes that have occurred during the illness and an effort should be made to discount the features of a previous anxious disposition. If a phobic patient has averted anxiety by restriction of activity to avoid the phobic stimulus this should be rated, based on the severity of restriction.

*'Have you been feeling nervous, anxious, or frightened? Have you felt tense or found it hard to relax? Have you had a feeling of dread, as though something terrible were about to happen?'*

0 = *Absent.*
1 = *Mild.* Complaints of out of the ordinary and inappropriate worries or tension states, which are mild but persistent though not occupying most of the patient's time.
2 = *Moderate.* Persisting and fairly frequent symptoms of greater intensity, and concerning patient for much of the time.
3 = *Marked.* Phobias with avoidance and risk of panic.
4 = *Severe.* Persistent state of intense anxiety, or near panic, dominating patient's mental life and talk at interview. Frequent panic attacks or severe impairment due to phobic avoidance.

(11)  Anxiety (Somatic Symptoms) (0-4)

These consist of the well-recognised effects of autonomic over-activity in the respiratory, cardiovascular, gastrointestinal and urinary systems. Patients may also complain of attacks of giddiness, blurring of vision and tinnitus.

These last three symptoms appear to be more common in women than in men.

*'Have you suffered from any of the following: trembling, shakiness, excessive sweating, feelings of suffocation or choking, attacks of shortness of breath, dizziness, palpitations, faintness, headaches, pain at the back of the neck, butterflies or tightness in the stomach? How often? How badly?'*

0 = *Absent*.

1 = *Mild*. One or two physical symptoms definite but mild, occurring less than twice a week.

2 = *Moderate*. Increased severity, more symptoms, occurring more than twice a week.

3 = *Marked*. Persisting, and frequent, e.g. everyday. Occasional severe episodic symptom, which incapacitates while it lasts.

4 = *Severe*. Several persisting and very frequent symptoms, resulting in disabling attacks.


(12) Gastrointestinal symptoms (0-2)

The characteristic symptom in depression is loss of appetite and this occurs very frequently. Constipation also occurs, but is relatively uncommon. On rare occasions patients will complain of 'heavy feelings' in the abdomen. Symptoms of indigestion, wind and pain, etc. are rated under anxiety.

*'How has your appetite been? Have you suffered from constipation?'*

0 = Normal appetite for patient.

1 = *Mild*. Loss of interest in food averaged over period in question or change of bowel movement in direction of constipation.

2 = *Moderate to severe*. Noticeable diminution in food intake or definite constipation requiring unusual use of laxatives.


(13) General somatic symptoms (0-2)

These fall into two groups: the first is fatigability, which may reach the point where the patients feel tired all the time. In addition, patients complain of 'loss of energy' which appears to be related to difficulty in starting up an activity. The other type of symptom consists of diffuse muscular achings, ill-defined and often difficult to locate, but frequently in the back and sometimes in the limbs; these may also feel 'heavy'.

It is not uncommon for women to complain of backache and to ascribe it to a pelvic disorder. This symptom requires careful questioning.

*'Do you feel tired easily? All the time? Have you much energy? Is it an effort to do anything? Do you spend a lot of time resting? In bed?'*

0 = *Absent.*

1 = *Mild.* Definite disproportionate fatigue. More time than usual spent sitting down leading to some interference with day-to-day activity. Diffuse physical malaise.

2 = *Moderate to severe.* Marked complaints requiring frequent rests after bursts of physical activity. Difficult 'to get going'. Body feels heavy. Exhausted.

### (14) Loss of libido (0-2)

This is a common and characteristic symptom of depression, but it is difficult to assess in older men and especially those whose sexual activity is usually at a low level, e.g. single people. The assessment is based on a pathological change, i.e. deterioration obviously related to the patient's illness. Inadequate or no information should be rated as zero.

*'Has there been any change in your interest in sex during the past month? Have you lost interest in the opposite sex recently? Have you had less sexual drive than usual? Sexual relations less often?'*

0 = *Absent.* Normal level of activity for the individual.

1 = *Mild.* Some loss of interest, or decrease in activity.

2 = *Moderate to severe.* Total absence of interest or activity.

### (15) Hypochondriasis (0-4)

The severe states of this symptom, concerning delusions and hallucinations of rotting and blockages, are extremely uncommon in men. Excessive preoccupation with bodily functions is the essence of a hypochondriacal attitude.

0 = *Absent.*

1 = *Mild.* Excessive preoccupation with bodily functions or minor symptoms, e.g. patient talks in these terms when asked but does not return to topic spontaneously.

2 = *Moderate.* Much preoccupation with physical symptoms and thoughts of organic disease, which are volunteered.

3 = *Marked.* Strong irrational convictions of the presence of physical disease, accounting for the patient's condition.

4 = *Severe.* Delusions of disease (rotting, blockage, riddled with tumour).

(16) Loss of weight (0-2)
The simplest way to rate this would be to record the amount of loss, but many patients do not know their normal weight. (It is assumed that most weighing machines are fallible.)
0 = *Absent*, or claimed loss of less than 4 lb.
1 = *Mild*. 4-14 lb over previous 8 weeks or clothes slack around waist.
2 = *Marked*. Over 14 lb in previous 8 weeks or noticeable thinning.

(17) Loss of insight (0-2)
This is not necessarily present when the patient denies that he is suffering from mental disorder. It may be that he is denying that he is insane and may willingly recognise that he has a 'nervous' illness. In case of doubt, enquiries should be directed to the patient's attitude to his symptoms of guilt and hypochondriasis.
  *'What do you think is the matter with you?'*
0 = Full appreciation of situation.
1 = *Partial loss*. Admits reluctantly to possibility of nervous condition.
2 = *Full loss*. Denies completely the possibility of mental illness or nervous disorder.

## The Beck Depression Inventory (BDI)

The BDI was first developed as an interview scale where the interviewer read out loud each item to the patient while the patient reads their own copy of the scale, and gives their choice. It is now more widely used as a self-rating scale.

It consists of 21 items, each containing 4 or 5 items ranked in order of severity. The patient chooses the statement closest to his/her present state.

The split-half reliability is around 0.9, and its test-retest reliability is approximately 0.75. It has consistently been found to correlate well with clinicians' ratings of severity of depression, as well as with other scales of depression. It has the advantage of being useful across a great range of severity levels and in both clinical and analogue populations, and has been extensively used in subclinical and student populations.

Like the Hamilton, it cannot be used to diagnose depression in the absence of a prior diagnosis − it is only a measure of severity once the clinical diagnosis has been made. This is an important point, for subjects may have an inflated BDI score for a number of reasons (e.g.

bereavement reaction, chronic low self-esteem) without a diagnosis of depression being warranted. In this sense the generalisability of many research findings in 'mildly depressed' students to clinically depressed populations may be called into question (see Depue and Monroe, 1978). However, this is a reflection on the use of the scale, rather than on the scale itself, which remains probably the best all-round scale of its type.

*Scoring*

Assign score of 0 to 3 for each item, ignoring 'a' and 'b' when scoring any item. Minimum score 0, Maximum 63. Normative data suggest the following categories of severity level: Mild, 14-20; Moderate, 21-26; Severe, >26.

Here are some statements regarding the way people feel or think. The statements are grouped in 21 sections from A to U. One statement must be chosen from each section. You are requested to put a circle round the number of the statement which best fits the way you feel *at this moment*. Be sure to read all statements in each group before making your choice.

A. 0   I do not feel sad
   1   I feel blue or sad
   2a  I am blue or sad all the time and I can't snap out of it
   2b  I am so sad or unhappy that it is quite painful
   3   I am so sad or unhappy that I can't stand it
B. 0   I am not particularly pessimistic or discouraged about the future
   1a  I feel discouraged about the future
   2a  I feel I have nothing to look forward to
   2b  I feel that I won't ever get over my troubles
   3   I feel that the future is hopeless and that things cannot improve
C. 0   I do not feel like a failure
   1   I feel I have failed more than the average person
   2a  I feel I have accomplished very little that is worthwhile or that means anything
   2b  As I look back on life all I can see is a lot of failures
   3   I feel I am a complete failure as a person (parent, husband, wife)
D. 0   I am not particularly dissatisfied
   1a  I feel bored most of the time
   1b  I don't enjoy things the way I used to

2    I don't get satisfaction out of anything any more
3    I am dissatisfied with everything
E. 0    I don't feel particularly guilty
1    I feel bad or unworthy a good part of the time
2a    I feel quite guilty
2b    I feel bad or unworthy practically all the time now
3    I feel as though I am very bad or worthless
F. 0    I don't feel I am being punished
1    I have a feeling that something bad may happen to me
2    I feel I am being punished or will be punished
3a    I feel I deserve to be punished
3b    I want to be punished
G. 0    I don't feel disappointed in myself
1a    I am disappointed in myself
1b    I don't like myself
2a    I am disgusted with myself
3    I hate myself
H. 0    I don't feel I am any worse than anybody else
1    I am critical of myself for my weaknesses or mistakes
2    I blame myself for my faults
3    I blame myself for everything bad that happens
I. 0    I don't have any thoughts of harming myself
1    I have thoughts of harming myself but I would not carry them out
2a    I feel I would be better off dead
2b    I feel my family would be better off if I were dead
3a    I have definite plans about committing suicide
3b    I would kill myself if I could
J. 0    I don't cry any more than usual
1    I cry more now than I used to
2    I cry all the time now. I can't stop it
3    I used to be able to cry but now I can't cry at all even though I want to
K. 0    I am no more irritated now than I ever am
1    I get annoyed or irritated more easily than I used to
2    I feel irritated all the time
3    I don't get irritated at all at the things that used to irritate me
L. 0    I have not lost interest in other people
1    I am less interested in other people now than I used to be
2    I have lost most of my interest in other people and have little feeling for them

3   I have lost all my interest in other people and don't care about them at all

M. 0   I make decisions about as well as ever

1   I try to put off making decisions

2   I have great difficulty in making decisions

3   I can't make any decisions at all any more

N. 0   I don't feel I look any worse than I used to

1   I am worried that I am looking old or unattractive

2   I feel that there are permanent changes in my appearance and they make me look unattractive

3   I feel that I am ugly or repulsive looking

O. 0   I can work about as well as before

1a   It takes extra effort to get started at doing something

1b   I don't work as well as I used to

2   I have to push myself very hard to do anything

3   I can't do any work at all

P. 0   I can sleep as well as usual

1   I wake up more tired in the morning than I used to

2   I wake up 1-2 hours earlier than usual and find it hard to get back to sleep

3   I wake up early every day and can't get more than 5 hours sleep

Q. 0   I don't get any more tired than usual

1   I get tired more easily than I used to

2   I get tired from doing anything

3   I get too tired to do anything

R. 0   My appetite is no worse than usual

1   My appetite is not as good as it used to be

2   My appetite is much worse now

3   I have no appetite at all any more

S. 0   I haven't lost much weight, if any, lately

1   I have lost more than 5 pounds

2   I have lost more than 10 pounds

3   I have lost more than 15 pounds

T. 0   I am no more concerned about my health than usual

1   I am concerned about aches and pains or upset stomach or constipation

2   I am so concerned with how I feel or what I feel that it's hard to think of much else

3   I am completely absorbed in what I feel

U. 0   I have not noticed any recent changes in my interest in sex

1   I am less interested in sex than I used to be

2   I am much less interested in sex now
3   I have lost interest in sex completely

## The Assessment of Behaviour

### General Behavioural Assessment

The following assessment format follows closely that used by Liberman and Roberts (1976) at the Oxnard Mental Health Centre. It may be used as a structured interview or as a checklist and corroborative evidence may be sought from spouse, relatives or friends where necessary and appropriate.

I.    *Background data*
      Who lives with patient?
      Previous psychiatric treatment (including hospitalisations) and results
      Age, marital status, family status, social class

II.   *Problems*
      Onset, current frequency, intensity, duration, inappropriate form, inappropriate occasions
      (a)  behavioural excesses (motivation to reduce?)
      (b)  behavioural deficits (motivation to increase?)
      Which of these most bothers the patient? Which would they like like to work on first?

III.  *Assets and strengths* (i, now; ii, in recent past; iii, distant past)
      (a)  Appearance, dress, etc.
      (b)  Self-help skills
      (c)  Social (including conversation, recreation, friendship, clubs, church?)
      (d)  Work
      (e)  Educational, vocational training

IV.  *Functional analysis of problems*
      (a)  What are consequences of current problems? (What would difference be if problem did not exist?) (Therapist notes potential loss of rewarding consequences if problem removed)
      (b)  Who persuaded patient into treatment? – or was it self-initiated? Does patient acknowledge problems and desire treatment?
      (c)  What are the $S^D$'s (discriminative stimuli: conditions, settings) which serve as occasions for occurrence of prob-

lems? Where? When? With whom? (Alternative strategy: when does problem *not* occur — Where? When? With whom?)

V.    *Reinforcement survey*

What does the patient find rewarding?

People-places-things-food-activities [now-past]

What does patient find aversive?

People-places-things-food-activities [now-past]

[NB. Take into account observations of patient by you and significant others and not only self-report.]

VI.   *Medical*

(a)  Medical/surgical problems and limitations to activity

(b)  Date of last physical examination

(c)  Name/address of General Practitioner

(d)  Current medical treatment and drugs (psychotropic and others)

(e)  Family history of significant psychological problems.

VII.  *Socio-cultural*

(a)  Recent changes in milieu (change job, house, intergenerational conflict in family)

(b)  Recent changes in social relationships (friend leaves area, etc. as well as separation, divorce), deaths

(c)  Other recent traumas and stresses

[What *losses* has the patient sustained in his own mind, even if not in reality?]

VIII. *Patient's own view of problems*

How have they explained their problems to themselves? What is their theory? How have they come to that conclusion? How much do they know about clinical depression? What has been their source of information — books, family, friends, voluntary help agency, GP's, former psychiatrists. Therapist to evaluate extent to which patient is clinging to previous advice and formulations they have been given, e.g. that they have a 'biochemical depression'. How much do they know about cognitive-behavioural theories and strategies?

IX.   *Formulation of behavioural goals* — (be specific)

(a)  Which desirable behaviour to increase (include strengthening assets)?

short term (1 month)      long term (3 months)

(b)  Which undesirable behaviours to decrease (include self-talk component)?

short term      long term

(c) Treatment techniques and interventions (see Chapters 4, 5 and 6)
(d) Recording and monitoring procedure:
diaries, etc.
self-report inventories?
observational (by therapist or spouse/friend)?

*Note*: Clearly some of these issues will need to be explored more extensively than others, and supplementary questions asked. The nature of the questioning will vary depending on the psychological sophistication of the patient. To avoid seeming inquisitorial, the therapist may move freely between topics, rather than follow the scheduled question in set order. However, it will be useful to check with this assessment format after assessment session(s) to see what has been missed and needs to be asked next session.

### Behavioural Diary

Most cognitive-behaviour therapists find it useful to supplement within-session assessment by asking patients to keep a daily dairy. The items to be included in such a diary will depend on individual therapist and patient. I have found the format in Table 3.1 to be useful because it includes self-ratings of feelings (Questions 1 and 2), somatic symptoms (3 and 4), and target behaviours (5-7).

### Assessment of Specific Behaviours (for in-patient, ward-based observations only)

Williams, Barlow and Agras (1972) developed this observer-rated scale for the assessment of depressed inpatients. Their aim was to develop an objective system of observing and recording depressive behaviour which could be administered by an auxiliary nurse in a general hospital psychiatric unit. For this purpose, subtle or low frequency behaviours are not assessed. Rather the authors sought consistent behavioural cues to depressed affect that were either present or absent without question at any point in time.

Their assessment allows a fairly precise, longitudinal record of the patient's depressed behaviour which correlates satisfactorily with the Beck (0.67) and Hamilton (0.71) in the ten depressed patients in their study. The inter-rater reliability was satisfactory at 96 per cent.

*The Scale.*   The authors' observations of their depressed patients sug-

Table 3.1: Diary (to be completed each night before going to bed)

---

Name . . . . . . . . . . . . . . . . . . . . . ., . . . . . . . . . .Today's date . . . . . . . . . . . . . . .

(1)   How anxious/tense have you been today?
      0   1   2   3   4   5   6   7   8   9   10
      Not at all          Moderately              Extremely

(2)   How depressed have you been today?
      0   1   2   3   4   5   6   7   8   9   10
      Not at all          Moderately              Extremely

(3)   How has your appetite been today?
      0   1   2   3   4   5   6   7   8   9   10
      Very poor          Moderate               Very good

(4)   How did you sleep *last* night?
      0   1   2   3   4   5   6   7   8   9   10
      Very badly          Moderately             Very well

(5)   How long did you spend . . . . . . . . . . . . . . . . .today? . . . . . . . . . . . . .
      (or) How many times did you . . . . . . . . . . . . .today? . . . . . . . . . . . . .
      How did you cope with . . . . . . . . . . . . . . . . . .today? . . . . . . . . . . . %

(6)   How long did you spend . . . . . . . . . . . . . . . . .today? . . . . . . . . . . . . .
      (or) How many times did you . . . . . . . . . . . . .today? . . . . . . . . . . . . .
      How did you cope with . . . . . . . . . . . . . . . . . .today? . . . . . . . . . . . %

(7)   How long did you spend . . . . . . . . . . . . . . . . .today? . . . . . . . . . . . . .
      (or) How many times did you . . . . . . . . . . . . .today? . . . . . . . . . . . . .
      How did you cope with . . . . . . . . . . . . . . . . . .today? . . . . . . . . . . . %

Any other comments

---

gested that when depressed, patients talked little, avoided social inter-action (often by withdrawing to their rooms), smiled infrequently and showed diminished motor activity. Each of these behaviours is assessed for presence or absence once (on average) every ½ hour for 8 hours each day.

|                        | No  | Yes |
|------------------------|-----|-----|
| (1) Talking            | 0   | 1   |
| (2) Smiling            | 0   | 1   |
| (3) Motor activity     | 0   | 1   |
| (4) Time out of room   | 0   | 1   |

Rate each behaviour once in every ½ hour block from 8 a.m. to 4 p.m. (16 times in all, per day). (Williams *et al.* made the rating at any time within the ½ hour, determined at random. This meant that the exact time of observation differed from day to day, avoiding regular rest times, etc.)

*Definitions.* Because the intention of this type of assessment is to be as objective as possible, precise definitions of the behaviour to be rated are given as follows:

*Talking:* must be directed towards another person
*Smiling:* if indistinct, rate Yes if corners of mouth turn up. Teeth may or may not show.
*Motor activities:* the following are 'activities'.
(a)  in room with visitor or another patient
(b)  at card table talking, reading or sewing
(c)  in T.V. lounge talking, reading or sewing
(d)  in room dressing or tidying
(e)  taking shower
(f)  in physical/occupational/group therapy (or preparing to go)
(g)  sitting watching T.V.
(h)  patient at card table/T.V. lounge with another patient or patients (even though not actually talking at that particular minute observed).
(i)  drinking coffee
(j)  alone in T.V. room, T.V. set off, reading, sewing, knitting
The following are *not* activities
(a)  in room alone, sitting, lying down, looking out of window
(b)  alone in T.V. room, with set off.
*Time out of room:* Patient not inside room at time he is checked.

*Scoring.* Williams *et al.* report that the 4 behaviours are highly correlated with each other (Kendall's coefficient of concordance: W = 0.70, p < 0.001), so scores for each behaviour may be summed into daily totals with minimum 0 and maximum 16 x 4 = 64. Average scores for the initial 3 days of hospitalisation on this measure are given graphically in the Williams *et al.* study for five patients = 20, 22, 17, 32 and 22. The final (3 days average) scores for these patients were 30, 38, 17, 51 and 42.

Clearly, this form of longitudinal assessment is more suited to research trials where careful and objective assessment is important.

On the other hand, Williams *et al.* suggest the assessment is of potential clinical value as a prognostic indicator. They found that this scale was more sensitive than either the Beck or the Hamilton in this respect. For example, the three patients who had relapsed one year following discharge had shown initial improvement in all measures, but only the behavioural measure showed a worsening prior to discharge in all three patients.

## The Assessment of the Cognitive Component of Depression

*The Assessment of General Cognitive Style: (a) The Cognitive Style Test*

This scale consists of thirty short descriptions of everyday events. Subjects are asked to choose one of four possible cognitive responses to the situation. It can be presented in written format or using a card format which enables randomisation of the types of events. In the latter case, the experimenter reads the situation aloud and then presents the responses visually which are pointed on the reverse side of the same card.

*The events* are classified into three themes which relate to Beck's cognitive triad of self (events of an interpersonal nature, relating particularly to self-image), world (situations which are more task orientated) and future (dealing with anticipated responses and plans). Within each of the three categories, half the items are pleasant/rewarding situations and half are unpleasant/punishing. Each positive item is roughly counterbalanced with a negative item. Thus the overall structure of the test yields six types of events (SP; SU; WP; WU; FP; FU) with five items in each type.

*The responses* are chosen to represent degrees of depressive distortion. The extreme responses include cognitive errors listed by Beck — arbitrary inference, selective abstraction, overgeneralisation, magnification/minimisation/personalisation — though not systematically, since in practice these categories are not independent of each other.

The statements are listed in random order for degree of positive and negative attitude: 4 = very negative; 3 = negative with some qualification; 1 = very positive.

The test in its present form is a further development of the test reported by Wilkinson and Blackburn (1981).

The validity and reliability of both the original scale and the present version have been found to be satisfactory.

The final version of the scale is to be published, so potential users are asked to refer for use of the scale to Dr. Ivy Blackburn in Edinburgh.[2]

*Norms. Depressed group* (N = 20), (Mean age 46 years, s.d. 13.0), Mean CST (Total) = 70.3 (s.d. 10.8)

    *Nondepressed group* (N = 20), (Mean age 47 years, s.d. 13.0), Mean CST (Total) = 58.6 (s.d. 8.4) (Blackburn, pers. comm., 1983) (Scoring key reproduced at end of scale.)

*Instructions.* On the following pages you will find a series of descriptions of everyday events. After each situation are alternative ways that people might think about it, marked A, B, C and D. I would like you to imagine that these events are happening to you. Then choose the alternative that best describes how you would think about the situation. (If your reaction is different from the alternatives provided choose the thought that is nearest to your own. If you agree with more than one, choose the one which would run through your mind most often.) When you have chosen the thought, put a circle around the letter next to it, like this:

There are no right or wrong answers.

Work through the questions quite quickly and try to pick the thought that is nearest to your *immediate* reaction to the situation.

(1) You are about to go into hospital for an operation on your back which has been giving you pain.

I think:  A. It may not work

        B. It should work, but there may still be some pain

        C. I don't think there's much chance of it working

        D. It will be a success and I will be able to do all the things I used to do

(2) Some close friends will be moving away to a different town.

I think:  A. With some effort we can still be friends

        B. It's likely that we won't be so friendly now

        C. It won't change anything

D. I shall never see them again

(3)  You meet friends whom you haven't seen for a long time.

I think:  A. I wonder if they still like me

B. It's good to see old friends

C. They won't like me any more

D. They like me a lot

(4)  You manage to deal with a difficult problem at work.

I think:  A. I am a capable person

B. I wonder how I managed it

C. I have some abilities

D. This was just luck

(5)  Somthing goes wrong with your work.

I think:  A. Nobody will mind, it happens to everyone

B. This job is too difficult for me

C. It was just a mistake, I can correct it

D. I must be more careful

(6)  You are promised a large pay rise next year.

I think:  A. I look forward to it eagerly

B. It will probably not happen

C. If it happens I shall be pleased

D. It's better not to make plans as it might not happen

(7)  Next year you will have saved enough money for your dream holiday.

I think:  A. It should be good fun

B. I don't think it's going to be enjoyable

C. It may be a disappointment

D. I will have a fabulous time

(8)  You fall out with friends over some minor matters.

I think:  A. They still like me

B. I don't have the knack to keep friends

C. I should be more careful with friends

D. They probably won't mind

(9)  You attend a family reunion.

I think:  A. It is nice to see some of the family again

B. This may not be a good idea

C. Family reunions are generally disastrous

D. They are very happy to see me

(10)You are told that you won't get a pay increase this year.

I think:  A. I will probably lose my job

B. I will get one next year

C. I may not have one for a long time

D. I wonder when I will get one

(11)  A person you admire tells you he/she likes you.

I think:  A. I am glad he/she likes me

B. People sometimes say that without really meaning it

C. I am a very likeable person

D. I cannot believe that I am likeable

(12)  You go out with some new people and you have a marvellous time.

I think:  A. I did not contribute much

B. It was all because of them

C. I might have contributed something

D. I helped to make it go alright

(13)  You cannot go on holiday because of unforeseen circumstances.

I think:  A. This is an unfortunate coincidence

B. Why do problems like this happen to me

C. It really does not matter

D. There are always obstacles in my way whatever I want to do

(14)  A close friend has an argument with you.

I think:  A. This is a major blow to our friendship

B. Our friendship will suffer a bit temporarily

C. It won't make any difference to our friendship

D. This friendship is ruined for good

(15)  The roof of your house starts leaking.

I think:  A. There are too many problems for me to deal with

B. It will be no problem to get it repaired

C. This is another problem which I must try to deal with

D. Maybe it could be repaired soon

(16)  You will have to meet some relatives whom you don't get on with.

I think:  A. This is going to be absolutely awful

B. It shouldn't be too bad

C. We shall probably get on better this time

D. This will be rather uncomfortable

(17)  You are unable to deal with a problem at work and have to ask for help.

I think:  A. I often find it difficult to cope with problems

B. I find it difficult to cope with some problems

C. I am a failure

D. These sorts of problems are always easier with help

(18)  You do not manage to finish a piece of work on time.

I think:  A. I should have tried harder

        B. I am just lazy and inept

        C. I have tried my best

        D. Maybe I could have tried harder

(19)  Things are going well at work.

I think:  A. This job is just right for me

        B. This job is not interesting

        C. This job may be right for me

        D. This job may be too easy

(20)  You are obliged to move out of your home and you are looking for a new flat/house.

I think:  A. I shall soon find what I'm looking for

        B. I'll never find anything as good as what I've got

        C. I may have to settle for something less than I want

        D. It's unlikely that I'll find something suitable

(21)  You will be starting a new job which involves work you've always wanted to do.

I think:  A. I will probably annoy people when I can't do it right straight away

        B. It may take a little while to settle in, but it will be OK

        C. I doubt that I will be able to do the work

        D. Everything should go smoothly

(22)  You help friends to do their garden. The next time you visit, they thank you enthusiastically.

I think:  A. I am very good at this sort of thing

        B. They don't mean it

        C. Maybe I have some skills

        D. I don't deserve that much praise

(23)  A special dinner gets spoilt because the main dish is slightly burnt.

I think:  A. Nothing ever goes right for me

        B. It can be easily remedied

        C. It had to happen today and nothing can be done about it

        D. Maybe it could be saved somehow

(24)  You invite some new friends round to your home for a meal.

I think:  A. They probably won't enjoy it

        B. It may turn out well

        C. It will be nice to get to know them better

        D. It will be a good evening

(25)  You can at last make plans to redecorate your house.

I think:  A. There are bound to be problems

        B. It will be beautiful when it's finished

    C. Something may interfere with the plans
    D. It should turn out nice
(26) You try to make friends with some new neighbours, but they do not seem to care much.
I think: A. I may not be their type
         B. I have done all I can
         C. I am not a likeable person
         D. They may not like me
(27) The other members of a local club choose you to be the new club secretary.
I think: A. This is a mixed blessing
         B. This is an impossible task/position
         C. It is an important and interesting position
         D. This position may be too difficult
(28) You spill your drink over friend's new carpet.
I think: A. I am always a clumsy person
         B. It could have happened to anybody
         C. I can be so clumsy at times
         D. I am not usually so clumsy
(29) A surprise party is arranged by friends for your birthday.
I think: A. They meant well, but I have reservations
         B. This is a wonderful idea
         C. This is more trouble than it's worth
         D. Birthday parties are never enjoyable
(30) You have planned to do certain jobs on Saturday and some old friends turn up unexpectedly to see you.
I think: A. This has completely ruined my plans
         B. This is great
         C. It is not a very suitable time
         D. It is a bit untimely but it's nice to see them

*Cognitive Style Test – Scoring Key*

Consists of 30 statements: 10 relating to view of the world, 10 to view of self and 10 to view of the future. Each group of statements consists of 5 pleasant and 5 unpleasant situations. The situations are randomly listed.

In the list below: S = self; W = world; F = future; U = unpleasant; P = pleasant.

| (1) F/U | (2) F/U | (3) S/P | (4) S/P |
|---------|---------|---------|---------|
| A.   3  | A.   2  | A.   3  | A.   1  |
| B.   2  | B.   3  | B.   2  | B.   3  |
| C.   4  | C.   1  | C.   4  | C.   2  |
| D.   1  | D.   4  | D.   1  | D.   4  |

| (5) W/U | (6) F/P | (7) F/P | (8) S/U |
|---------|---------|---------|---------|
| A.   1  | A.   1  | A.   2  | A.   1  |
| B.   4  | B.   4  | B.   4  | B.   4  |
| C.   2  | C.   2  | C.   3  | C.   3  |
| D.   3  | D.   3  | D.   1  | D.   2  |

| (9) W/P | (10) F/U | (11) S/P | (12) S/P |
|---------|----------|----------|----------|
| A.   2  | A.   4   | A.   2   | A.   3   |
| B.   3  | B.   1   | B.   3   | B.   4   |
| C.   4  | C.   2   | C.   1   | C.   2   |
| D.   1  | D.   3   | D.   4   | D.   1   |

| (13) W/U | (14) W/U | (15) W/U | (16) F/U |
|----------|----------|----------|----------|
| A.   2   | A.   3   | A.   4   | A.   4   |
| B.   3   | B.   2   | B.   1   | B.   2   |
| C.   1   | C.   1   | C.   3   | C.   1   |
| D.   1   | D.   4   | D.   2   | D.   3   |

| (17) S/U | (18) S/U | (19) W/P | (20) F/U |
|----------|----------|----------|----------|
| A.   3   | A.   3   | A.   1   | A.   1   |
| B.   2   | B.   4   | B.   4   | B.   4   |
| C.   4   | C.   1   | C.   2   | C.   2   |
| D.   1   | D.   2   | D.   3   | D.   3   |

| (21) F/P | (22) S/P | (23) W/U | (24) F/P |
|----------|----------|----------|----------|
| A.   3   | A.   1   | A.   4   | A.   4   |
| B.   2   | B.   4   | B.   1   | B.   3   |
| C.   4   | C.   2   | C.   3   | C.   2   |
| D.   1   | D.   3   | D.   2   | D.   1   |

| (25) F/P | (26) S/U | (27) W/P | (28) S/U |
|----------|----------|----------|----------|
| A.   4   | A.   2   | A.   2   | A.   4   |
| B.   1   | B.   1   | B.   4   | B.   1   |
| C.   3   | C.   4   | C.   1   | C.   3   |
| D.   2   | D.   3   | D.   3   | D.   2   |

| (29) W/P | (30) W/P |
|----------|----------|
| A.   2   | A.   4   |
| B.   1   | B.   1   |
| C.   3   | C.   3   |
| D.   4   | D.   2   |

*(b) Hopelessness Scale* (Beck *et al.*, 1974)

This scale, developed by A.T. Beck and colleagues, measures the patient's view of the future, or degree of hopelessness. A depressed patient or other potentially suicidal patient can tolerate his illness provided they have some hope for the future. When they begin to view the future in totally negative terms, life becomes pointless and intolerable, and the patient becomes a high suicide risk. This risk exists particularly if the patient is depressed, but occasionally hopelessness does occur in patients who do not have the physical symptoms of depression.

(A further factor for the therapist to consider is whether the patient has an impulsive nature, which increases suicide risk also.)

*Procedure.* The scale is self explanatory and can usually be filled in by the patient. If not, it can be read to him/her, asking 'true or false?' after each statement.

*Scoring Information:* For matching answers score 1 point:

| (1) F  | (8) F  | (15) F |
|--------|--------|--------|
| (2) T  | (9) T  | (16) T |
| (3) F  | (10) F | (17) T |
| (4) T  | (11) T | (18) T |
| (5) F  | (12) T | (19) F |
| (6) F  | (13) F | (20) T |
| (7) T  | (14) T |        |

*Tentative Cut-off Scores.* Each patient in a sample of suicide attempts in Beck's clinic was rated independently by a clinician for depth of hopelessness. This scale was also administered. The standard deviations and means for the groups categorised by clinician's ratings of hopelessness were computed, and the following tentative cut-off points for each category established.

| 0 - 3 | None or minimal |
|-------|-----------------|
| 4 - 8 | Mild |
| 9-14  | Moderate: May not be in immediate danger but requires frequent regular monitoring. Is the life situation stable? |
| 15+   | Severe: Definite suicidal risk |

Beck *et al.* (1975) reported a mean score of 9.0 (s.d. = 6.1) for 384 suicide attempts. Greene (1981) has reported a mean score of 4.45 (s.d. = 3.09) in a normal population (39.6 randomly selected adults). Further detailed data are given in a paper by Nekanda-Trepka, Bishop and Blackburn (1983).

This questionnaire consists of a list of twenty statements (sentences). Please read the statements carefully one by one.

If the statement describes your attitude *for the past week, including today*, write down TRUE next to it. If the statement is false for you, write FALSE next to it. You may simply write T for TRUE and F for FALSE. Please be sure to read each sentence.

—A. I look forward to the future with hope and enthusiasm.
—B. I might as well give up because there's nothing I can do about making things better for myself.
—C. When things are going badly, I am helped by knowing that they can't stay that way forever.
—D. I can't imagine what my life would be like in ten years.
—E. I have enough time to accomplish the things I most want to do.
—F. In the future I expect to succeed in what concerns me most.
—G. My future seems dark to me.
—H. I happen to be particularly lucky and I expect to get more of the good things in life than the average person.
—I. I just don't get the breaks, and there's no reason to believe that I will in the future.
—J. My past experiences have prepared me well for my future.
—K. All I can see ahead of me is unpleasantness rather than pleasantness.
—L. I don't expect to get what I really want.
—M. When I look ahead to the future I expect I will be happier than I am now.
—N. Things just won't work out the way I want them to.
—O. I have great faith in the future.
—P. I never get what I want so it's foolish to want anything.
—Q. It is very unlikely that I will get any real satisfaction in the future.
—R. The future seems vague and uncertain to me.
—S. I can look forward to more good times than bad times.
—T. There's no use in really trying to get something I want because I probably won't get it.

## Assessment of Specific Thought Content

*Dairies/Thought Forms:* Tables 3.2 and 3.3 give two examples of forms which can be used by patients.

The first is based on Beck *et al's* (1979) Dysfunctional Thought Form, and asks patients to list the situation, the emotion, the negative thought, a rational alternative thought, and emotional outcome. Beck *et al's* form also asks patients to rate on a scale 1-100 how much they believe in the negative thought and its rational alternative as well as rerating belief in the original negative thought when rerating the emotional outcome. Patients are asked to fill the form in whenever they have a negative thought, or whenever they feel low.

Table 3.2: Thought-diary

| Date | Situation | Emotions | Negative thought(s) |
|------|-----------|----------|---------------------|
| | Describe (1) Actual event leading to unpleasant emotion, or (2) Stream of thoughts, daydreams or recollection, leading to unpleasant emotion. | (1) Specify sad/anxious/ angry, etc. (2) Rate degree of emotion, 1-100. | (1) Write automatic thought(s) that preceded emotion(s). (2) Rate belief in automatic thought(s) 0-100%. |
| | *Rational response* | | *Outcome* |
| | (1) Write rational response to automatic thought(s). (2) Rate belief in rational response, 0-100%. | | (1) Re-rate belief in automatic thought(s), 0-100%. (2) Specify and rate subsequent emotions, 0-100. |

There is no doubt that some patients find the full version of the form difficult to complete, and therapists may need to tailor the form to individual requirements. For example, rating strength of belief may be thought unnecessary at the early stages of treatment. Similarly, finding alternative rational explanations and interpretations may be too hard a struggle at the outset and ought to be left until the patient is familiar with the practice of thought-catching for his negative thoughts. Some colleagues have also pointed out that since the essence of the diary is to 'catch' the negative thought, perhaps the thought or the emotion ought to be noted first, with details of the situation noted afterwards. Other problems with thought-catching are dealt with in Chapter 5 on cognitive techniques (p. 117). It is worth stating here, though, that unlike therapy for anxiety and phobic states in which competence at diary keeping may be assumed from early on in therapy, such competence at thought-diary keeping cannot be assumed for many depressed patients. As such, competency at filling in the full Thought Form may be conceived as a reasonable *goal* of therapy, since the aim of therapy is to make the patient more objective about his/her self-talk, in a way which should make the form filling easier.

## Table 3.3: Activity and Thoughts Diary

We would like you to complete this diary during the next week. Fill out a diary
page each day, preferably a little bit at a time, several times during the day.
Indicate the major activity you were doing within each 2-hour block.
PLEASE EXAMINE THE EXAMPLE ILLUSTRATED
In the activity section please indicate what you have been doing during the
time indicated. Write down M (for mastery) if you got any sense of accomplishment, and/or P (for pleasure) if you obtained enjoyment during the time concerned. In the thoughts and feelings section write down how you felt during
the period and what thoughts have been going through your mind.

|  | Activity | M or P | Thoughts and feelings |
|---|---|---|---|
| 12 - 2 a.m. | Sleep | | |
| 2 - 4 a.m. | Sleep | | |
| 4 - 6 a.m. | Woke up at 4.15 a.m. and got up to let cat out | M | Felt half-awake and unreal |
| 6 - 8 a.m. | Woke hour before alarm | | Worrying about Len's (son's) problem with his boss |
| 8 - 10 a.m. | Made breakfast, woke family (burnt toast) | M | Why can't I do anything right |
| 10 - 12 a.m. | Took bus to town shopped in market. Bought flowers. | M<br>P | Managed to shop without feeling anxious like I normally do |
| 12 - 2 p.m. | Had lunch in town with Vera (friend) window-shopped | M | Enjoyed Vera's company at first but then had argument about her children's behaviour. Made me miserable. |
| 2 - 4 p.m. | Took Metro home. Sat and did nothing | | Wished I didn't always brood after arguments |
| 4 - 6 p.m. | Collected Sara from school. Made her tea. Prepared Joe's (husband's) meal | M | Felt empty even though I did everything right |
| 6 - 8 p.m. | Had meal with Joe and Len. Talked about moving | M | I wish he would listen for once to my point of view |
| 8 - 10 p.m. | Watched TV for hour, after reading story to Sara | M | Wish my life was like these stories |
| 10 - 12 p.m. | Crotcheted shawl for niece's christening. Bed at 11.00 p.m. | M<br>P | Made good progress. Joe in a good mood and this helped me. |

The second (Table 3.3) is an activity, thoughts and feelings diary
developed by Stephen Tyrer in Newcastle. It has the advantage of
simplicity and understandability. Beck's concept of Mastery and

Pleasure is included. No attempt is made to separate thoughts from feelings, but since many patients themselves do not easily make this distinction, especially at the start of therapy, this is not necessarily a disadvantage of the scale. It has the advantage of covering 24 hours, important in view of the idiosyncratic sleeping patterns of some patients with early, middle or late insomnia.

Its lack of specificity which allows it to be straightforward may also be a disadvantage later on in therapy when therapist and patient need to be more precise about thought/affect connections and rational alternative explanations. It may be appropriate therefore to use the Tyrer scale early on in therapy and introduce the Beck *et al's* form after the patient has shown him/herself able to complete the simpler scale competently. In any event, no diary at all should be given to patients without the patient having shown themselves able to grasp, within the session, what counts as an 'activity', 'thought/feeling', 'mastery' and 'pleasure'.

*Rating Frequency of Negative Thoughts.* Table 3.4 lists sample negative thoughts in the patient's day to day experience. This is especially useful if the patient finds it difficult to identify spontaneously when a negative thought occurs. The patient may not clearly recall having had a depressing thought in the past hour, session, or day, yet may recognise having had a particular thought if it is shown to him/her.

Table 3.4: List of Negative Thoughts for Frequency Ratings

| | |
|---|---|
| (1) | It seems such an effort to do anything |
| (2) | I feel pessimistic about the future |
| (3) | I have too many bad things in my life |
| (4) | I have very little to look forward to |
| (5) | I'm drained of energy, worn out |
| (6) | I'm not as successful as other people |
| (7) | Everything seems futile and pointless |
| (8) | I just want to curl up and go to sleep |
| (9) | There are things about me that I don't like |
| (10) | It's too much effort even to move |
| (11) | I'm absolutely exhausted |
| (12) | The future seems just one string of problems |
| (13) | My thoughts keep drifting away |
| (14) | I get no satisfaction from the things I do |
| (15) | I've made so many mistakes in the past |
| (16) | I've got to really concentrate just to keep my eyes open |
| (17) | Everything I do turns out badly |
| (18) | My whole body has slowed down |
| (19) | I regret some of the things I've done |

(20)   I can't make the effort to liven up myself
(21)   I feel depressed with the way things are going
(22)   I haven't any real friends anymore
(23)   I do have a number of problems
(24)   There's no-one I can feel really close to
(25)   I wish I were somebody else
(26)   I'm annoyed at myself for being bad at making decisions
(27)   I don't make a good impression on other people
(28)   The future looks hopeless
(29)   I don't get the same satisfaction out of things these days
(30)   I wish something would happen to make me feel better

---

The clinician may ask the patient how frequently each thought has occurred in the past hour, day, few days or week. If the precise frequency is difficult for the patient to estimate, then a card with a 5-point scale written on it may be shown: 0 - not at all; 1 - sometimes; 2 - moderately often; 3 - often; 4 - all the time.

In my own clinical work, I have used items based on Velten's Mood Induction Procedure (Velten, 1968) for this assessment. Each item in Table 3.4 is typed on a separate card, and 16-20 cards selected for any one patient. I have sometimes found the use of this procedure encourages the patient to think of their thoughts as psychological events rather than as necessarily reflecting reality, a procedure which encourages 'distancing', and thus useful as a therapeutic procedure as well as for assessment (Williams, 1981).

## Notes

1. Professor Hamilton has made it clear to me that any reader may use or adapt his scale for their own clinical and/or research use without having to seek his permission.

2. MRC Brain Metabolism Unit, Thomas Clouston Clinic, 153 Morningside Drive, Edinburgh, U.K.

# 4 BEHAVIOURAL TECHNIQUES

The following techniques are linked by the common underlying theme that depressive behaviour is the result of environmental contingencies, maintained by its consequences, and that changing the contingencies will change the behaviour. There are several ways in which the description of these techniques could be arranged. I have decided to start with a description of those in which the therapist attempts to control most environmental contingencies (token economy), to those in which the patient is left to determine his/her own pattern of rewards and punishments (see Table 4.1).

Table 4.1: Behavioural Techniques Categorised by Degree of Control over Contingencies Attempted

|  | | Degree of Control | | |
|  | Great | Moderate | Little | None |
|---|---|---|---|---|
| Technique | Token economy Contingency management | Reinforcement by spouse, relatives, friends. Premack principle | Self-reinforcement | Activity scheduling, Desensitisation |

In each case, the techniques are described within the following format:

Title of technique
Rationale of technique
Aim of technique
Procedure
Example (where necessary to clarify the use of a technique)
Comment

In selecting these techniques to describe, I have attempted to include those which are used most frequently in the outcome studies reviewed in Chapter 2. The exception is Contingency Management and Token Economy techniques which are included not on the basis of their frequent use, but because they form an important part of the groundwork on which later techniques have been built. As was made clear in Chapter 2, most controlled studies of the efficacy of psychological treatments of depression have used packages of techniques. The individual techniques by themselves have received little attention. It is worth bearing in mind, then, that few of the techniques to be described are likely to be efficacious in isolation. Which combination to use with which patient at what point in the course of depression (discussed also in Chapter 2) is ultimately a matter for the clinician's own judgement.

## Contingency Management

### Rationale

Depressive behaviours *per se* constitute the disorder. They can be manipulated by encouraging the performance of positive behaviours (by a token economy or contingency management scheme) which are incompatible with symptomatic manifestation.

### Aims of Treatment

To increase frequency of work behaviour, coping strategies and interpersonal efficiency which will be incompatible with depressive behaviour.

### Procedure

The treatment is usually carried out in an inpatient or daypatient setting, where staff can observe and interact with patients over a long period each day, and where many of a patient's daily living activities, such as cooking, cleaning, personal hygiene and social interaction, can be made the focus of treatment. Typically the patient consents to participate in a scheme which is running for a whole ward or unit. (Some therapists maintain that programmes for individuals within a normal ward are impractical, non-cost-effective, and more difficult to control. However, there is nothing in principle to stop therapists from adapting these procedures for use with individuals in normal inpatient or daypatient settings.)

*Stage 1. Introducing the Patient to the Scheme.* At this stage a great deal of didactic explanation of principles underlying the scheme is thought to be essential. Some patients and relatives may readily accept the philosophy, others may not. The following is the information given on a form to patients participating in Liberman and Roberts' Day Treatment Centre (Coupon Incentive Scheme) (Liberman and Roberts, 1976).

The form gives the following information:

(1) Emphasises that active participation in the programme is the 'best therapy'.
(2) Gives brief description of way the unit is run – meals, recreation, therapy, etc.
(3) Introduces 'token economy' concept. Tokens given on predetermined basis at a set rate for jobs around unit.
(4) Gives procedure for exchange of tokens (snacks, coffee, recreation, etc.).
(5) Gives procedure for monthly renewal of tokens and 'fresh start'.
(6) Explains management of token economy by patients themselves chosen by all patients weekly, with staff members in support.
(7) Includes a consent section to sign.

These details give something of the 'flavour' of the coupon incentive scheme, and although not appropriate for many settings, it may be modified for use in some centres. Note that it is explicitly behavioural-educational, but that the patients run many aspects of the scheme themselves. One important aspect of the approach is that, in Liberman and Roberts' Centre, the token economy was not the only therapy strategy operating. Each patient was assigned to a therapist (nurse, psychological technician, rehabilitation worker – ten in all) who worked out individual strategies for each case, including homework assignments.

*Other activities* during the day included workshops (with again the emphasis on education) which taught skills in community living (human economics?) and personal finance, as well as conversational skills, use of public agencies, etc.

*Example*

More details of the actual procedures employed are given by Liberman and Roberts (1976) using the example of Sarah Jane, a 30-year-old married ex-secretary with 3 children. On admission to their Day Treatment Centre she had a history of loss of interest in everything, 'feeling like a nothing', staying in bed for long hours, failure to cope with housework and childcare. On previous admissions to other units she had been described as agitated, tremulous and apathetic. Her diagnosis was 'neurotic depression'. Psychotherapy had been tried on a previous admission to no avail.

Table 4.2 gives a good example of the specification of problems and of goals for the individual case of Sarah Jane.

Table 4.2: Specification of Problems and Goals for Sarah Jane

| Problems | Goals |
| --- | --- |
| *Deficits* | *Behaviour to strengthen* |
| (1)  Fails to perform housework and childcare | Cleaning, clothes washing, making beds, going shopping, cooking meals, making snacks for children. |
| (2)  Poor grooming | Fix hair more stylishly, wear more colourful clothes, iron clothes so they are not baggy or wrinkled. |
| (3)  Infrequent conversation with husband and children | At least 15 minutes of conversing with husband each day, reading to children in evening. |
| *Excesses* | *Behaviour to decrease* |
| (1)  Complains about helplessness and worthlessness | Verbalisations about feeling sick, helpless, worthless, 'like a nothing'. |
| (2)  Retreating to bed | Time spent in bed during daytime and before 11 p.m. each evening. |

The staff at the Centre where Sarah Jane was a daypatient ignored the patient's negative self-references, and gave social approval for improved grooming (as per contract in Table 4.2). The treatment of the excess sleeping and deficient housework was carried out by pairing the two in a contingency self-management programme which will be described in a later section. Sarah Jane was taken off the medication she had been taking on admission (Doxepin and Chlorpromazine) (on the grounds that 'the scientific literature reveals no clear benefit of medication in neurotic depression'). She and her therapist met daily to review the contents of her daily diary. During these sessions also, the therapist ignored remarks about how difficult her housework duties were, and instead enquired further into the details of Sarah Jane's accomplishments in her assignments.

After one month of this intensive Day Treatment, conjoint marital therapy (one session per week) was started, though it seems that the patient continued to attend the Centre on some days until three or four months — by which time she was doing a 3-day-a-week volunteer job. A three year follow-up revealed that she and her husband had decided to separate by mutual decision. She was leading an extremely happy and fulfilled life.

*Comment*

A number of things are notable about the original contracts that were made. Firstly, many may object that it is sexist. 'Adaptive' behaviours seem to be geared to increasing comfort with the housewife and 'sexually attractive wife' role. This may be so, though the importance is to be laid on a *negotiated* contract between therapist and patient, with neither side being able to impose a philosophy on the other. (In fact, the authors were well aware that the causes of this patient's depression had much to do with her husband's behaviour, and arranged for marital therapy to take place.) Secondly, in common with much behaviourist formulation, there is no place for 'reasons'. 'Verbalisations about feeling sick' are to be decreased with, it seems, scant regard for what prompts the verbalisation (e.g. actually *feeling* sick). On the other hand, the indications are that such contracts are willingly negotiated and in some patients there is *relief* that the focus of treatment is so observable. No therapist could wish to impose such a programme on an unwilling party.

Note also, that in this case the token economy scheme was very much a 'background' against which these other treatments were implemented. The coupons were given for helping out around the unit, but the modification of particular depressive behaviours (e.g. deficient grooming) were individually tailored for each patient. This individually specific assessment and treatment formulation differs from other token economy programmes. In that of Hersen *et al.* (1973), for example, patients were awarded blue index cards contingently upon completion of target behaviours in four categories — personal hygiene, responsibility, occupational therapy attendance and work (all off the ward). These assignments were administered by hospital personnel, nonpsychiatric staff. Even within this more rigid system, however, individuals took responsibility for planning their day each morning during the unit's 'banking hours'. The indications are that both practices can work well. It is up to individual practitioners to decide which approach they prefer.

## Using Spouse as Source of Reinforcement

*Rationale*

Depressive states are associated with a failure to control one's interpersonal environment (McLean *et al.*, 1973) with the result that adaptive ('performing') behaviour is extinguished and depressive behaviour is reinforced (Burgess, 1969).

*Aim of Treatment*

To reverse (using spouse as ally) the progressive extinction of performing behaviours and reverse the acquisition/maintenance of depressive
behaviour. This is attempted by teaching both patient and spouse about
reinforcement principles, instructing the spouse to selectively ignore
and reinforce aspects of patients behaviour (Burgess, 1969; Lewinsohn
*et al.*, 1969) or by modification of the verbal interaction style between
partners (McLean *et al.*, 1973).

*Reinforcement of Patient by Spouse*

*Procedure.*

(1) *Assessment*: takes place according to principles on p. 67 at an
initial interview. Emphasis is on discovering the things which client is
*not* now doing that (s)he used to do; finding out what (s)he used to
find most rewarding and which of these activities are still currently
available (see list p. 102); specifying ways in which the depressive
behaviours are being inadvertently maintained and reinforced; getting
a complete description of symptoms, and a breakdown of any recent
life events.

(2) *Explanation to Patient*: Burgess (1969) emphasised to her patients
that a major effect of depression was its tendency to inhibit the completion of tasks. These little failures (a) themselves arouse further mood
disturbance and (b) represent an interruption in the smooth flow of
behaviour, a disruption which is often socially reinforced (e.g. someone
else finishes the task, sympathises with the patient, etc.).

(3) *Treatment*: At the most straightforward level, treatment consists of
selecting simple, easily executed tasks for which the probability of
completion is high, and instructing the spouse to reward completion
with attention and praise. Note that in this treatment, the couple is told
that successful completion of a task is in itself the goal, and that the
nature and value of the task itself does not matter. It is important to
instruct the spouse to give reward only according to prescribed contingencies – for completion of tasks, not for complaints of how difficult
the task is (see p. 100 for activity scheduling procedures).

*Example.* Burgess gives two examples of patients whose spouses were
involved in treatment. Both found the simplest tasks very difficult,
showed sleep disturbance, decreased sexual interest, failed to attend
work, decreased interest in interacting with others, suicidal ideation and
ruminated about their own worthlessness. The first was a 26-year-old
graduate who, having recently changed his job, was having difficulty

adjusting. He blamed all of these difficulties onto his own failures and deficiencies. Task assignment started at the most simple level with making telephone calls, mowing the lawn, drying dishes, etc. and progressed to complex tasks such as job interviews, taking employment tests, and writing CV's. The client's wife rewarded him only for completion of a prescribed activity with attention and praise, and ignored the depressive behaviour. Burgess reported very quick improvement (2 weeks) although it is to be noted that the patient was seen *daily* for the first week, thus demanding a great deal of therapist time.

The second was a 40-year-old sociologist who had recently lost his job and was in the process of selling two properties. Again he was seen daily at the outset. His assigned tasks included receiving telephone calls, reading 20 pages of a textbook, eating dinner with the family and keeping a log of tasks performed (time spent, others reactions, his own level of mood disturbance). Husband and wife were subsequently seen together once a week. It seems that instructions to the wife about rewarding, ignoring and coping with depressive behaviour respectively had not been sufficient to change the wife's negative style towards him, or the family's reinforcement of his depressive behaviour. Follow-up data suggested that this treatment was producing gradual changes in the desired direction.

*Conjoint Therapy – Mutual Reinforcement by Patient and Spouse*

*Procedure*
(1) *Assessment* (Lewinsohn's procedures for assessing interaction patterns): This is done by a one-hour session conducted at the outset in the patient's own home with all the family present (there is a similar session conducted at the middle and end of treatment). During this home session, the behaviour emitted by the client, and its consequences, are carefully monitored. Lewinsohn has produced a manual for how to do this ('*A manual for instructions for the behavioural ratings used for the observation of interpersonal behaviour*', unpublished MS, University of Oregon). McLean *et al.* (1973) adapted these assessments for twenty couples with the following form:

(a) Instruct the couple to conduct a conversation, at home, about some of their problems, lasting half an hour, and to tape record it (by themselves).
(b) Analyse the tape recording by splitting it up into 60 x 30 second intervals, and
(c) Code the interaction according to whether, during that period, an

individual was *initiating* or *reacting to* conversation in a *positive* or *negative* manner.
(d)  Average the scores across patient and spouse and
(e)  Express negative interaction score as the proportion of total interaction for each tape session.

*Reliability*:  McLean *et al.* (1973) report inter-scorer agreement between 73 and 97 per cent (average 88 per cent).

*Sub-categories of Verbal Interactions*

|  | Action | Reaction |  |
|---|---|---|---|
| Negative | a | b | a & b |
| Positive | c | d | c & d |
| Total | a & c | b & d | a & b & c & d |

Clearly, one can concentrate either on total negative actions and reactions within an interaction, or only on the actions and reactions of the patient.

(Lewinsohn then uses the interaction data to define treatment goals. Such analysis following home observation may reveal very one-sided interactions or that the client does not reinforce behaviour directed at him/her. It may also become clear that the *topics* of conversations in the home are of little interest to one or other partner.)

(2)  *Explanation to Patient*: McLean *et al.* (1973) focus explicitly on the relationship. They emphasise to patients the punishment aspect of these interactions, and how, very quickly, depressed behaviour by one partner leads to (and is then further caused by) ignoring or criticism of a behaviour. It is explained how often couples take appropriate behaviour for granted, and reserve feedback for behaviour which is not appreciated. Eventually, the couple may decide that 'it doesn't pay to talk about it' and thus condemn each other to continue to make the same mistakes.

*Treatment.*  Treatment consists of 8 one-hour weekly conjoint sessions with male and female co-therapists.

(1)  At the outset, depression is explained to the couple in social learning theory terms. Three aspects are emphasised:
(a)  That alienation and apathy can grow up in a relationship over a long period due to the couple not rewarding each other for appropriate behaviour. If one individual does not behave in a way which elicits a

positive reaction from the other, a downward spiral in the relationship may begin.

(b) As the level of adaptive, appropriate behaviour gets less and less, the couple will tend to turn to coercive techniques to try and elicit the desired behaviour. The coercive techniques tend actually to lower the probability of the very behaviour it aims to increase, in the long run. This leaves both partners feeling powerless. (Seligman's learned helplessness theory is used here to illustrate the wide ranging effect of such feelings of powerlessness.)

(c) Such a sequence of events may lead to cognitive, somatic and behavioural manifestations of depression in one or both partners. In the early stages, there are pay-offs for depressive behaviour which reinforces the non-coping behavioural style — sympathy, lessening of criticism by spouse, etc.

(2) A ban is put, by the therapists, on 'blameful' statements by either partners.

(3) The co-therapists emphasise the importance of avoiding 'bringing up the past' to explain or justify the current situation.

(4) The differential effect of positive and negative reinforcement on behaviour and emotions is discussed. Emphasis is placed on *being specific* about behavioural goals each wants to achieve in him/herself or the partner. The major facet of therapy consists in the use of reciprocal behavioural contracts, practised throughout the eight sessions (for further details of this approach see Patterson and Hops (1972)). In this scheme, the patient and spouse are taught to make specific requests about the behaviours they would like each other to change. If it is agreeable to the spouse, each requests the change in the other's behaviour.

*Example.* The example of reciprocal contracting shown in Table 4.3 is given by Liberman and Roberts (1976) in their marital treatment with Sarah Jane and her husband, Jack.

*Comment.* Note that Liberman and Roberts were implementing this strategy following Sarah Jane's progress in making use of behavioural contracts as part of the Day Unit (see p. 87). It was explained that, though the receipts were very artificial, they at least kept both patients aware of the contractual agreement into which they had entered for the purposes of therapy. It also represented some observable reminder to give more general reinforcement (attention, praise, etc.) to the other. The couple is assured that the receipts will be dropped when

Table 4.3: Contingency contracts negotiated by Sarah Jane and Jack during marital therapy

| Sarah Jane's responsibilities | Jack's responsibilities |
| --- | --- |
| *Contract I* | |
| Sit and talk with husband during breakfast, Monday to Friday | Arise from bed by 10 a.m. on Saturday and Sunday |
| Clean the living room for two hours each week | Engage in some mutual activity with Sarah Jane 10-11 p.m. on Tuesday, Thursday, Saturday and Sunday |
| *Contract II* | |
| Same as above plus the following: | |
| Dress in clothes that appeal to husband | Arrive at home by 5.30 p.m. each day |
| Initiate affection (kisses, hugs, hand-holding, caresses) reward husband | Avoid expressing hostility or 'uptightness' (coldness, rejection), annoyance, silence, withdrawal) when wife asks not to pursue sexual relations |

This contract shall be monitored by a medium of exchange. Sarah Jane shall give Jack a receipt for each successful completion of his terms of the contract. Jack shall give a receipt to Sarah Jane for her successful completion of each term of her part of the contract. Each receipt will have the recipient's name, the date, and what was done to earn it. The receipts earned by each shall be brought to the therapy session each week.

both feel settled in the new pattern of interacting.

In McLean's use of this technique, the couple are instructed to comply with their side of the bargain whether or not their own requests are being met, for the first 3 weeks of the 8-week treatment. Thereafter, they are obliged only to carry out their behavioural target (e.g. coming home on time) if their partner carries out theirs (e.g. dressing attractively).

## Application of Premack Principle

### Rationale

Occurrence of high frequency behaviour should have reinforcing value for low frequency behaviours (Premack, 1959).

### Aim of Technique

To make occurrence of a high frequency behaviour contingent upon a low frequency behaviour.

*Procedure and Examples*

*When Therapist Controls Contingency*. Lewinsohn *et al*. (1969) present the case of a 22-year-old divorced male who was in financial problems, would ruminate on his marital and other failures, showed suicidal ideation and lack of grooming.

*Step 1*: identify high frequency behaviour to be reduced (depressive talk)

*Step 2*: identify low frequency behaviour to be increased, i.e. establish series of targets which patient agrees are achievable in principle (e.g. for Lewinsohn's patient, talking to tutor, making arrangements to recover from his financial plight, making enquiries into availability of various jobs).

*Step 3*: therapist makes available more time to listen to 'depressive' talk (if client wishes to talk) *only* if some prescribed positive steps are taken between sessions. Each interview begins with report on progress patients had made. If all prearranged targets met, a full hour session is made available. If little had been accomplished, the therapist is polite but brief, and ends session within 10 or 15 minutes, suggesting that the client return 3 or 4 days later.

In the case in question, within a few weeks the client had made and acted upon many decisions, had found a job and arranged a loan to ameliorate his financial embarrassment.

*Comment*.   There are several points that deserve comment. Firstly theoretical: given that all behaviours are multiply determined, it is doubtful whether a clear contingency between the high probability behaviour and low probability behaviour was established in this case. Activity scheduling itself has been used clinically without making opportunity for occurrence of depressive talk contingent upon it, and may thus have been the effective component. Secondly practical: many therapists would be unwilling, (a) to terminate a session prematurely for any reason other than by mutual agreement of both parties, or (b) to let the longer session wander aimlessly, directed only by the client's wish to discuss self-critical topics. Nevertheless, for some patients who seem to find therapy sessions an end in themselves, and in whom there is evidence of low motivation to pursue targets because of a fear of termination of therapy, this principle may be applicable. In these cases, it can be made clear to the client that you want to meet weekly to monitor midweek progress, and that there is no point in meeting if no homework has been attempted.

*When Patient Applies Premack to Him/Herself.* In Liberman and Roberts treatment of Sarah Jane, they included a self-managed Premack technique which the patient operated herself at home. Together, the therapist and patient prepared a notebook for use as a behavioural diary, dividing each page into 2 columns. One column was headed 'constructive activity' (low frequency behaviour which they had decided to try and increase). The other column was for recording the particular depressive high frequency activity they had decided to try and decrease – in Sarah Jane's case, the time spent lying down during the day (approximately 5 hours at the outset). The patient was urged to go to bed during the day *only* after she had completed a predetermined amount of adaptive, constructive activity (e.g. housework, shopping, interactions with children). Sarah Jane herself produced the list of constructive activities which would be subject to this scheme. The idea is that as the frequency of constructive activities increases, they gain their own reinforcing qualities independently of the inappropriate activities. Thus, it is hoped, mood will improve and gradually the desire to, for example, take to bed will decrease. This is what occurred in the case of Sarah Jane. By the end of 7 weeks the 'time in bed' earned by the completion of constructive activities consistently exceeded the time in bed actually taken up.

*Comment.* The use of the Premack principle in this way seems to avoid the disadvantage of the use of the principle by the therapist. It is self-managed and is therefore easier to make plain to the patient exactly what the purpose of it is. Furthermore, it *gives permission for the depressive behaviour to take place.* My own impression is that depressed clients have often become very immune to attempts by spouses, family and friends to spur them into action. Often spouses have tried both positive and negative approaches in attempts to prevent the patient lying down on the bed (for example) for a great part of the day – to no 'avail. The patient themselves are often extremely frustrated and puzzled by their own lack of energy and listlessness. A therapy which allows any amount of this to happen, so long as some (at first) minimal constructive activity has taken place has a lot to commend it.

A variant of the Premack principle is used in *coverent conditioning.* In this procedure, a list of positive self-descriptions are drawn up by the patient with the therapist's help. The items are written on cards, and the patient instructed to read through the list before engaging in a high probability behaviour (e.g. smoking, drinking coffee, tea, using the toilet, etc.). The aim is an increase in spontaneous use of such positive verbalisations as a result of these 'conditioning' trials, but no attempt to decrease the high probability behaviour itself is implied.

## Teaching the Individual to Self-reinforce

*Rationale*

Depression results where a person's behaviour has become ineffective in securing positive reinforcers from his/her environment, because of alterations in the reinforcement schedule or changes in significant discriminative stimuli under which behaviours were typically emitted. This leads depressed people to have overly high criteria for positive reinforcement, and too low criteria for self-punishment. However, with many individuals it is not possible to remedy this situation by harnessing environmental influences. The individual may have few friends or other people available, willing or able to give social reinforcement appropriately.

*Aim of Treatment*

To teach the patient to administer rewards to him/herself contingent upon performing a pre-established response, in the absence of direct social influence.

*Procedure*

*Assessment Phase*:
(a)  Behavioural assessment (see p. 67)
(b)  List everyday tasks
(c)  Select one item which is performed frequently and client considers important
*Baseline Phase*: (10 days): Instruct client to keep 3 records (completed each night before retiring):
(a)  Total amount of time that day spent doing any subcomponent of selected task.
(b)  Rate depression according to client's own criterion on a point scale.
(c)  Record number of rewards client self-administers for that task.
(Definition of reward: 'praising yourself, doing something you like, feeling contented as a consequence of doing activity'.)
*Treatment Phase*:
(a)  Explain to client the role of self-reinforcement in general, and particularly its role in maintaining behaviour for which external rewards

are available only infrequently.

(b)  Split up selected task into subcomponents – take each separately and help client to outline what help (s)he wants to accomplish. What does 'completion' of that component mean? How long do you estimate it will take?

(c)  Help client to set appropriate (often lower!) goals, in order to maximise the chances of successful completion.

(d)  Instruct patient to write down each goal (being specific about what the performance criteria are) before starting the task (these diaries are useful for later reference by client).

(e)  Instruct patient to assess performance in light of what (s)he had set out to do (see diary).

(f)  If goals matched (or surpassed) told to do something pleasant immediately. If there is a need to ensure that this self-reward takes place, give patient packet of counters or poker chips. Instruct patient to take as many as (s)he feels (s)he deserves up to 10, and to record number taken.

(g)  Continue to monitor behaviour and mood (as baseline phase).

(h)  Later sessions: generalise scheme to other behaviours. Drop use of counters/chips when patient efficient at self-evaluating and self-rewarding.

*Example*

Jackson (1972) gives the example of a 22-year-old housewife, who, since getting married 2 years before had been depressed, suffered feelings of worthlessness, was inactive, and constantly made self-derogatory statements. Despite this she was, by her husband's account, a 'meticulous housewife and excellent cook'. On questioning, the client herself 'knew' rationally that she did do things comparable to or better than her peers, but this knowledge was insufficient to shift her low moods. Even compliments by others had become discriminative stimuli for self-criticism.[1]

The patient's list of activities to be increased were: relating to people; housekeeping; reading; talking to husband; watching T.V.; drawing.

She decided to select *housekeeping* as a *frequent* but *important* task. Splitting this up into subcomponents, she recorded how long she spent in washing dishes, drying dishes, dusting, and so on; for 10 days. She also recorded frequency of self-reward, and the mood, each day.

In the treatment phase, therapist and patient decided that 'self-reward' should consist of doing something from a list of 'pleasant' or 'positive' things. For example she would compliment herself, or telephone an interesting friend, or have a cigarette. She was given a box of poker chips to start off with.

An appointment was arranged on Day 4 and Day 10 of the treatment phase to check progress. Gradually, the patient found that she was doing housework more efficiently, and had adopted a more easy-going attitude to it. This resulted in spending less time doing the housework. On her own initiative she started to apply the same principles of socialising, inviting friends to a meal, etc. by deciding exactly what goals she wanted to accomplish and then self-evaluating and self-reinforcing. At a follow-up two months later, the depression had subsided and the effects of the specific treatment technique had generalised to other areas of her life.

## Comment

This technique is particularly appropriate if clients live alone or the partner is unavailable or unable to dispense rewards appropriately. That is not to say that it would work well if the partner was in some way hostile to the technique.

Note that in Jackson's example, the self-monitoring (SM) phase (10 days baseline) did not itself produce any improvement in mood, (though some clinicians would argue that SM is itself therapeutic). Of course, it is quite possible that the treatment phase would have been ineffective if it had not followed a period of SM.

Jackson considered two aspects of the treatment essential:

(a) requiring the person to administer the *tangible* reinforcer (points or tokens) at the same time as positive self-talk. He contends that 'it encourages the person to engage deliberately and overtly in the act of self-evaluation and self-reinforcement, and also provides the means of recording these behaviours'.

(b) presenting ordered task assignments in which the probability of successful completion is maximised. In this respect, Jackson is following the behavioural therapists, though differing from the Cognitive Therapy approach somewhat which emphasises the collection of thought-data whether the task succeeded or failed.

One problem that often arises, not discussed by Jackson, is where the patient persistently refuses to self-reinforce, explaining away successes as being 'too easy', or 'anyone could have done that'. In these cases it is necessary to remind the patient that their goal was successful completion of that subcomponent. That is what then deserves the pre-arranged self-reward. It may be necessary to renegotiate the tasks that are going to be attempted — respecifying the behaviours so there is less room for ambiguity over the outcome. It may also be necessary to remind the patient that often depression affects these little tasks most, so that being able to compare them is an important step.

Finally, this technique is obviously more appropriate for those patients who have maintained *some* basic behaviours but who find them a great *effort*, rather than those who have stopped these altogether. For other techniques which aim to increase activity see 'Activity Scheduling', p. 104; 'Anticipation Training', p. 140; and 'Systematic Resensitisation', p. 145.

### Activity Scheduling — Lewinsohn's Technique

*Rationale*

As for contingency management procedures (above) depression is seen as being associated with schedules of positive reinforcement which are inadequate to maintain adaptive behaviour. Thus therapy needs to restore the level, quality and range of activities and interactions for the patient. Whereas contingency management did so by attempting to gain control of reinforcers, activity scheduling seeks to select carefully those activities of demonstrated reinforcement potential for that individual.

*Aim of Treatment*

To increase the patient's frequency of engaging in activities that are likely to be reinforced by others or are intrinsically reinforcing for the patient.

*Procedure*

*Assessment Phase*: (a) Either, (i) ask the patient to list activities which were enjoyable, interesting, or gave a sense of accomplishment in the past, or (ii) use a previously derived activities list (see Table 4.4) or Pleasant Events Schedule (MacPhillamy and Lewinsohn, 1971).
(b) Rate each item on list for pleasantness and frequency over past month.
(c) Select items from list which are rated as at least slightly pleasant, or use whole list if not too long.

*Baseline Phase*: Instruct patient (i) to use list as basis of diary to be

Table 4.4: Sample List of Activities for Activity Scheduling

| Activity | Past Frequency | Past Enjoyment | Present Enjoyment | Present Frequency |
|---|---|---|---|---|
| (1) Buying new clothes | | | | |
| (2) Cooking a meal | | | | |
| (3) Gardening | | | | |
| (4) Going for bike ride | | | | |
| (5) Going for drive/ride | | | | |
| (6) Going for walk | | | | |
| (7) Going on the Metro | | | | |
| (8) Going out for a meal | | | | |
| (9) Going shopping | | | | |
| (10) Going to bingo | | | | |
| (11) Going to football match | | | | |
| (12) Going to pictures | | | | |
| (13) Going to pub/club | | | | |
| (14) Going to rugby match | | | | |
| (15) Jogging | | | | |
| (16) Knitting, sewing | | | | |
| (17) Playing musical instrument | | | | |
| (18) Reading | | | | |
| (19) Swimming | | | | |
| (20) Telling a joke | | | | |
| (21) Visiting friends | | | | |
| (22) Visiting relatives | | | | |
| (23) Watching T.V. | | | | |
| (24) Patient's own ideas for activities | | | | |
| (25) | | | | |
| (26) | | | | |
| (27) | | | | |
| (28) | | | | |
| (29) | | | | |
| (30) | | | | |
| (31) | | | | |
| (32) | | | | |
| (33) | | | | |
| (34) | | | | |
| (35) | | | | |

completed each evening before retiring. Tick each item which (s)he has done if (and only if) it was at least slightly pleasant; (ii) to rate mood at same time as completing diary.

*Treatment Phase*: (a) Compute correlation between Daily Pleasant Activity Score and Daily Mood Rating.
(b) Select those activities which are most frequently associated with

good mood to use as targets.

(c) Instruct patient to engage in as many of these activities per day/ week as possible.

*Alternative*

(a) Select targets from list used in Assessment Phase which patient is able to endorse as having *once* been pleasant and enjoyable. (Lewinsohn's own list may be particularly helpful here, see Table 4.5.)

Table 4.5: Activities found by Lewinsohn to be associated with mood for 10 per cent of his sample (Lewinsohn and Graf, 1973)

---

*Social Interaction*

(1)  Being with happy people
(2)  Having people show interest in what you have said
(3)  Being with friends
(4)  Being noticed as sexually attractive
(5)  Kissing
(6)  Watching people
(7)  Having a frank and open conversation
(8)  Being told I am loved
(9)  Expressing my love to someone
(10) Petting, necking
(11) Being with someone I love
(12) Complimenting or praising someone
(13) Having coffee, tea, a coke, and so on with friends
(14) Being popular at a gathering
(15) Having a lively talk
(16) Listening to the radio
(17) Seeing old friends
(18) Being asked for my help or advice
(19) Amusing people
(20) Having sexual relationships with a partner of the opposite sex
(21) Meeting someone new of the same sex

*Incompatible Affect*

(22) Laughing
(23) Being relaxed
(24) Thinking about something good in the future
(25) Thinking about people I like
(26) Seeing beautiful scenery
(27) Breathing clean air
(28) Having peace and quiet
(29) Sitting in the sun
(30) Wearing clean clothes
(31) Having spare time
(32) Sleeping soundly at night
(33) Listening to music
(34) Smiling at people

(35) Seeing good things happen to my family or friends
(36) Feeling the presence of the Lord in my life
(37) Watching wild animals

Self-efficacy

(38) Doing a project in my own way
(39) Reading stories, novels, poems or plays
(40) Planning or organizing something
(41) Driving skilfully
(42) Saying something clearly
(43) Planning trips or vacations
(44) Learning to do something new
(45) Being complimented or told I have done well
(46) Doing a job well

*Miscellaneous*

(47) Eating good meals
(48) Going to a restaurant
(49) Being with animals

---

## Comment

Activity scheduling of some sort is the most commonly used technique in the cognitive-behavioural therapist's armoury. Notice how Lewinsohn and his colleagues take great trouble to establish the correlations between activity and mood before starting treatment.

For most clinical purposes it may not be necessary to go to such lengths, especially since it requires that a patient may go through a list of fifty activities each day, checking which he has done and found pleasurable. Over several days (Lewinsohn's baseline period is 30) a computer or calculator is needed to give quick answers to the question of whether there is a correlation between mood and activity at all, and then, which activities are associated most with pleasant mood. There are usually only 10-20 activities which are mood-related for any given subject. Lewinsohn reports that, in his studies, the average correlation between total number of pleasant activities and mood over a 30-day period is about 0.3-0.4, but he also reports wide individual variation in the level of correlation from 0 to −0.75. Importantly, he then insists that *increasing pleasant activity can only be expected to alleviate mood in those individuals in whom a reasonable level of activity/mood correlation has been found* (Lewinsohn, 1975). What is the level at which one should proceed? Lewinsohn suggests levels of >0.3. But this is not the only restriction in using instructions to increase pleasant events as a treatment for depression. For clearly if someone is depressed and yet is engaging in a reasonable number of events from which they derive some pleasure, increasing these events may not have any effect. They *already* do these activities, yet their depression remains. In fact, Lewinsohn argues that increasing pleasant activities is only likely to work in those whose pleasant activities score emerges at 1 or 2 s.d. below the mean of a normal control group. Such a rule may be useful in research, but clinicians do not have normal data at their disposal with which to compare their patient's score. In any case, if one's activity list is individually tailored for the client, this precludes the use of any control data. Perhaps then the clinician should take the message that if, in their judgement, their patient is engaging in very few pleasant activities, then the opportunity may exist to use Lewinsohn's technique in therapy.

A final word about the Activities List in Table 4.5. Lewinsohn has found these to be associated with mood for 10 per cent of his sample, and has observed that they fall into three categories — social, incompatible affect, and ego-supportive (self-efficacy). Note that some of these activities are essentially passive, e.g. 'being complimented'. It may be thought difficult for a patient to actively procure 'being complimented', especially for those whose problem is that they instantly seek for reassurance. On the other hand, these items may lead to a discussion of where one is likely to be in a situation where one will be noticed, complimented, etc. 'Where did you used to go where you felt noticed?' Answers to this sort of question may lead to new targets being negotiated in order to maximise the chance of these events occurring. Secondly, other items on the list are not easy to actively procure, e.g. 'sleeping soundly at night'. Nevertheless this item is still useful as a diary measure. If it demonstrates a correlation with mood, it can show the patient how getting overtired can contribute to a problem, or how sleeping too much during the day often leads to bad nights which may lead to poor work next day.

### Activity Scheduling — Other Methods

*Rationale* (As above)

*Aim of Treatment*

Also as above, but often without the very careful baseline observations of Lewinsohn.

*Procedure*

(a) Ask patient to provide lists of activities which they used to enjoy, or use lists in Tables 4.3 and 4.4.

(b) Choose, with patient, one or two activities as targets for the week.

The following method of generating pleasant activities from a client's own experience was used by Anton *et al.* (1976).

### ACTIVITY LOG

Name_____  Date_____

*Direction*: Take a few minutes and think back over what you did today. Select the eight[2] most important activities of the day and list them below. If it seemed important to you, for whatever reasons, put it down. What seems like an important activity on one day may seem unimportant on another day. Don't worry about that. For each day, select the eight activities which seemed most important on that day, regardless of how they compare to activities on other days. After you have listed the activities, rate each activity using the seven-point scale

| Extremely | 1  2  3  4  5  6  7 | Extremely |
|-----------|---------------------|-----------|
| Unpleasant |                    | Pleasant  |

*Activity*                        *Rating*

(1)
(2)
(3)
(4)
etc.

### Graded Task Assignment

Many therapy strategies urge caution in choosing activities as targets. Some (e.g. contingency management, self-reinforcement) suggest that targets be chosen to maximise the probability of successful completion. 'Grading' tasks involves choosing targets in order of difficulty so that the patient starts with the easiest. However for some patients, even the most simple tasks seem too difficult in which case the task must be split into subcomponents, with targeted activity being the completion of only one component. Ingenuity is often required to split tasks satisfactorily. In general, a task can be split in terms of *time* (e.g. only do 10 minutes dusting and stop then no matter how much/little you have done) in terms of *place* (only clean in one room on that day, no matter how you feel about the other rooms), in terms of *proportion* (don't try and do the dishes immediately after lunch, but aim to clear the table and pile the dishes neatly by the sink ready for washing).

It is sometimes useful for patients to write down the target just before starting the task, to reinforce the idea that they are to reward themselves following completion of a target *as defined previously* (rather than indulging in self-criticism for 'only' clearing the table, and for not doing all the dishes).

Cognitive therapy (see p. 122) also makes use of Graded Task Assignment to test out a person's negative thoughts.

### Desensitisation

*Rationale*

Depression is sometimes associated with phobic reactions, and anxiety about certain situations may block progress by preventing the patient from engaging in activities which are potential reinforcers. Desensitisation may thus be useful in conjunction with other techniques.

*Aim of Treatment*

To alter phobic response patterns which restrict the patient's progress, by pairing feared situations (in imagination or *in vivo*) with relaxation.

*Procedure*

(a) Behavioural Assessment — addition of a Fear Survey Schedule where patient can use to help him/her list fears and phobias (see Table 4.6).

(b) Select target situations which are to become focus of treatment, and discuss '*in vivo*' vs. 'imaginal' options with patient.

(c) Construct hierarchy of anxiety-provoking situations or subcomponents/aspects of situation.

(d) Teach relaxation method.

(e) Present situations/scenes in imagination or *in vivo* telling patient to relax when (s)he signals experiencing any anxiety and continue imagining scene until patient can successfully imagine coping with the scene.

*Comment*

Many variants of these procedures have been developed, some emphasising the *induction* of anxiety followed by practising the *management* of that elicited anxiety. Others emphasise the importance of only allowing a minimal amount of anxiety to be experienced at all. There is no general rule to help choose between them. Some researchers maintain that neither relaxation nor the hierarchy are essential requirements for

Table 4.6: A Fear Survey Schedule

---

FEARS YOU MAY HAVE

(A)  *Leaving home or travelling*

(1)  Going into the street or open places
(2)  Going shopping
(3)  Travelling by tube train
(4)  Travelling by surface train
(5)  Travelling by ship
(6)  Travelling by bus
(7)  Travelling by car
(8)  Travelling in aeroplane
(9)  Other situations?  (Specify) . . .

(B)  *Crowded or confined spaces*

(10) Crowded shops
(11) Cinema, theatre or church
(12) Tunnels
(13) Football match
(14) Lifts
(15) Going to the hairdresser
(16) Other situations?  (Specify) . . .

(C)  *Heights and water*

(17) High places
(18) Bridges
(19) Deep water
(20) Having a bath
(21) Other situations?  (Specify) . . .

(D)  *Animals*

(22) Dogs
(23) Cats
(24) Snakes
(25) Worms
(26) Bees or wasps
(27) Rats or mice
(28) Spiders
(29) Birds
(30) Other animals?  (Specify) . . .

(E)  *Social situations*

(31) Speaking or acting to an audience
(32) Being stared at
(33) Meeting someone of the opposite sex
(34) Meeting authority
(35) Arguing with someone
(36) Being criticised
(37) Signing your name in front of someone
(38) Going to parties
(39) Eating or drinking with other people
(40) Talking to someone you don't know well
(41) Seeing others vomit or vomiting yourself

(42) Other situations?  (Specify) . . .

(F)  *Illness, injury, disease*

(43) Hospitals
(44) Germs
(45) Surgical operations
(46) The sight of blood
(47) The thought of dying
(48) Sharp objects — needles, knives, glass
(49) Being mentally ill
(50) Fear of suffocation
(51) Going to the dentist
(52) Fear of fainting
(53) Fear of certain illness   (Specify) . . .
(54) Fear of heart stopping
(55) Other situations?   (Specify) . . .

(G)  *Other fears*

(56) Thunder and lightning ı
(57) Strong winds or storms
(58) Darkness
(59) Being left alone for a few hours
(60) Failing in some task or exam
(61) Urinating in a public toilet
(62) Other situations . . .

---

successful treatment. On the other hand, many therapists prefer to use both, since they seem very *plausible* to the client (and may thereby enhance expectancy based improvement). In addition, relaxation training may have more general benefits on other aspects of the patients functioning (e.g. sleep).

It must be said that there is no good evidence that relaxation treatment is by itself effective as a technique for primary depression. McLean and Hakstian (1979) in a very careful evaluation of behavioural and drug treatment in depression, used relaxation as a 'no treatment' control, and the results seemed to justify this decision. Many therapists who have vainly tried to relax depressed patients would agree with this conclusion. Nevertheless, there is little doubt that *some* patients do benefit (see Sammons' procedure p. 145), so it ought to be kept in mind if the behavioural analysis reveals avoidance of anxiety provoking material as a major component of the problem.

## Social Skills (Assertion) Training

There are now a number of very good guides to assertion training, some of which are listed below. For this reason I shall not go into detail here. Suffice it to say that the therapist needs to constantly bear in mind that a problem of interpersonal skills deficit may have caused or be maintaining the depressive state and in such cases assertion training may be appropriate. Where it is appropriate, the therapist must then choose whether to concentrate on very specific components of interpersonal skills (e.g. voice volume) or take a more holistic approach and teach complete strategies of social interaction.

*Bibliography on Social Skills/Assertion Training*

The following are recommended as guides to the use of these techniques:
(1) Liberman, R.P., King, L.W., Derisi, W.J. and McCann, M. (1977) *Personal Effectiveness: Guiding People to Assert Themselves and Improve Their Social Skills*, Research Press, Illinois
Although now some years old, an excellent guide with many practical suggestions on techniques to use within therapy sessions.
(2) Trower, P., Bryant, B. and Argyle, M. (1978) *Social Skills and Mental Health*, Methuen & Co. Ltd. London
A good text with reviews of research and outcome literature on social skills training.
(3) Spence, S. and Shepherd, G. (eds) (1983) *Developments in Social Skills Training*, Academic Press, New York
An up to date account of the application of these methods to different client groups. The main section of the book covers work with different adult and child client groups, with a third section on new developments.

## Notes

1. Jackson gives no instance of this, but an example would be a man telling his wife how nice the gravy tasted, and the wife thinking to herself 'what's wrong with the rest of the meal'. Or a wife complimenting husband on his tie eliciting the thought 'what's wrong with my shirt'. Beck might call this 'arbitrary inference'. The important point to note in Jackson's patient (as in many depressed patients) that self-derogatory statements are often made following rewards by others. One can see, therefore, how families learn very early that it is better not to be complimentary, and the cycle of nonreward twists again. This sequence ought to be explained carefully to the client. Note also that most therapists could not ignore the association in Jackson's example, between getting married and becoming depressed, nor between the depressed mood and being seen as a 'meticulous housewife'. Careful assessment of these issues, including assessment of the woman's satisfaction regarding the marital/housewife role, would be required.
2. Or any number the therapist thinks appropriate. Three may be the most you can select for the more depressed patient.

# 5 COGNITIVE TECHNIQUES

## Overview of the 'Cognitive Therapy Package'

There has recently been a large growth in interest in Beck's Cognitive Therapy (CT). This comparative recency is surprising in the light of the fact that Beck himself has been writing about a cognitive theory of affective disorders for some years (Beck, 1963; 1964; 1967), but interest in the techniques was fairly limited, at least in the UK. Many factors have probably contributed to the sudden large growth of interest, but two seem to be of especial importance. Firstly, psychologists working with *anxious* patients began to describe the importance of taking the 'thoughts' or 'self-talk' of patients into account (Lang, 1971; Meichenbaum, 1974; Rachman, 1976), and cognitive-behaviour modification for these clients became respectable (Meichenbaum, 1977). Secondly, Seligman's theory of learned helplessness, the origins of which had been animal experiments in 1967 (Overmier and Seligman, 1967; Seligman and Maier, 1967), but whose theory was most fully propounded in his book in 1975, gave a coherent 'cognitive' account of some depressive states. Most of Seligman's early work was experimental rather than clinical, and the clinical implications of helplessness theory poorly worked out. Suggestions such as giving patients a sense of control, through, for example, success experience, were made, but (a) much of the evidence was from studies using analogue student populations; (b) therapeutic strategies were not outlined in sufficient detail to be of practical use to clinicians, and (c) none of the suggestions, if successful, would have uniquely supported the theory on which they were based, so the impetus to carry out detailed clinical anti-helplessness work may have been lacking. None of this hindered helplessness theory itself from becoming a very widely known, accepted and extensively researched set of concepts (see Abramson *et al.* (1978) for a review). Against the background of an attractive theory with few therapy strategies linked to it, psychologists were bound to look with greater urgency to existing approaches for the treatment of depression, and Beck's cognitive therapy was there to fill the vacuum. (See Seligman (1981) for his account of the overlap and differences between anti-helplessness interventions and CT.)

The underlying assumption of cognitive theory of depression is that the patient's emotional disturbance follows from distortions in thinking, so that change in the patient will be long-lasting only if changes in thinking patterns occur during treatment. In other treatments, this change may occur incidentally (as a side-effect of psychodynamic or pharmacological intervention), but in CT the thinking of style is met and dealt with 'head on'. A range of behavioural and cognitive techniques are used for this purpose. The term 'cognitive therapy' is misleading in that it sounds like one specific therapy; it is not. Many of the techniques are very familiar to the behavioural therapist (assertive training, task assignment). It is the way they are introduced to the patient and used in therapy which provides a common and distinctive theme to the therapy sessions and to the techniques which are to be reviewed here.

Several core techniques are used to serve the common purpose of: (a) eliciting the patient's thoughts, self-talk, and interpretations of events; (b) gathering with the patient, evidence for or against the interpretations; and (c) setting up experiments (homework) to test out the validity of the interpretations and gather more data for discussion.

Particularly, CT focuses on errors in thinking which habitually occur in depressives, for example:

*Dichotomous Thinking* (black/white, all or nothing thinking), where there is no perceived middle path − just the extremes.

*Selective Abstraction*, the selecting out of small parts of a situation and ignoring others, e.g. a tutor's report on your essay gives much praise, but mentions at one point that the Introduction was too long. 'He doesn't like my essay' would be selective abstraction.

*Arbitrary Inference*, where a conclusion is inferred from irrelevant evidence, e.g. you phone your boy/girl friend and no-one answers '(S)he's probably out with another partner' would be arbitrary inference (if inferred on those grounds alone).

*Overgeneralisation*, to conclude from one specific negative event that another negative event is thereby more likely, e.g. failure at maths means failure at everything.

*Catastrophising*, to think the very worst of a situation. Each of the above examples would suffice.

It is an active therapy in which the therapist deliberately seeks to collaborate with the patient, with therapy concentrating mainly on the 'here and now'. The past is introduced only so far as it helps to explain habitual modes of thinking and behaviour in the present.

*Indications for Use*

Beck *et al.* (1979) recommend standard physical treatments for bipolar depressives, highly regressed or highly suicidal patients. Although it has been used with depressed inpatients, research in both the USA and UK (Blackburn *et al.*, 1981) has so far concentrated on unipolar non-psychotic outpatients and primary care patients (though many of Blackburn's Edinburgh patients were 'endogenous' depressives by Spitzer's criteria (see p. 40).

*Overall Strategy*

CT is normally limited to 15-20 sessions of 50 minutes each, once weekly, though for more severely depressed patients sessions are held twice weekly for the first 4-5 weeks. It is interesting to note that in Blackburn *et al's* study, patients were considered 'nonresponders' if their Beck *or* Hamilton Scores had not dropped by 50 per cent after 12 weeks of treatment.

*Outline Plan of Therapy*

Figure 5.1: Diagrammatic representation of relative proportion of cognitive and behavioural techniques used as a function of stage in therapy and/or severity of depression

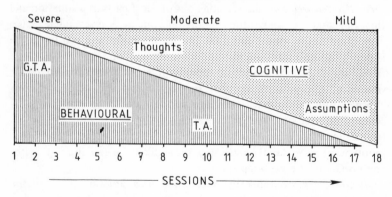

Note:   G.T.A. = graded task assignment
        T.A. = task assignment

Figure 5.1 shows a general treatment plan. It conveys the idea that the overall approach is partly behavioural and partly cognitive and that the more severe the depression at the outset of therapy (as defined by clinical judgement or questionnaires such as Beck or Hamilton), the greater weight is given to behavioural techniques. A less severe depression would start straight away with both facets (e.g. equivalent of Session 6 in diagram). Finally, it illustrates that within each component, the progression is from discussion of the simple to discussion of the complex. Within the behavioural component, this involves grading tasks before assignment — splitting, for example 'housework' into cooking, dusting, ironing, mending, etc., and 'cooking' into buying ingredients, selecting recipe or choice of food for meal, cooking meal (simple to complex), and so on. Even within this list, 'buying ingredients' may itself have to be split up into subcomponents. Within the cognitive component, the progression is from discussion of simple 'thoughts' and obvious interpretive errors to more complex 'assumptions' on which the patient's attitudes are premised.

In the sections that follow, specific techniques are described in detail. The clinician who is new to cognitive therapy might also like to look at Chapter 7 where some training exercises are presented for use by themselves or in training groups.

*General Characteristics of Therapy Sessions*

There are certain *general characteristics* of cognitive therapy which give structure to each session.

First, the therapist *establishes an agenda*. The therapist reviews with the patient points that they wish to be discussed in that session. This may take up to *10 minutes* at the outset of the session, and may include review of previous week's homework. Substantive issues arising from homeworks may, however, form a major part of the entire session.

Second, the therapist *structures the therapy time*. This involves covering all the issues on the agenda, and assigning time next session for discussion of those issues not discussed. The therapist attempts to keep a balance between central and peripheral issues so that the latter don't predominate.

Third, the therapist *summarises periodically* during the interview, and elicits patient's reactions to the summary. The therapist deliberately seeks the patient's guidance on where he/she may have misinterpreted any aspect of the patient's problem.

Fourth, the session is dominated by a *questioning approach* by the therapist. Statements of fact or offering advice are not thought to be therapeutic.

Finally, the therapist does two things:
(a) *assigns homework* based on topics that have emerged during the session as problematic.
(b) asks patient to *sum up the session* and go over what the homework assignment is. The patient is encouraged to indicate any points at which the topics discussed had been (in)appropriate, hurtful or helpful.

There are many techniques used in CT[1] which are used in other treatments — task assignment, assertive training, relaxation, role-play, reattribution training, etc. The distinctive and uniting thing about CT is the *way* in which the techniques are used. Cognitive therapists call the overall strategy: 'collaborative empiricism'. In reading through the techniques below, be aware of the ways in which the cognitive therapist attempts to keep the collaboration in the forefront of the discussion, and keeps the entire interaction *empirical*.

In the following description of core techniques the format differs slightly from the 'behavioural techniques' section. Here, the rationale and aims of treatment are followed by a section on 'Procedure' which itself may include some examples. Unlike the behaviour descriptions, examples are given by way of extracts from clinical sessions rather than more general case descriptions. Rather than make general comments about the procedures, where appropriate several 'Problems' are raised and suggestions offered.

For *assessments* which may be used prior to implementing any of these techniques — see Chapter 3.

### Thought-catching

*Rationale*

(1) That by recording thoughts the connection between thought, feeling and behaviour will be demonstrated.
(2) That the act of recording will itself help to break the thought-affect link by making the thought seem less real.
(3) That data for therapist and patient to formulate hypotheses for reality testing is provided.

*Aim of Technique*

To enable patients to accurately monitor and record their own self-talk whenever they feel upset in any way.

*Procedure*

*Explaining the link between thought, feeling and behaviour.* It is important that the framework within which the therapist is working is com-
municated to the patient early in therapy. The patient who has long
seen their 'bad thoughts' as being secondary to their (biological) depression may be surprised and threatened to find a therapist who is interested in recording and modifying the thoughts themselves. For these
clients, the way in which their thoughts and interpretations *maintain*
the depressive cycle, no matter what initiated it, may need to be carefully explained. But even if understanding the theory, a patient may
not be able to readily identify 'thoughts' as separate entities. Beck *el al*.
(1979) find it useful to use a patient's thought as they waited in the
waiting room before their first appointment as an example. The question would be: 'what thoughts were running through your head just
before you came in to see me?'. The client may well reply 'I thought
you might say I was unsuitable for treatment', or 'What am I doing
here seeing a psychotherapist!'. The therapist may then ask 'What did
you feel when these thoughts were occurring to you?'. From this situation, the therapist extracts a model for other situations. But the identi-
fication of the patient's self-talk as thought rather than as reality may
have to be constantly made throughout the early sessions. The way the
therapist asks the questions during the sessions can become a model
for the patient's own use.

*Example*   Consider the following interchange: The patient is upset and
puzzled by her failure to overcome her procrastination:

   **Patient:**  I always put off and put off until there's just no . . . I can't
be bothered
   **Therapist:**  You *always* do that?
   **Patient:**  Yes — I didn't used to.
   **Therapist:**  Or you *feel* like doing that?
   **Patient:**  Oh, I feel like doing that, yeah. And that's wrong. To me it
is wrong. But I still do it.
   **Therapist:**  What do you feel like when you say 'it's wrong'? What
does that make you feel?
[Therapist attempting to identify 'it's wrong' as a 'thought' rather than
'reality', to draw out thought and affect connections]
   **Patient:**   That I should pull my socks up. (Patient replies with
another thought).
   **Therapist:**  O.K. Well what do you feel when you say 'I should pull

my socks up?'

**Patient:** Ashamed of myself.

**Therapist:** What about your feelings? What does it make you feel?

**Patient:** Guilty, ashamed, depressed.

**Therapist:** Would you like to change those things? Would you like to do something in the morning instead of the afternoon, or the afternoon instead of the evening?

**Patient:** I'd just like to keep on doing things instead of having to make such a tremendous effort — supreme effort — all the time.

**Therapist:** You'd like to keep 'ticking over'?

**Patient:** Yes I would, but at the moment I'm just not.

**Therapist:** How likely is it that you'll keep 'ticking over' when you feel guilty?

**Patient:** From past experience, no likelihood at all, but it's the guilt that drives me on.

**Therapist:** The guilt drives you on, but it also inhibits you — is that what you're saying?

**Patient:** (After a pause) It inhibits me, yes.

Here the therapist, through questions, attempts to make the relationship between thoughts, feelings and behaviour the central subject of the discussion. The question is not whether it actually *is* wrong for the patient to procrastinate, but what effect that thought has on her feelings (guilt, shame, depression) and behaviour (procrastination followed by intense activity).

*Instructing patient to monitor thoughts.* When the therapist feels that the patient is able to begin to identify such thoughts within the session, (and use of the Thought List on p. 83 may help in this process), (s)he can ask the patient to monitor their own thoughts between sessions.

*Example*

**Therapist:** In the session today we've talked about several recent situations which have made you feel upset or depressed. In these cases, we saw how the things that ran through your mind at the time seemed to make things worse. In fact, it is rare that people feel upset without there being thought behind it. Between now and next session I want you to be on the look-out for feelings of upset and depression and 'catch' the thoughts that go along with these moods.

A form (see p. 81) is given to the patient on which they may complete date, situation, feeling, and thought. (S)he may complete it in the actual situation, or later when alone. If later, it is useful to advise the patient to note down the thought on a scrap of paper as soon as possible after it has occurred.[2] If this is not done, valuable data may be lost; nor will there be the opportunity for the technique of thought-catching to help to 'distance' the thought itself in a therapeutic way.

## Comment and Problems

The examples of items taken from thought forms on p. 163, reveal the *variable quality* of material produced when a patient is asked to record thoughts. A number of problems may arise the most common of which seem to be:

(1) *The patient feels that it will make him/her worse to concentrate on their negative thoughts.*   From the patient's perspective this seems a very reasonable prediction, especially if they have been consciously trying to put some thoughts out of their head. The therapist may ask whether trying to exclude the thoughts has worked, or whether they just pop up again regardless of the patient's attempts. In this case the therapist may point out the possible advantages of meeting the thoughts 'head on' so to speak and to deal with them directly. Another useful strategy is to admit that it may cause some distress or it may not; that some find it surprisingly therapeutic, and that there is no way of knowing which category your patient falls into until they try it. This approach emphasises the collaborative and experimental nature of the therapy, in which the therapist does not set himself up as knowing the answers, but as the collaborator of the patient in finding out.

(2) *The patient believes he/she has no thoughts.*   In this case, it may be possible to use the thought-list (p. 83). Some patients are unable to recall negative thoughts on demand, but can easily recognise them. An example of using this technique follows:

Miss H. was a 41-year-old shop assistant who lived with her married sister and family. She first presented three years before with 'depression in the context of a chronically anxious personality'. She had been admitted five times and had received a large number of medications to no effect. She was the least attaining in her family (of which she was constantly reminded by living with her sister) and seemed to feel that life had passed her by in her prime. On assessment, her responses revealed her attempts to ignore any thoughts she might have: 'There is nothing', 'I've trained myself to feel nothing', 'I'm cut off from everything', 'I can smile, but it means nothing'. Interestingly, although she *thought* she was feeling nothing, and thinking nothing, she was clearly being very upset by some aspect of her mental state. Sixteen items from the list of self-statements (p. 83) were used, and she was asked to rate frequency of occurrence over the last 24-hour period on a 10 point scale (0 – not occurred at all; 10 – occurred almost constantly). She found she could rate the frequency of the thoughts. Indeed, five of the sixteen she rated as 'very frequent', and she was able to appreciate that, in fact, far from blotting out thoughts, she was bombarded with them for the most part of the day.

Giving specific examples of thoughts was an aid to identifying naturally occurring depressive cognitions in a patient unable or unwilling to do this for herself.

(3) *The negative thoughts come so fast and with such intensity that the patient feels unable to write them down.* Beck *et al.* recommend that if thoughts are just too intense to 'catch', then short-term *distraction* techniques are appropriate. Such diversionary tactics may consist of focusing all attention on some object in the immediate environment and describing it to themselves in great detail, counting numbers of marks, scratches, patterns, etc. Some patients find it helpful to count backwards from 100. If this does not demand all available attention, then the patient may count backwards in 3s or 7s. Of course, there are some general diversionary tactics like reading or taking a walk which can be advised, but many patients may have tried these to no effect. In general, emphasise that mood alleviation due to distraction may only be short-lived in the first instance, but they will become more practised. Patients may like to note down how long it worked for, and discuss this next therapy session.

## Reality Testing

### Reality Testing Within Session

*Rationale.* That testing out thoughts may help them to be seen as 'psychological' phenomena, not identical with reality, and that many reactions are based on interpretations rather than fact. Making the patient aware of, and distanced from their erroneous thinking style may make it more likely (s)he will hesistate when making a similar error in future.

*Aim*. To seek, with patient's help, evidence for and against the negative thoughts and assumptions.

*Procedure*. (a) Identify thoughts and statements made by patient which are negative or associated with bad feelings.

(b) Ask patient how much they believe that statement is true, or how likely it is that this negative event will come about

(c) Check feelings associated with statement, 'When you say that to yourself, what does it make you feel?'

(d) Leaving the validity of the statement as an open question, gently probe the evidence, e.g. past outcomes of similar situations; alternative outcomes and their frequencies, times when same situation has had (i) worse consequences than at present envisaged[3], or (ii) better consequences than envisaged.

(e) If patient catastrophises about the future, ask them to rate actual probability, e.g. if patient says 'I'll never find another friend like him', ask them how probable that state of affairs actually is — one chance in a million, one in a hundred, 10 per cent or 40 per cent chance.

(f) Throughout the interchange, emphasise that it is not a glowing positive interpretation which is being encouraged, but challenging thoughts with *reality*.

(g) Check how much patient *now* believes the original statement is true.

*Example*. This patient had the habit of biting her nails down to the quick, when she felt very stressed and upset. This in turn upset her, even after the precipitating event had passed, when she saw what she had done to 'her appearance'. She believed everyone would immediately notice that her nails were bitten, that they would know that she was 'still a child' (she was 28 years old). After a nail-biting bout, she said in one session, 'my whole life is affected', 'I can never pull myself together at all after doing this'.

**Therapist:** When you say to yourself 'my whole life is affected', how does it leave you feeling?

**Patient:** Helpless and depressed.

**Therapist:** How true do you think it really is that it affects everything in your life?

**Patient:** It always affects everything. It takes me ages to get over it.

**Therapist:**  So if I asked you to rate your percentage belief in those statements 'it always affects everything' and 'it takes me ages to get over it', what would your rating be?

**Patient:**  One hundred per cent.

**Therapist:**  Can you tell me about a time when you bit your nails and it seemed your whole life fell apart?[3]

(Note here that the therapist does not ignore patient's claim that everything is affected. The patient gave such a description, and then therapist asked: Can you remember a time when you bit your nails when it hasn't been quite so bad afterwards?)

**Patient:**  Well, I suppose there have been times, at home, not this year, but at other times when I've pulled myself together.

**Therapist:**  Well, give me a couple of examples. . . remind me of a couple of times when you've bitten your nails, been really down, and then you've recovered quite quickly.

(Interestingly, at this point in the interview, the patient can remember that there *have* been times when the consequences haven't been so catastrophic, but struggles to find particular examples.)

**Patient:**  There have been times . . . (pause)
. . . nothing shines up, but there have been times when I have got really low, and I've just decided the next morning that I've got to make the best of this bad situation.

**Therapist:**  Do you remember such a time?

**Patient:**  Well . . . there was that [pause] Oh, I know!

(At this point the mood rapidly lifted, as the patient went on to recall an *actual* event. This mood lifting had not occurred when the patient merely remembered that these events *had* occurred. This illustrates the importance of being particular in the incident recalled as part of the reality testing procedure. After the discussion of this event . . .)

**Therapist:**  So it seems that when you've been biting your nails, you feel pretty fed up and depressed, and much of the time this seems to get you right down, but at other times you manage to cope pretty well. You know at the start of this discussion you said 'It *always* affects everything' and 'It takes me ages to get over it'. How much do you now believe that that statement is true?

**Patient:**  Well it's pretty bad. Well, about 60 per cent.

(Note that it is rare to find a patient in whom reality testing within the session allows them totally to reject their negative thoughts. Furthermore, Beck *et al.* stress, and the clinical impressions of myself and colleagues confirm, that the therapist has to go through the same sort of procedure again and again throughout therapy before the patient starts to go through the same procedure themselves spontaneously.

*Problems: The patient does not understand 'rating degree of belief as a percentage'.* Because some patients think in extremes ('It's either true or false') it may be difficult for them to understand the request to rate degree of belief. Drawing out a scale on paper or a blackboard, using analogues such as temperature on a thermometer, reducing the scale to five points and putting words to each point, may be useful, e.g.:

| *Thought* | Disagree strongly | Disagree | Neutral, uncertain | Agree | Strongly agree |
|---|---|---|---|---|---|
| 'So far in my life everything's gone wrong for me' | — — | — | 0 | + | ++ |

*The patient gets depressed when thinking of good times.* Some patients constantly remind themselves of when times were better and become upset in so doing (the upset being perhaps caused by the focusing on the *loss* of past rewards, and the implicit or explicit thought, 'I'm never going to have such happiness again' or 'I shouldn't be like this when I've got such a good home and family', etc.). Note then how thoughts about 'good times' are themselves ambiguous. They may be associated with a preoccupation of loss, or used by the therapist and patient to challenge current feelings of hopelessness. In either case, the therapist and patient may collaborate in an attempt to identify what is different about current circumstances or attitudes which are acting as a 'roadblock' to getting the rewards the patient once obtained.

*The patient cannot think of better times.* If a patient says that nothing gives them satisfaction at present, it may be little use challenging the notion by mere argument. A therapist who says to patients 'You're wrong, surely. There must be something which gave/gives you pleasure', will quickly lose rapport and trust of the patient. If the patient feels the therapist is belittling the problems in some way, they are less likely to collaborate. Instead a therapist may ask about things the person did when they were young, members of their family or friends with whom they were close, hobbies or pastimes they may have had (did they ever have a pet?). The therapist may rephrase the questions to ask about the times when the depression is not so intense (it is sometimes better to ask about specific time intervals, e.g. the last month, week, or yesterday). Finally, the therapist can ask the patient to keep a diary of activities for the next week on which (s)he can mark with an M (for mastery) anything which gives a slight sense of accomplishment and a P (for pleasure) anything which gives a sense of pleasure. The idea of rating both M and P is that some tasks (e.g. clearing out a cupboard, mowing the lawn) may give little pleasure but some sense of accomplishment. By contrast, other tasks (e.g. watching T.V.) may give pleasure without accomplishment. The therapist and patient may discuss how to increase both facets. The less depressed or more 'rating conscious' patient may rate M and P on a five or ten point scale. The next session may be taken up with discussion of the diary and to what extent the patient's prediction that 'nothing gives me pleasure' has turned out to be true.

## Reality Testing by Task Assignment

*Rationale.* Virtually all cognitive behavioural approaches to depression incorporate task assignment in one form or other as a means of increasing the patient's activities, interactions and range of rewards. In CT, the role of task assignment is extended to that of 'data collection' as a means of confirming or refuting an hypothesis based on a negative thought. So in addition to the beneficial effects of activity *per se*, the aim is also to make the patient view their thoughts as hypotheses to be tested out — something which initiates and stimulates action rather than inhibits it.

*Aim of Technique.* To come to agreement with patient regarding between-session targets which will test out a negative thought as if it was an hypothesis ('hunch', 'idea').

*Procedure.* (a) Identify within session an idea or thought which is upsetting — ask patient to rate degree of belief.
(b) Define, with the patient, the implications of the statement — what does it predict will happen?
(c) Discuss ways of testing out the truth of the statement.
(d) Set up a between-session 'homework' to test out statement — agree on criteria by which homework will be evaluated.
(e) Emphasise a 'data gathering' approach to task assignment rather than 'success/failure' approach, i.e. 'try it out, see how far you get, and keep a note of your thoughts and feelings for us to talk about next time'. 'It doesn't matter how far you get — if you come across a 'road-

block' we can talk about it next time – just note down what happens'. The implicit emphasis of the therapist is not 'You can do it if you try' (relatives and friends may have been saying that for some time to no avail). Rather it is 'you may find it *more* difficult than you imagine or *less* difficult than you imagine, I don't know. So let's try it out to see exactly what the difficulties are, then we can discuss them next time and get to work on them'. The therapist shares his *ignorance* of the outcome with the patient, thus subtly challenging the patient's view that 'it's bound to make me feel worse'.

(f) Next session, discuss the outcome of the homework (see (d) above), remembering to come back to the specific purpose of the assignment, i.e. to test out a negative thought.

*Example*. This patient had said during one session 'my friends are sick of me'. Within that session the therapist had discussed this thought and discovered that the evidence on which it was based was that she and her friends had not been in contact with each other for 2-3 weeks. In fact, when examining the reason for this, it had occurred to her that she had been out of the area for three weekends out of four. Despite this evidence, she still felt they were probably sick of her as well. Patient and therapist discussed how it could be tested out between sessions. She decided she would phone some friends and, together, therapist and patient made up a list of people to contact.

In discussing the homework in the next session the following interchange occurred:

**Therapist**: What was the point of doing this?

**Patient**: To find out whether my friends were sick of me or not.

**Therapist**: Why should we want to find out whether your friends were sick of you or not? Why did we select that as being something we should look at?

**Patient**: Because I had not heard from them for a fortnight to three weeks.

(Note, here, the therapist is trying to remind the patient that this thought was selected because it was upsetting her and they wanted to test out the upsetting thought.)

**Therapist**: And why had you not heard from them?

**Patient**: Well (a) I had been out of the district, and (b) I'd just lost all confidence altogether.

**Therapist**: O.K. So you'd been out of the district and you'd lost confidence and you hadn't heard from them. What were you saying to yourself?

**Patient:** That I really am an awful person to be with.

**Therapist:** So what did you decide to do to test it out?

**Patient:** Well first of all, I rang Marilyn, no, I rang Simon, but he was at work, and it wasn't convenient. And then I rang Marilyn, a girl I got to know through church and she lives near the hospital and she said 'Bring Veronica along'. So we went to see 'The Jazz Singer', and I really enjoyed it; I was glad of the company.

**Therapist:** So what was the target, what was the homework to do?

**Patient:** It was to see if my friends were sick of me, now Marilyn wanted to go out, she desperately wanted to go out with me . . . we had quite a nice evening actually . . . she wasn't sick of me.

*Problem.* The patient fails to carry out assignment nor keeps record of any attempts to do so[4].

*Possible Reasons.* (a) *Therapist has not emphasised* that homework is a part of the treatment, not an 'optional extra'.

(b) *Therapist has not explained* the reason for that particular assignment (get patient to restate reasons and assignments in own words).

(c) *Therapist has not allowed* enough time in session in which the homework was set up for patient to voice objections to it.

(d) *Task too complex* — needs to be graded.

(e) *Patient did not understand the 'try anyway' message.*

(f) *Patient questions whether 'merely doing it' will help his depression.* This is a common underlying feeling. It may be explained to the patient that concentrating on the smaller simple parts of a task is an important forerunner to contemplating some complex activity. Mountaineers often plan their climb by a series of 'camps'. At any one time, all effort will be concentrated on getting to the next camp. Straining to see the summit, the eventual goal, might be a dangerous distraction. So what are the patient's 'camps' on the way to the solution of this or that problem? It may also help to explain that depression is a disorder which affects ability to carry out minor tasks as much or more than the major ones.

(g) *Patient feels therapist is trying to control him and boss him around.* Emphasise patient's freedom to choose methods to help him/her. Discuss a *range* of homeworks and let patient choose.

(h) *Patient feels the depressed behaviour is inevitable.* Discuss depressive behaviour and its consequences on mood. Discuss alternative strategies and their probable consequences. Emphasise that patient is free to choose either and set up homework instructing them to choose *either* strategy and follow it through. For example, Beck *et al.* quote the case of a patient who went back to bed and stayed there for long periods every time her boyfriend left her following a visit. Attempts to schedule alternative activity seemed to have been unsuccessful; the therapist suggested to the patient that she could operate Plan A (going back to bed) *or* Plan B (getting up and doing a, b and c). The between-session instruction was to choose one of the strategies on future occasions, and follow it through. In this case, the depressive behaviour actually became part of the homework assignment, but by 'free choice'. In such cases, once the patients believe that the behaviour (whichever is chosen) is under their own control, this may relieve the burden of the thought 'I am the victim of my moods'; and may opt for the more adaptive strategy. See Premack principle (p. 94) for the use of high frequency (depressive) behaviours as reinforcers for low frequency (constructive) behaviours.

*Reality Testing – by finding alternative responses to negative thoughts (between sessions)*

*Rationale.* A major problem with automatic negative thoughts is that they seem indisputable and incontrovertible. If the patient learns to write them down, this may itself dampen their impact because it makes them seem like 'thoughts' rather than 'reality'. Producing alternative, realistic responses is a further stage in weakening the hold the automatic negative thought has on the person's mood and behaviour.

*Aim of Technique.* To teach patient to automatically answer their own automatic thoughts with believable rational responses.

*Procedure.* (a) After discussing the automatic negative thoughts the patient has collected between sessions, ask them for other possible interpretations of the situation.
(b) Collect and write down other interpretations (but without regard at this stage for whether they would upset the patient *more* or *less*).
(c) Demonstrate the range of alternatives in order to show that the original interpretation was one among a few.
(d) Begin testing the evidence for or against the alternatives – keep an open mind on which alternative the evidence will turn out to support.
(e) If the evidence supports the more negative alternatives, review with patient 'Is it as bad as it seems'.
(f) Give patient full 'Thought Record Form' (see p. 81) and ask them

to note down Situation, Emotion (rate intensity), Negative Thought (rate belief), Alternative Thought Interpretation (rate belief), Subsequent Emotion (rate intensity) plus rate final belief in Negative Thought. (If all these ratings overcomplicate matters for a particular patient, then they may be omitted, but careful demonstration, with examples, will help to alleviate confusion.)

*Problem. The patient can't think of any rational responses – 'there are no rational response to this predicament'.* This common problem is not resolved by the therapist merely suggesting that the negative thought is wrong, and suggesting alternatives him or herself. More realistic responses may have to be *shaped* (i.e. therapist gradually rewards for successive approximation to a realistic response). The therapist must ensure that (s)he is as empirical with the rational responses as the negative responses. That is, if the patient's only rational response is 'It'll all turn out right in the end' there may be as little evidence for this over-optimistic view as for the pessimistic view it is supposed to replace. Try evaluating the evidence for things turning out alright in the end.

Another approach is to ask the patient what they would say to a friend with a similar problem or perspective. This may take the form of a more formal role-play in which patient and therapist take on different roles. Or the therapist may ask the patient what they would say to themselves 'on a good day'.

Alternatively, the therapist may suggest that the patient concentrates attention on the negative thought itself, analyse it, make sure it truly represents the situation, categorise it (over-generalisation, selective abstraction, etc.). If it is a statement about the past, has there *never* been a counter-instance? If it is a statement about the future write down the *actual* probability. If it is a general statement like 'I always . . .', 'I can never . . .', and if this is based on valid evidence, then the statement may be changed to 'In the past, I have been unable . . .'. This ties the statement down more to a specific time period and makes it easier to evaluate.

Finally, the therapist may suggest a *number* of possible alternative thoughts and ask the patient to *choose* one which is least inappropriate. Ask how much they could believe in that. Remember that small belief in the rational response is most unlikely to shift the belief in the negative thought, leaving the mood just as intense. So if someone says that writing alternative rational responses 'doesn't work', examine the responses to see how believable they really are. Bland expressions of optimism are rarely sufficient to reduce the impact of a negative automatic thought (see Training Exercise, p. 163).

### Cognitive Rehearsal

*Rationale*. If a patient has stopped many activities they used to perform, it sometimes becomes difficult to even *imagine* doing the task successfully. The entire task (even the simplest) seems a great effort without the patient being aware of what it is about the task they find difficult. Cognitive rehearsal provides useful data on these questions. Each newly discovered 'roadblock' may become a target in itself. Furthermore, if the patient can imagine successfully *completing* the task, and something of the feeling of accomplishment that this involves, it may enhance motivation to attempt the task or some aspect of it between sessions (see also Anticipation Training, p. 140; Systematic Resensitisation p. 145).

*Aim of Technique*. To identify 'roadblocks' in progress and thoughts/feelings associated with doing activities by imagining doing them in every detail during the session.

*Procedure*. (a) Identify a task with which the patient has particular difficulty, or that they used to do but say 'I couldn't possibly do that now'.
(b) Check whether it is the sort of activity which *would* give mastery or pleasure to them if it could be done.
(c) Check that initiating the task or its successful completion is not crucially dependent on anyone or anything *other* than the patient (e.g. I can only decorate that room when we can afford it, or when my wife/husband chooses the wallpaper), though these 'reasons' in themselves may be the subject of enquiry and challenge in some cases.
(d) Ask patient to imagine doing the activity starting with *planning* stage, buying, preparing any materials/ingredients, starting activity, middle of activity, end of activity, immediately afterwards, own feelings, others' reactions, etc.
(e) During cognitive rehearsal, identify points which patient finds difficult, ask patient to imagine all aspects of that difficulty, then suggest that any particular 'roadblock' is passed so they may continue the task. Do this with each block until patient imagines successful completion.
(f) Discuss with patient roadblocks and/or whole task with a view to setting up between-session assignments.

*Example.* This patient was a 26-year-old secretary who had been referred for psychological treatment of depression and failure to cope at work. It became clear during therapy that a major underlying problem was the patient's inability to deal with her mother, who lived elsewhere in the locality, and whom she felt to be imposing on her. She was also concerned about, though jealous of, her brother who still lived with the widowed mother, but who himself got very anxious and unstable at times. The patient felt duty-bound to phone her mother each week. She found that this left her feeling upset, but she did not know why. Cognitive rehearsal was used for this situation. The patient closed her eyes and imagined vividly going to the telephone, and dialling her mother's number. She was instructed to talk aloud her thoughts as the phone call progressed. These are extracts from what she said:

> 'It's mother on the line'
> 'He's been getting at her again'
> 'Why should she suffer this again'
> 'She's upset'
> 'She's alone – she can't escape – she's a bit paralysed'
> 'My mind builds this image – my mind has a field day with the most . . .'
> 'This is silly, I shouldn't be reacting like this'
> 'It's absolutely true'
> 'How long before Martin (brother) really cracks up!'
> 'I feel churned up. I can't talk about nice things'
> 'Giving her suggestions doesn't help'. 'I can't make her feel good'
> 'I can't tell her about me'. 'It doesn't help'
> 'For God's sake shut up, I can't stand listening'

A number of issues emerged from this session of cognitive rehearsal. On reviewing the statements made, the patient was able to clarify the reasons why she found the phone situation so upsetting (e.g. having to listen to mother's problems, having to listen to mother's preoccupation with brother (jealousy?), feeling there was nothing she could do about mother's situation, being reminded that she couldn't confide in mother because her mother was not strong enough, being reminded of the apparent insolubility of her own problems). Note the statement 'I can't tell her about me', this was seen by the patient to explain a lot of her feelings.

In this way, a great number of thoughts were brought to the surface and examined. Those that were seen to be important formed the basis of further discussion. Meanwhile the difficulty of the phone situation itself was not lost sight of, and a search for alternative strategies (see next section) implemented to enable the patient to have some tactics for coping. Methods of closing the telephone conversation (she felt particularly guilty about closing conversations) were practised, and between session homework set up for her to practise phoning her mother up for a short conversation which the patient herself would terminate. The next session revealed that she had been able to terminate such calls more easily than anticipated, using some of her strategies, and had not felt so guilty or upset after the phone call.

*Comment.* Note (1) that the way in which cognitive rehearsal is used varies depending upon therapist preference, characteristics of the patient and of the situation being imagined. Sometimes it is used as a more formal procedure where the aims and rationale are explained, the patient was instructed to relax and/or close their eyes, and attempt to vividly imagine being in the particular situation. Alternatively, the technique may be informally applied as a more implicit component of a normal therapy session. Here the therapist merely asks the patient (for example) 'If you were now, at this moment, sitting at your desk trying to work — what thoughts would be going through your mind — what would you be feeling — what would you do?' The latter procedure is more appropriate if the patient is more restless and agitated, or for some other reason may find relaxing and closing eyes very difficult. There is no definite prescription for how formal to be. It is a matter of judgement for the therapist.

Note (2) that throughout, the therapist uses all the skills at his disposal to elicit from the patient an entire range of real and imagined roadblocks to progress. For some patients, this is a very easy process — it will be obvious what the problems are, which can then be the subject of individual task assignments. For others, it will not be at all clear. Some, for example say 'I should be able to get to the shops without any bother — I'm so stupid' or 'I have a lovely home and family — there's no reason for me to be depressed', 'There's lots of people worse off than I am'. Individual therapists have their own way of dealing with these sort of comments. Some may ask what the patient *feels* when (s)he says that to her(him)self. The therapist may point out how that thought itself seems to lead to feelings of depression and try to raise the patient's curiosity as to why thinking a seemingly *positive* thought, 'I've got a lovely home', leads to feelings of depression. Are there any other examples of remembering or imagining positive events which lead to bad feelings (e.g. I used to be athletic, I had such good times at school, my family believe in me)? In what situations do these thoughts occur? (A further opportunity for cognitive rehearsal.) Follow through the *sequence* of thoughts and feelings. It will often be the case that it is not the 'lovely home' thought itself that causes the dysphoria, rather the subsequent thought 'I should be grateful' or 'I should not feel like this'. The patient may be reassured to know that many people feel this way when they are depressed. It may help to demonstrate how such thoughts bring to mind the *discrepancy* between the patient's ideal and what they think they really are, and the thought of the discrepancy itself produces a negative mood. A similar effect is discussed in relation to Systematic Resensitisation (p. 145) part of the rationale of which is that the enjoyment a depressed patient often obtains from current activities is inversely related to the pleasure obtained before they were depressed. Thus a lady who had loved knitting, but had always found sewing rather a bore found that, when depressed, all she could do was sew, whereas even *looking* at her knitting bag made her feel drained and hopeless.

Each of the above thoughts, feelings and situations reported by the patient may become the target for formal or informal cognitive rehearsal within the therapy session to enable therapist and patient get a clearer idea of the context in which the thoughts and feelings occur, and the blocks which inhibit behavioural progress.

### The Search for Alternatives (Alternative Therapy)

*Rationale.*   Inducing depressed mood under controlled conditions of therapy may itself distance and objectify the depressing situation, allowing the patient to feel more in control of their mood. Searching for alternative behaviours increases possible response options allowing patients to feel more in control of their environment.

*Aim of Technique.*   To ask patient to imagine being in a situation likely to induce depressed mood, then to generate alternative solutions to the situation.

*Procedure.*   (a) Ask patient to imagine a typically desperate situation (perhaps one that has actually occurred in the past week or is likely to occur in next few days).
(b) Encourage patient to experience, right now, the usual despair; the

whole range of negative thoughts and feelings.

(c) Attempt to collaborate with patient in generating solutions to the situation. During or after generating some options, develop each possible course of action in great detail to discover roadblocks.

*Example.* This patient (age 23 years, married, no children) was attending weekly sessions for relaxation treatment, in addition to regular cognitive-behaviour therapy. While attending one such relaxation session she had felt very depressed and hopeless and took an overdose.

In the CT session which followed, and after some initial general discussion, it was decided to use 'alternative therapy'. After the situation had been graphically described, patient and therapist went through some of the apparent alternative strategies. The therapist then asked the patient to summarise these alternatives by writing them down. This is what she wrote:

| OPTIONS | CONSEQUENCES |
|---|---|
| *Stayed at Hospital* | |
| Remained in day room | Inability to talk to other members of group. Did not want them to realise how desperate I felt. |
| Gone to recreation room | Someone would probably have come to find me, either staff or group member. Did not want to draw attention to myself. Did not want to remain alone, yet at same time I could not cope with other people. I remember that this choice did occur to me. |
| Talk to a member of staff | No-one I feel at ease with, unable to confide in them. Would have to seek them out. This has gone on for 3 years – continuing 'nuisance value' to others. I repeat myself and feel that doctors and nurses would say the same old things which offer neither solution nor help. |
| Continue with the day | Probably one of the easiest options. Could not do it feeling as I did – could not keep up appearance – this eventually becomes such a strain that I just crack. |
| *Left Hospital* | |
| Rung G.P. | Have done this before – means putting strain on her. Last time she felt obliged to contact other agencies – don't want to put her in that position again. I feel I am burdening her with my problems. |
| Gone to see Priest | Again the feeling of his reaction being 'Not again' – I will appear a failure because I can't cope again. I should be able to cope. |
| Gone home | If Mike (husband) at home. Don't want to upset or annoy him. If Mike not there – lonely – |

| | |
|---|---|
| | wouldn't have helped. Same end result. |
| Gone for a walk/drive | But feeling the way I did (or worse) I would have wandered, thinking, getting more upset — trying to find answer, solution, way out. |
| Gone shopping | No spare cash. Already done weekly shopping. Don't particularly enjoy shopping — especially when depressed. Need to be organised to shop — don't like seeing all the other shoppers coping quite adequately. |

Notice here how the therapist has not just encouraged the patient to list all the options, but also to list reasons why they might not have seemed genuine options at the time. For example, on first generating options, 'shopping' appeared a clearly available choice. It was only after going through 'cognitive rehearsal' strategies to examine this seemingly viable option that some obvious roadblocks became evident (e.g. I'd already done the weekly shopping, I had no money, etc.).

Thus the search for alternatives is a technique used in close association with cognitive rehearsal in which the apparent options are explored. The reader may find it instructive to go back to this patient's 'options' and think about what their own therapeutic strategies would have been.

*Problem. Patient fails to generate alternatives — believes nothing will help solve this situation.* In these cases, the therapist's own ideas may be of little use, merely serving further to alienate the client. Instead, the therapist might (a) list advantages of behaviour and (b) ask about the sort of options available if the patient were *not* depressed. Consider this example of another patient:

**Patient:** I went back home to my parents to sort out some of my stuff. I couldn't face it. I felt so depressed.

**Therapist:** Has this happened before when you've tried to sort it out?

**Patient:** Oh yes, it happens all the time. I get so low. It's no use.

[Therapist asks more questions to make situation clear. It becomes evident that being in the family home is rather difficult anyway, but that attempts to sort out belongings has produced depressed mood of suicidal proportions].

[Therapist decides to focus on task].

**Therapist:** You mention that you need to sort out your stuff because of moving into this new flat. Let's list all the reasons why it might be good to sort it out — what would the advantages be?

[Lists on paper/blackboard].

And now what are the disadvantages/problems.[5]
[Lists as before: e.g. 'too much stuff to go into new flat', my clothes won't fit now I've put on weight', 'my new flatmates might not want to use my cups and plates'].

Note how this procedure elicits negative thoughts which may tend to occur when patient thinks of clearing up her belongings. The therapist may also bear in mind less explicit thoughts which *may* be affecting patient's mood such as 'If I move all my stuff out, I won't have anything left in my old home' (i.e. guilt and anger about abandonment of (and by) parents). Each of these thoughts may need to be subjected to reality testing. If there seems to be too many to test individually, the therapist may identify a theme (e.g. possible rejection) to discuss with the patient, or may select one salient thought to test out.

**Therapist:** Now, we've got a list of reasons for sorting out your stuff and some disadvantages too. Let's take these disadvantages — these roadblocks — one by one and see if we can think of a way of coping. Imagine, for example, that the only problem was that your clothes might not fit, everything else is O.K., but you're really worried about the clothes not fitting.
**Patient:** It's such a long time. I've put on so much weight.
**Therapist:** So nothing will fit you?
**Patient:** Well there may be some things.
**Therapist:** Give me an example of something you know won't fit you — definitely — without doubt.
**Patient:** My blue skirt — it was always a bit tight.
**Therapist:** And is there anything which you're fairly sure will still fit?
**Patient:** I made a large cape for myself when I was at college. I suppose that would fit me.
**Therapist:** So it seems likely that some clothes won't fit, and others will. What proportion of your clothes do you think won't fit you anymore.
**Patient:** About 60 per cent.
**Therapist:** Now let's suppose you weren't concerned about anything else but your clothes not fitting. How would you cope with sorting out your stuff?
**Patient:** I suppose I would get a couple of boxes and a suitcase, and sort it out.
**Therapist:** And then?

**Patient**:   Well, one box could go to a jumble sale – another could stay there in case I lose weight again – and I could take the suitcase back to the flat . . .

Note how already the patient begins to think about practical coping strategies. She seems to be beginning to think through the problem, imagining herself up in the attic with the boxes. In the same way the therapist may take her through the other 'roadblocks'. In each case a coping strategy may suggest itself. At the end of the session, therapist and patient may end up with a short list of possible strategies which could form the basis of a homework assignment. At this point, before terminating the session, the therapist may wish to return to the patient's belief that 'there is no solution', and discuss the homework targets as an attempt to test this idea out.

## Concluding Remarks

Beck *et al.* (1979) take pains to point out that cognitive therapy techniques must be used in the context of a therapy session in which accurate empathy, warmth and genuineness are evidence on the part of the clinician. The therapeutic strategies are not 'mechanical devices' in which the turning of the right screw will have predictable consequences. Rapport between patient and therapist in which collaboration and mutual understanding are the keynote is essential.

As emphasised in Chapter 2, cognitive therapy has used a blend of cognitive and behaviour techniques. Prospective users may refer to that chapter to find information on which techniques have been found most useful in what combinations. (That chapter also has a section on drug interactions which may be of interest.) The cognitive behaviour therapist does not attempt to stick rigidly to any one technique, but will select from a range of techniques the one which seems most appropriate at any time. The range is large, but the evidence suggests that the core techniques here described, when taken together with some core behavioural techniques (e.g. task assignment) should form a sound basis on which to proceed with many depressed patients. There are also many supplementary cognitive behavioural techniques and a sample of these are described in the next chapter.

## Notes

1. For listing of all techniques typically used in the CT 'package' see Tables 2.1 and 2.2 on pp. 27 and 29.

2. It is sometimes necessary to be specific about the number of negative automatic thoughts you expect the patient to note during each day (e.g. at least 4).

3. Note here a sometimes useful therapeutic technique of being prepared to consider *worse* situations than the patient, to get away from the 'I'm sure its OK really' attitude.

4. Beck *et al.* (1979) have a questionnaire for the patient to fill in giving possible reasons for not doing self-help assignments, (p. 408).

5. This 'double column' technique is a commonly used adjunctive technique in cognitive therapy.

# 6 OTHER TREATMENT STRATEGIES

**The Treatment of Initial Insomnia** (Borkovec and Boudewyns, 1976)

*Rationale*

Although some sleep disturbance associated with depression is undoubtedly biochemically based, sleep disturbance may, once initiated, be maintained by the maladaptive strategies the patient uses to try and cope. These may be amenable to psychological intervention.

*Aim of Treatment*

To teach patients methods of coping to
  (a)  bring sleep under appropriate stimulus control
  (b)  distract the patient from interfering thoughts
  (c)  decrease arousal

*Procedure*

*Assessment Phase.* (a) Assessment of alternative explanations for sleep disturbance — life crises, primary depression, fears and phobias, etc.
(b) Assessment of sleep pattern. Use questionnaire or structured interview to ask about the following:

*Background*
(1)  Duration of disorder — when first noticed?
(2)  Life circumstances at that time
(3)  Previous attempts to control sleeping
        activities during day
        activities when retiring
        medication past and present
(4)  Any ideas as to what might be causing current problem

*Actual Sleep*
(1)  (a)  No. of nights per week initial insomnia experienced
     (b)  How long does it take to fall asleep?
(2)  (a)  No. of nights per week middle insomnia experienced
     (b)  How many times in night?
     (c)  What proportion of times is there difficulty in getting back to sleep?

(3) Rate (10 point scale) difficulty of getting off to sleep
(4) Rate (10 point scale) how rested you feel in the morning
(5) How often do you feel tired during the day because of poor sleep on the preceding night?
(6) Specify disruption in daily living caused by insomnia

*Situational Factors*
(1) Time of retiring
(2) Time of awakening (self or alarm)
(3) Bedroom (own or shared)
(4) Bed (own or shared)
(5) Noise/light level during the night
(6) Use of bed for non-sleep activities:
   studying, eating, listening to music, reading, resting during day, watching TV, listening to radio, (plus sexual activity)
(7) Taking of naps during the day — how often, where.

*Cognitive Physiological Problems*
(1) Intrusive or repetitive thoughts — specify content
(2) Recurring dreams/nightmares
(3) Bodily sensations (heartbeat/muscle tension)

*Treatment* (ten weekly, 50 minute sessions)

The purpose of the assessment is to build up a picture of the factors preventing sleep, especially the environment in which he/she attempts to sleep and the cognitive and physiological events which distract from sleep. Often, individuals (perhaps as an earlier attempt to cope with insomnia) take snacks to bed, or watch TV, or read. These then become conditioned to the bed situation and distract from sleep. That is, the 'bed stimuli' elicit 'non-sleep responses'. A similar outcome follows changing hours of retiring and arising too often.

*Treatment Strategy 1.* is therefore to instruct the patient to:
(a) stop all non-sleep related activities in the bedroom or on the bed (if in a bedsitter). If they must be in the bedroom during the day for a long period, avoid visual or physical contact with the bed if possible . . . 'beds are for sleeping'. Borkovec goes further and
(b) asks the patients to start treatment by rearranging the bedroom furniture to create stimulus conditions which are different from their past insomnia.
(c) Instruct patient to keep to fixed retiring and arising times, and to

change daytime schedules to fit in with their new sleeping schedules.
(d) Instruct patient not to take naps during the day. Relax by reading or listening to music instead, but do not lie down.
(e) Instruct patient to reduce external distractors — noises and lights — which may maintain insomnia.

In conjunction with this, therapist should use:

*Treatment Strategy 2* which is to teach progressive muscular relaxation and encourage twice daily practice at home over the ten weeks of treatment, the second practice session to be on retiring (when there will be no need to get up again). Emphasise to the patient (a) that 'overarousal' is often associated with insomnia, and that a specific means of relaxing is required to combat this; and (b) that concentrating on pleasant internal sensations will help to distract away from intrusive and repetitive thoughts which are often associated with insomnia.

*Treatment Strategy 3* which accompanies the above, may be used specifically for those who are mainly bothered by worrying or repetitive thoughts. Many patients find themselves going over the events of the day in their mind, or planning tomorrow, or next week, or are just bombarded with random thoughts.
(a) Instruct patient to leave the bedroom if he has not fallen asleep after 10 or 15 minutes. The aim of this is to associate the bedroom with the rapid onset of sleep (Bootzin, 1973).
(b) Allocate Worry Time to solve problems, plan next day, etc., at a separate time (from bedtime) and a separate place (from the bedroom). Teach the rule to engage in such planning/worrying activities at this scheduled time and place. Do not retire until this activity is complete, and a specific time has been set aside for the same activity the next day.
(c) Use desensitisation for worrying in bed. Imagine lying on a bed and the mind begins racing. Imagine switching off the thoughts and concentrating on relaxing (Geer and Katkin, 1966). Desensitisation may also be used to combat recurrent nightmares, with components of the nightmare forming the hierarchy.

Finally, treatment progress is monitored with daily diaries completed on rising from sleep. Monitor time taken to get off to sleep and middle insomnia; presence of distracting stimuli, internal or external; and degree of success at practising relaxation techniques.

*Example*

Mrs S. was a 35-year-old lady, married with one son, aged eight. Her husband worked night shift, so that the time she went to bed each night was under her own control. Even though her depression had responded to pharmacological treatment, she was referred for psychological assessment and treatment for initial insomnia. This insomnia (lying awake for 2–3 hours after her first attempts to go to sleep) was controllable with hypnotic medication, but she sought psychological help because she was afraid of long term dependency on the sleeping pills.

Initial assessment revealed a very maladaptive pattern of behaviour. Because her husband was out she would often retire to her bedroom just after she had put her son to bed (about 8 p.m.) and would sew, knit, read, watch television or listen to the radio in her bedroom. She would have mid- and late-evening snacks in her bedroom also. At 10.30 p.m. she would put off the light and lie down, to try and sleep.

Treatment consisted of three components: (a) explanation of the probable cause of her present insomnia problems; (b) behavioural management – staying downstairs until bedtime being the main change initiated; and (c) relaxation training. The hypnotic medication was gradually reduced as the patient became more accomplished at relaxing.

At the end of eight weeks of treatment she was symptom free and not dependent on hypnotics. She had also allowed her son to stay the night with a friend (unthinkable previously) and she coped well by herself.

*Comments*

In Borkovec and Boudewyns' original paper, they do not address the question of sexual activity, which is likely to be a frequent non-sleep activity performed in the bedroom. Instructions to the client will depend on whether sleep disturbance is associated with sexual activity or not, on assessment. If it is unreasonable to suggest a different time (e.g. mornings) or place for sex to take place, then therapy will have to concentrate on the other potential distractors such as eating, watching TV, and ignore the sex distractor. It is still possible to instruct the patient to do the relaxation practice following sex, rather than before.

As for using relaxation techniques, the comments made when these techniques were discussed in Chapter 4 are relevant here. There is not a great deal of optimism that depressed clients find relaxation a useful technique in general. However, several workers have found it useful for some clients and some stages in the treatment programme, so it ought to be borne in mind.

The caveat about the insomnia being secondary to life crises or primary depression, implied in Assessment subsection (a) needs emphasising. To treat the symptom of insomnia without enquiring about other symptoms of depression or life circumstances is very bad therapeutic practice. Nevertheless, this book assumes that depression has already been identified as a major problem, and will probably be under active pharmacological and/or psychological treatment when the question of treating the insomnia is raised. In any event, it is worth bearing in mind that insomnia, however initiated, may thereafter become established and hard to eliminate because of the 'bad habits' acquired by the patient, which these strategies aim to treat.

Finally, therapists who have worked long in this area advise never to instruct patients to suddenly give up their medication. First, withdrawal effects will almost certainly be evident, and disrupt the treatment progress. Second, drugs may form a useful aid to psychological treatment methods in the early stages, and can be reduced gradually as sleep patterns respond to psychological strategies. Third, the clients' doctor may be using the same psychotropic medication for a dual purpose. For example, amitriptyline, taken before retiring, has a hypnotic effect although its primary action is antidepressant. If the therapist is not responsible for the patient's drug regimen, it is essential to consult the physician who is before recommending changes. On the other hand, putting sleep back into the patient's own control, without the use of drugs, is the ultimate aim of these treatment strategies.

### Anticipation Training (Anton *et al.* 1976)

*Rationale*

Although increasing the quantity of reinforcement may be achieved by increasing the number of pleasant events the person experiences, depressed patients very often anticipate a negative outcome of such experiences, and direct their attention to the negative side of otherwise potentially pleasant events.

*Aim of Treatment*

To modify the negative anticipations of depressed patients.

*Procedure*

*Session One.* (a) Behavioural Assessment (see p. 67).
(b) Give 'Activity Log' to the patient to be completed each night before retiring (see p. 105).

*Session Two*. (a) Focus on arranging for pleasant activities to happen. Patient to select 6 pleasant activities to be performed over the next 2 weeks. Three to involve the patient alone, three to involve other people. Each task to take at least 10–15 minutes to perform. Each task to be able to be performed most days.

(b) Patient then constructs three positive anticipation statements for first scheduled activity (see Table 6.1). Instructed to close eyes, relax, imagine activity as if it were actually happening. Rehearse in mind 3 statements and create a vivid image of the feelings associated with the statements.

(c) Continue repeating imagery and statements (covertly) until patient can identify a positive feeling while doing so.

Table 6.1: Activity Schedule

---

(1) Select 6 pleasant activities. The aim is to do these over the next 2 weeks. Three of these must be activities you do by yourself, and three activities you will do with someone else. Each should take more than 10/15 minutes to perform, but should be easily performed within the day.

(2) Complete the following form for each activity.

Activity planned: . . . . . . . . . . . . . . . . . . . . . . . . . . . . . . . . . . .
Date planned for: . . . . . . . . . . . . . . . . . . . . . . . . . . . . . . . . . . .

(3) Now complete the following sentences with 3 different statements.

I will enjoy. . . . . . . . . . . . . . . . . . . . . . . . . . . . . . . . . . . . . . .
. . . . . . . . . . . . . . . . . . . . . . . . . . . . . . . . . . . . . . . . . . . . . . .
I will enjoy. . . . . . . . . . . . . . . . . . . . . . . . . . . . . . . . . . . . . . .
. . . . . . . . . . . . . . . . . . . . . . . . . . . . . . . . . . . . . . . . . . . . . . .
I will enjoy. . . . . . . . . . . . . . . . . . . . . . . . . . . . . . . . . . . . . . .
. . . . . . . . . . . . . . . . . . . . . . . . . . . . . . . . . . . . . . . . . . . . . . .

(4) Three times a day (morning, afternoon and before retiring), find a comfortable quiet place, relax, and imagine doing the planned activity. Say each of the three statements to yourself, and create a vivid image for each statement. Do this every day until the activity has been performed.

---

(d) Instructed to do this for Activities 1 and 2 at home. First activity scheduled to occur before:

*Session Three*. (a) Activity 1 discussed and any problems associated with anticipation sequence reviewed.

(b) Schedule activity 3 and discuss anticipation statements. Patient to construct statement for Activity 4 themselves.

(c)  Activities 2 and 3 occur before:

*Session Four.*  (a) Activities 2 and 3 anticipation practice reviewed.
(b)  Activity 5 scheduled; patient to construct own anticipation statements for Activity 5 and 6, and actually schedule Activity 6 without
assistance.

*Session Five.*  Review of anticipations and scheduling. If difficulty in
motivation, instruct patient to image task *completed* and associated
feelings.

*Session Six.*  Review of progress and of generalisation of anticipation
training to other behaviours.

Anton *et al.* provide some examples of the use of this technique with
some depressed women. It may be interesting to see their examples of
activities planned by their clients during treatment.

| *Alone* | *With someone* |
| --- | --- |
| Have hair done | Go to a film |
| Spend an afternoon in town | Phone parents |
| Browse in antique shops | Take a friend to lunch |
| Spend three hours reading | Play tennis |
| Prepare a Chinese meal | Go out to dinner |
| Buy new towels | Have friend to dinner |
| Ride bicycle | Visit an Art Museum |
| Work in the garden | Go to the city |
| Drive to the beach | Take children to the zoo |
| Go to a lecture | Go to a concert |
| Buy a new plant | Spend an evening playing with the children |
| Browse in a bookshop | Go to a Health Club |
| Take a long walk | |

Other activities, should the patient not be able to select any, could
be selected from Lewinsohn's List (p. 102).

*Example*

This is how a colleague of mine introduced Anticipation Training to a
client. He was a 26-year-old chartered surveyor who had been referred
specifically for cognitive-behaviour therapy for depression. His Beck
score was 22, and he had particular problems with sleeping, loss of
energy, fatigue, psychomotor agitation, loss of interest in sex, hobbies
and social contacts, and a diminished ability to concentrate.

**Therapist** What I'd like you to do first is to make a list of things you used to do that you got pleasure from – that you're not doing now. Let's choose some that your pleasure doesn't depend on other people getting pleasure from it – we can't control how other people will react.

**Patient** The first thing is going out for a drink in the evening. I used to do it a lot when I was a student.

**Therapist** That's a good one.

**Patient** I find I can't sit down and relax to watch T.V. – I do, but I can't switch off my negative feelings.

[Patient and therapist finally decide on three activities for next week].

(1) A night in with my wife – just spending some time together
(2) A night out at the cinema
(3) Go out to a local football match

**Therapist** What I would like you to do is to prepare yourself for these activities – so that you set yourself up to enjoy them rather than setting yourself up not to enjoy them.

Let's think about the football match (scheduled first). You've mentioned two things that could dampen it; one, you feel you ought to be working for your exams, and two, you feel bad about going out without your wife.

Have there been any other negative thoughts about going?

**Patient** Yes. The two friends who've invited me have already passed the exam I'm struggling with – I've thought that I hope they don't talk shop.

**Therapist** What I want you to do with this first activity is to practice a technique that I'd like you to apply to the other two activities later on. First of all, can you list three things that you will enjoy about going to the match. Start off with 'I will enjoy'.

**Patient** The company of other friends; watching the football.

**Therapist** Finally, 'I will enjoy . . .'

**Patient** An evening away from work.

**Therapist** Now what I'd like you to do in the next five minutes is to get as relaxed as you can – and to imagine all the things that are going to happen tonight. At any point when you get to any of the things that you've listed you will enjoy (being with friends, watching the football and not thinking about your work) let it enhance the scene. Imagine feeling the pleasure.

[The patient was encouraged to use the technique at home, and it was discussed at subsequent sessions. Over the ensuing weeks, the following activities were successfully instituted using this method (3 enjoyment statements listed in each case].

*To go out for a drink with wife*
   (1)  I will enjoy the company of just the two of us.
   (2)  I will enjoy being able to relax.
   (3)  I will enjoy a change of environment.

*To stay in one night with Frances – just spend
the evening in each others' company*
   (1)  I will enjoy an evening in with Frances.
   (2)  I will enjoy each others' company.
   (3)  I will enjoy making love together.

*Staying in to watch TV – no revision*
   (1)  I will enjoy doing nothing that evening.
   (2)  I will enjoy watching TV without thinking about work.
   (3)  I will enjoy being able to relax with just my own company.

*Going to a film with Frances*
   (1)  I will enjoy an evening out of the house.
   (2)  I will enjoy getting absorbed with the film.
   (3)  I will enjoy Frances being with me.

*Going to football match*
   (1)  I will enjoy the company of other friends.
   (2)  I will enjoy watching the football.
   (3)  I will enjoy the novelty of doing something other than work.

*Comment*

The problem with this strategy is what to do if the patient continually can't find the motivation, or push to *do* the actual targeted behaviour. This may need discussion in itself though some therapists have suggested making therapist time contingent upon completion of activities.

Anton *et al.* themselves point out that it is better to choose activities which do not rely too heavily on other people's reaction in order to be pleasant for the patient themselves. Furthermore, the client must be able to be fairly sure that the activity itself is one that has given pleasure in the past, rather than choosing something which (s)he is not sure will be pleasurable. However, in Anton's group of depressed clients (mean Lubin DACL score 66) a shift over 6 weeks to 49 (within nondepressed range) was noted.

It is doubtful whether Anticipation Training by itself would be sufficient to alleviate depression. In Anton *et al's* paper, many depressed clients asked for further counselling, despite the fact that the outcome measures showed a favourable response. It is not that such training is too short (though it may be) but that it is uncommon for the behavioural analysis (done at the Assessment stage) to reveal no other problem than anticipation of events. In the next section, on Systematic Resensitisation, pleasant events are again scheduled, but rather more carefully.

**Systematic Resensitisation** (Sammons, 1974)

*Rationale*

Depression is associated with low rate of response contingent positive reinforcement, but often, encouraging a patient to engage in a formerly enjoyable activity actually causes *more* frustration and depression. This may be because the person has tried the activity before while depressed and a counter-conditioning process has taken place so that the activity has become paired with depression. Indeed it may be that the more enjoyable an activity once was, the more *upset* an individual gets when he tries to do it when depressed.

*Aim of Treatment*

To resensitise the individual to previously enjoyed items in the same way as phobic patients are *de*sensitised to feared objects.

*Procedure*

(a) Behavioural assessment — focus especially on previously enjoyed activities and feelings that result when any of these are tried.

(b) Choose, with patient, one of these activities which is currently available to work on as a target.

(c) Develop, with patient, a hierarchy of scenes associated with the activity — e.g. making plans to do it, getting dressed up, getting equipment (if sport, etc.), travelling to activity, meeting friend outside, going to door, entering, meeting one friend inside, meeting three friends inside, meeting crowd of friends inside, doing activity. Ask client what was good about each stage of hierarchy.

(d) Teach patient progressive relaxation.

(e) Instruct patient to relax and form image of scenes at bottom of hierarchy. Attempt to get vivid image of anything that was good about this particular subcomponent — imagine pleasant feelings. Present scenes with a lot of 'positive suggestion' about 'feeling better'.

(f) If at any stage the patient feels upset or uncomfortable about a scene, the imagining is stopped immediately, and the previous scene is imagined.

(g) When patient can imagine the top of this hierarchy (i.e. the formerly *most* reinforcing aspect) without feeling uncomfortable, instruct patient to start *in vivo* work: first target: bottom of hierarchy, and so on up the hierarchy with instructions to leave the situation if there are any feelings of discomfort.

(h) Continue to instruct patient to try activities for longer (etc.) up hierarchy until pleasant feelings are gained for activity.

(i)  Introduce other activities in same imaginal – *in vivo* sequence.

*Example* (Sammons, 1974)

Sammons reports the use of this technique with a 39-year-old depressed man. He had been hospitalised on five separate occasions with the shortest hospitalisation being six months. During the past ten years, the patient had not remained out of hospital for more than nine months at a time. On initial assessment the patient was extremely lethargic, with no spontaneous speech and only seldom initiation of any activity.

Despite this he was able to list some things which had once been reinforcing for him. These included 'shooting pool' and since there was a pool hall at the hospital, the therapist suggested he might attend on a couple of occasions. At the next session, the patient reported feeling worse after having tried to carry out the assignment.

Although the patient was reluctant to begin relaxation training, he agreed, and found he enjoyed it. It was at this time that Sammons decided to attempt to use the relaxation to 'resensitise' the patient to the previous reinforcers. Together they developed a 'pool shooting' hierarchy which ended with a scene of the patient having completed three consecutive games of pool. After inducing relaxation, these scenes were presented along with positive suggestions of 'feeling good, feeling better than he had in a long time'. If at any time the patient began to feel uncomfortable or depressed, the scene was terminated and the previous scene repeated. Gradually, *in vivo* exposure was introduced. The patient was invited to try to play the game for as long as he felt good, but to leave the area for at least 30 minutes if he felt at all uncomfortable or depressed. It was impressed upon him that the duration of contact with the activity was not as important as his participating in the activity only for as long as it was pleasant.

The first day the patient spent 30 seconds in the pool hall, then left. The second day he spent nine minutes. By the end of seven days, he was spending one hour a day playing the game. By this time, Sammons had started to use the same approach with the patient's television watching. General recovery was rapid, and the patient was soon discharged. After 12 months the patient was still well and out of hospital.

*Comment*

There is little doubt that Sammons procedure contains an important insight – the inverse correlation that is found, for many patients, between former enjoyability of tasks and current enjoyability. This may be because nondepressed individuals tend to get most pleasure out of activities which take a lot of effort and concentration (two aspects which are most vulnerable to depressive breakdown). Or it may be that the more the expected enjoyment, the greater the frustration becomes a contributor to the low mood. In any event, it is not an uncommon phenomenon, and because it baffles patients, deserves to be explained to them. One patient of mine had used to love knitting before she became depressed, but as for sewing – she could 'take it or leave it' – finding it rather a bore. When I met her as a depressed in-patient, she found sewing her greatest ally – it was the only activity she found she could do. She reported that even looking at her knitting bag made her feel very low, and on the few occasions she had attempted to start knitting she had given up after a very few minutes, extremely frustrated and upset. Another patient, a young man who suffered bouts of severe depression and had made a very serious attempt on his life (it had failed only by accident), gave the following as his previously enjoyed activities: academic discussion (6), electronic gadgetry (4/5), travelling (10), countryside (8), special friend (8), girlfriend (10), being in good company (10), guitar (4/5), art in general (10).

The numbers in brackets represent a rating on a 10 point scale of how much pleasure he used to get out of each. When asked to rank the activities for how much he felt able/willing to do each *now*, the ranks showed a strong inverse correlation. When asked which of these he currently did, the answer was playing the guitar and fiddling with electronic gadgets. Note again how the activities most easily performed are the ones which were previously the less rewarding.

In both cases the individuals were very relieved to know that this was quite common – for they had both felt hopeless about ever getting better partly on the grounds that if they didn't even enjoy their favoured activity, what hope was there of getting pleasure out of anything else.

So systematic resensitisation contains a useful element. Furthermore this useful element may be exploited even if the patient does not find relaxation helpful. The hierarchical organisation of targets is reminiscent of graded task assignment (though GTA does not advocate leaving the situation if unpleasant feelings arise), and the suggestion of pleasant feelings while covertly rehearsing the target activity is reminiscent of Beck's cognitive rehearsal. It is maybe the way in which these techniques overlap which explains why systematic resensitisation has not, to my knowledge, been subject to an extensive clinical study.

## Evening Therapy (Benatov, 1981)

### Rationale

Memory is a basic determinant of consciousness, behaviour and future expectations. Many events each day do not pass the 'barrier' or 'filter' into long-term memory. This filter is biased negatively in depressed patients so that only depressive events tend to be remembered. This biasing maintains the disorder.

### Aim of Treatment

To redress the bias in what is selected from everyday events to pass into long-term memory.

### Procedure

Therapy consists of 60-90 minute sessions every evening or at least four times a week. A quiet room and a comfortable armchair (back to therapist) is the setting in which the patient is instructed to recall every detail of that day. Benatov talks of the 'reactivation of short-term memory', the aim being to 'restore STM's of the day in all details'.

The patient is led to concentrate on information from 'perception' rather than 'interpretation'. In early sessions, patients tend to begin with an 'egocentric structure of the facts', but later are able to pay more attention to all details of daily experiences.

### Comment

This is an interesting procedure which seems to share the aims of 'reality testing' of cognitive therapy. It is simple in concept, and has, of course, a great deal of experimental evidence to back up its rationale. Depressed individuals *do* tend to select out the negative feedback (see Chapter 1). Of course, the terms STM and LTM should not be taken as referring to the same constructs as in most cognitive psychology theories. If so, there would be some difficulty in the 'recovery' of material which was supposed to be 'lost'. Nevertheless it is true that for all people (depressed or nondepressed) remembering everything we have done in the last 24 hours is difficult, and this 'common frailty' allows a great deal of negative bias to creep in for a depressed individual who can easily believe that a long sequence of unpleasant things have happened to the exclusion of all else.

Because it needs to occur daily if possible, it seems very suitable for inpatient work. The role of therapist, could perhaps be played by any one (or more) members of the multidisciplinary team — nurse, psychiatrist, social worker or psychologist.

## Reattribution Training

### Rationale

Following a stressful experience, an individual will attempt to explain the occurrence, i.e. to attribute the event to various causes. It has been suggested that depressed individuals tend to have biased attributional styles in which aversive events are attributed to internal, stable and global causes, and positive events to external, unstable and specific causes (see Chapter 1).

### Aim of Treatment

To help the patient identify their maladaptive causal attributions and then to make more realistic and appropriate attributions of causality.

### Procedure

(a) *Assess* attributional style. Seligman and co-workers have devised a questionnaire measurement of attributional style — a sample item from which is reproduced below (Seligman *et al.*, 1979).

You have been looking for a job unsuccessfully for some time:
(1) Write down one major cause
(2) Is the cause of your unsuccessful job search due to something about you or something about other people or circumstances? (circle one number)

| Totally due to other people or circumstances | 1 2 3 4 5 6 7 | Totally due to me |

(3) In the future when looking for a job will this cause again be present? (circle one number)

| Will never again be present | 1 2 3 4 5 6 7 | Will always be present |

(4) Is this cause something that just influences looking for a job or does it also influence other areas of your life? (circle one number)

| Influences just this particular situation | 1 2 3 4 5 6 7 | Influences all situations in my life |

(5) How important would this situation be if it happened to you? (circle one number)

| Not at all important | 1 2 3 4 5 6 7 | Extremely important |

Alternatively, the cognitive style measure given on p. 73 could be used, with particular attention being paid to those items which reveal maladaptive attributional styles.

(b) *Explain* the importance of attribution to the patient. An example such as the following (Cleaver, 1981) may be used:

'Consider the case of an individual who fails a maths exam and attributes his failure to the fact that '(S)he is useless at everything (s)he attempts?' This is an *internal* attribution because it relates failure to *personal* incompetence; it is a stable attribution because it relates failure to an *unchanging* or *constant* feature of his functioning, namely, his 'uselessness'. And it is *global* because it may be used to explain his failure in a wide range of situations (e.g. the individual might use this attribution 'I am useless at everything I do' to explain why (s)he burnt their supper)'.

Such an attribution pattern would (if widely applied) tend to magnify all failures, and lead to hopelessness and depression, especially if the event was important. The example continues:

'Imagine that the individual had passed his exam, and had attributed it to the fact that the questions were particularly easy. Such an attribution is external because it relates success to a characteristic of the exam, not to a characteristic of the individual; it is unstable because easy questions cannot be regarded as a constant feature of exams, and it is specific because it cannot be used to explain success in any other setting.'

Such an attribution pattern (if widely applied) would tend to minimise all successes, and act to maintain hopelessness and depression.

(c) Choose hypothetical example and get patient to work out maladaptive and adaptive attributional style.

(d) Find particular example from the patient's recent past (preferably last week) and discuss attribution for that event.

(e) Examine with patient links between attribution for an event and mood.

(f) Discuss alternative attributions for the event in question.

*Example*

*Discussing hypothetical situations.* Cleaver (1981) devised a reattribution training technique which worked from discussion of hypothetical situations to actual situations explicitly within the framework of Abramson, Seligman and Teasdale's attributional reformulation of learned helplessness. That is, she attempted to teach patients what internal, stable, global attributions were, and how they could be modified.

*Stage One.* In the first stage, the following hypothetical situations are discussed with the patient.

(a) *A friend of yours has passed you by in the street and ignored you*

(i) So-and-so must be in a bad mood today − (s)he's ignoring his/her friends.

(ii) So-and-so must have been day dreaming − (s)he didn't see me.

(iii) So-and-so is a bit weird − he/she always ignores people he/she knows well.

(iv) So-and-so really ought to wear his/her glasses then (s)he might see me.

(b) *You're in a group learning to do something new and everybody seems to get the hang of it faster than you.*

(i) The other people have probably learnt something like this before.

(ii) The others are trying a lot harder than me.

(iii) They're probably just as confused as I am but too scared to admit it.

(iv) I've had a hard day.

(v) I'm probably a lot more tired than the others.

(vi) This really doesn't interest me.

(c) *You write to a friend asking if you can stay with her for a few days and you don't get a reply within a fortnight.*

Discuss possible attributions with patient.

(d) *You're in the pub with a group of friends and no-one is talking*

*to you.*
Discuss possible attributions with patient.

In each case, the patient's spontaneous attributions are elicited and analysed on the three dimensions of internality, stability and globality. For each dimension, the patient is praised for employing the 'adaptive' attribution, and it is pointed out what (s)he has done. Alternatives are called for and suggested if the 'maladaptive' attribution is offered.

Below is the format used by Cleaver (1981):

(1)  I want you to imagine that: (a), (b), (c) or (d) above

(2)  What would it be most natural for you to think was the reason for this happening?

(3)  (a) *Internal*, say:
Now, I'd like you to try and think of some other reasons which suggest that it is something about the other people not something about you.
*Examples*: (see above)
(b) If *External*, say:
Good, that's just the sort of thing we're looking for.
Some other reasons you could have given are . . .

(4)  (a) If *Stable*, say:
Now, try and think of a reason which suggests that things could change – could be different on another occasion.
*Example* (including internal, unstable attribution)
(b) If *Unstable*, say:
That's good, you've chosen something which suggests that things would be different on another occasion. Some other things you could have thought of are . . .

(5)  (a) If *Global*, say:
Now, you've chosen the sort of reason which could explain why things go badly on another occasion (explain why). What I want you to do is to think of a reason which applies only to the situation we're talking about.
(b) If *Specific*, say:
Good, you've chosen a reason which can only apply to this particular situation. Other suitable reasons would have been . . .

*Stage Two*. Elicit real negative events from patient with a view to discussing and changing maladaptive attributions for them. Go through same procedures as above using patients own examples. Cues: rejection, snubs, disappointments, accidents, etc.

*Stage Three*. Hypothetical 'success' situations: encourage Internal, Stable, Global attributions, e.g.
(a) You've been invited out to supper by a couple you know
(b) You've been successful in completing the crossword puzzle in a newspaper.
(c) You've been complimented on your appearance by a friend in the pub.
   Analyse attributions as before.

*Stage Four*. Elicit real positive events from patient with a view to discussing and changing maladaptive attributions.

*Comment*

There have been few systematic investigations of reattribution theory as a treatment of depressed patients in its own right, though both Seligman (1981) and Beck *et al.* (1979) claim that it is an important component of psychological treatment. It must be said that the theory on which it is based is constantly shifting, so it would be unwise to think that the attributional styles outlined here are always maladaptive and that modification of them will necessarily be beneficial. Many of these issues are discussed by Cleaver (1981) and referred to in Williams (1982b) as well as in other chapters in Antaki and Brewin's book *Attribution and Psychological Change* (1982).

A useful strategy may be to incorporate some elements of attributional modification into cognitive-behavioural therapy where it becomes clear that constant misinterpretation of events is a problem for the client. In such cases one could encourage them to keep a diary of their interpretations of events (perhaps taking one attributional dimension each week as a 'theme', e.g. look for internal attributions one week and stable attributions the next) and challenging themselves to try out other interpretations. Another useful strategy may be to encourage the person to see the consequences of his attributions on his behaviour, and how the behaviour then brings its own consequences (e.g. if people aren't talking to you in a pub, and you think this is because they don't like you, you may turn away slightly, making it even less likely that they will talk to you. The attribution may in this way become a self-fulfilling prophecy). Role-play may be used in the sessions to allow the person to practise acting on the consequences of alternative attributions (e.g. they're too shy to talk, so how can I break the ice). In these ways reattribution training may become a useful adjunct to psychological treatment. It needs a great deal more systematic investigation, however, before the extent of its usefulness may be properly assessed.

# 7 TRAINING EXERCISES

## Introduction

There are probably as many ways to improve one's skills in therapy as there are trainers and trainees. Whether one is fairly new to the practice of psychological treatment of depressed clients or have a great deal of experience, the improvement of skills remains an important component of one's job. To some extent we may apply the same model to our own skills as we ask our clients to apply in coping with their lives: we may learn to determine appropriate *goals* for our therapeutic practice, then decide what *strategies* will make those goals more likely. Within each general strategy, there will be specific *tactics* which will be optimal in attaining the desired goals. In order to improve these skills we shall need to do what we require of our clients: to self-monitor, self-evaluate, and self-reinforce. The first of these is easy to arrange. We can tape our interactions with some clients some of the time, and it may be useful to be specific in routinely scheduling this into our therapeutic practice. This can be a very revealing exercise. There is often no harsher critic of one's practice than oneself. On the other hand it has its drawbacks. We may be better at spotting our faults than knowing how to put them right. In this respect, it is often useful to hold group discussions on a regular basis with close colleagues who are grappling with the same issues. Such regular discussions will help the self-evaluation and self-reinforcement aspects of skill development. This section of the book aims to provide some material which individuals or groups may find helpful in their own skills training. Part I contains some case descriptions together with questions to direct the reader's attention to certain aspects of the material. The focus is on determining general therapeutic strategies. Part II becomes more particular, focusing on determining strategies within the therapy session. Part III is similarly specific, but focuses on between-session homeworks, diaries and thought forms. Finally, Part IV gives some suggested techniques for role induction, should a group wish to use role-play format as a training exercise.

None of this material is an adequate substitute for the reader's own clinical case material. Rather the material here included raises issues and illustrates points which may remind individuals and groups of clients they have seen to whom the same questions could be applied and with whom the course of therapy has raised similar issues.

Finally, in reading this material, guard against the assumption that the cases you read are 'obviously suitable for such and such an alternative therapy'. It is often easier to see other dynamics in case descriptions than it is making them the subject of therapeutic goals in practice. In many patients, many alternative techniques will have been tried, and they are being referred for cognitive-behaviour therapy precisely because the alternatives have not been successful.

### Part I: Deciding General Therapeutic Strategy

Read the following case descriptions as if you were to decide which therapeutic strategy you would prefer to initiate. It may be helpful to bear in mind two specific models and compare what further information you would need in order to initiate either. Let us therefore focus on contingency management and reality testing. What contingencies would you want to manage? What strategies of reality testing would you employ and what aspects of reality would you seek to test? To what extent do both techniques assume that the objective reality for the client is benign. If 'reality' is genuinely stressful, what follows for your therapeutic practice?

*Case 1*

Stephanie is a 23-year-old woman, who lives with her mother and father in a small private house near the city centre. She is their only child. She did moderately well at school until in her mid-teens when she got bored, and left at the earliest opportunity without taking any exams. She moved from job to job, never settling at anything for very long. She is now unemployed in an area where jobs are scarce, even for qualified youngsters.

The home situation has always been tense. Her mother and father have violent arguments. She takes her mother's part in these — feels she needs defending.

Her passion is dressmaking. Although limited by lack of finance she takes great care about selecting patterns and has done some designing herself.

Stephanie has always been a loner, but now she has been referred by her G.P. for treatment of depression. She lacks interest in anything except dressmaking; she cannot get to sleep at night; and finds it difficult to get up in the morning. She eats very little. She feels life is not worthwhile and has considered suicide.

> *Recent incident.* An interesting-looking job prospect has fallen through.

## Case 2

John is a 34-year-old man, married with two children, aged 6 and 4. He is referred for treatment of depression of 3 years' duration, the main characteristic of which is bouts of severe lethargy and depression (lasting 2-3 weeks) separated by up to a week of feeling 'perfectly O.K.'. During these 'good spells' he is not 'high', and shows no signs/symptoms of mania/hypomania.

Antidepressant drug and Lithium therapy have had no effect.

He was trained as a junior school teacher. The depression came to the attention of health care professionals when he took a large overdose and was admitted to general, then psychiatric hospital. Since then there have been three further overdoses.

He has quite a few friends through the children's school, and through church, but feels he is a burden to them. He often thinks of suicide, and sometimes drives out by himself intending to 'do something', but ends up feeling angry that he hasn't got the courage. 'They would be better off if I wasn't there.' The mornings are especially bad. He is tired, irritable and depressed.

The evenings are not much better — he often lies on the couch listlessly, or watches the television without really taking it in. On these occasions he finds it difficult to get to sleep, and the 4-year-old often wakes them in the night anyway, having recently started to wet the bed.

> *Recent incident.* Wife went out for night class and children were both ill and bad-tempered.

## Case 3

Carla is a 29-year-old unmarried woman who has been referred for psychological treatment of her depression. Before admission to the psychiatric unit she had lived in a flat with workmates (she is a trained physiotherapist). Her work had been punctuated by frequent absenteeism due to unspecified illnesses. She had found work stressful and had several times left the flat to go back to her family home. (Indeed, she had started training at a college away from home, but had returned after only two weeks, and completed her training from home.) She was a 'good worker' but her frequent absenteeism meant she could not be given responsibility, and juniors were promoted before her. Her absenteeism increased and she took three moderately severe overdoses during a 4 year period.

Her mother and father and younger sister still live at home. When she goes home she gets frustrated and her mood is extremely volatile. She feels she has no personality, that she has no 'guts' or 'stickability'. 'Everyone else is so composed', 'my friends are sick of me', 'I can't even hold down a job'.

*Recent incident.* Phoned home and parents too busy to talk, on same day as a friend did not keep a coffee appointment.

## Case 4

Patrick was referred for psychological treatment of depression, secondary to bouts of panic and anxiety he had suffered for some time. At the time of referral he had difficulty sleeping, had loss of energy, and increased tiredness, psychomotor agitation, loss of interest in usual activities including social contact and sex, and a diminished ability to think and concentrate.

He trained as a veterinary surgeon (the same profession as his father). He took a year out due to excessive anxiety which failed to respond to pharmacological treatment. He moved back to his home town where, as an inpatient he was successfully treated by relaxation methods, after which he moved back to college to finish his training.

After qualifying he started to work in his father's surgery, but missed the college social life and felt isolated in a country practice. He married and moved back to the city in which he had trained. The anxiety symptoms returned and he also became very depressed. He was referred for assessment for individual psychodynamic therapy but was felt to be too overcompliant/dependent and started in group psychotherapy instead. He felt uncomfortable with this arrangement and discharged himself after a few weeks, after which he was referred for cognitive-behaviour therapy.

*Recent incident.* Wife, who has been very supportive up until now, says she is getting tired of his behaviour. He feels she may get bored with him and leave.

## Part II: Choice Points Within the Therapy Session

When you listen to a tape of your therapy sessions you may be able to identify various points during the session where the course of therapy could have travelled in a number of directions. It becomes an interesting exercise for a therapist (perhaps with a group of colleagues) to listen to a tape and identify these choice points. Once these have been identified, you may discuss the range of options and why one was chosen rather than another. In this way, group members can sensitise themselves to the process of therapy interchange.

In the transcript that follows, I have cut up the session. At each stopping point, the reader may consider which way he or she would have directed the session, or whether they would have attempted to allow the client to decide. If you are doing this exercise in a group, each member may first make their decision, after which differences in member's conclusions may be discussed. If you find this particular transcript is not satisfactory for your group's needs, use one of your own tapes or transcripts and stop it at various intervals to try the same exercise.

The transcript extracts which follow were from a 22-year-old man who had been depressed since his final year at school. He had then given up his Advanced Levels (final year examinations) but had now gone back to a technical college to do some less advanced exams — to 'get back into the swing of it'. By the time this session was held, considerable progress in therapy had been made, though the patient believed this was due to a 'biochemical depression' which had now lifted. The therapist was concerned to investigate the patient's attribution of his success (biological factors vs. learning coping strategies) in order to discover his level of vulnerability to possible future stresses. The patient believes that everything he has achieved was really quite easy since his biological depression had lifted. What would your strategies have been at the choice points I have indicated?

**Therapist** So this is what you filled in 2 weeks ago. And we were doing this to see what activities you are involved in now. (Patient brought in 2 weeks activity schedules).

**Patient** Well I think it was to compare with the one I did right at the beginning.

**Therapist** That's right. Yes.

**Patient** I don't know how accurate the times are, because I tended to find I got to the end of the day and couldn't remember.

**Therapist** So you were filling it in at the end of the day retrospectively. It seems a lot busier, a lot more full than the other one we had, which we've got here (earlier activity schedule). The pleasure scores are quite high as well.

**Patient** Some are, some aren't, it depends.

**Therapist**  There are quite a few over 5, 5 out of 10.

**Patient**  Oh yes.

**Therapist**  Before you were finding things had little pleasure, or enjoyment, is that right?

**Patient**  I think some did, probably not everything.

**Therapist**  How's it been about getting up in the morning?

**Patient**  O.K.

**Therapist**  What sort of times have you been getting up?

**Patient**  Well it depends what time I have to get up. If I'm going to college for 9, I get up around 7.

**Therapist**  And is there any problem getting up at 7?

**Patient**  No.

**Therapist**  You don't find the old problems creeping back of lying in bed, thinking about getting up and not being able to do it, putting it off.

**Patient**  Not if I have to go to college for 9. If, say, I don't have to go until the afternoon, sometimes I do.

**Therapist**  What sort of thoughts do you have, if you've got college at 9; when you wake up, what thoughts run through your mind then?

**Patient**  Just that I'm going to college and I have to get up, and that's it. It isn't really all that difficult actually.

**Therapist**  How do you actually get up, how do you decide to get up? If you're thinking — there's nothing to get up for, it doesn't make any difference what time I get up, so I might as well lie in a bit longer — where does the change come before you actually decide to get up?

**Patient**  Possibly in the time. If it gets toward 10 o'clock — I feel I ought to get up.

**Therapist**  Um — so as it's getting later you feel slightly obliged.

**Patient**  Yeah.

**Therapist**  And that time's about 10 o'clock.

**Patient**  Yeah.

**Therapist**  Whereas before you were saying it could be midday, 1 o'clock in the afternoon, that you were lying in till, and you still didn't want to get up.

**Patient**  Yes, but I still might not want to get up at 10 o'clock.

**Therapist**  But you do.

**Patient**  But I do, yes.

**Therapist**  So that's a big contrast, isn't it?

**Patient**  Also I think, possibly, there are more things that I want to get done.

**Therapist** There are more things to get up for?

**Patient** Uh-uh.

**Therapist** Can you give me an example of what some of those things are?

**Patient** — Uhm, well I might have essays to write, I might have a book I've started, or I haven't taken the dog out — which I could put off, but the more you put them off, there's probably things that I'd want to do then anyway. I suppose there's less empty space.

**Therapist** Yes. So some of the things are the same things that you used to do before which seem to have a bit more meaning, like walking the dog or reading, they were the sort of things you were doing before-hand but you couldn't be bothered so much about.

**Patient** Yes, I think I could put them off longer.

**Therapist** And other things that you are doing are actually new things, that are part of your life now, that weren't before, to do with college. And they actually encourage you to get on with the day?

**Patient** Well I have to get them done, so — yes.

**Therapist** It seemed, at one stage, when we were talking about the problem of getting up, that you thought you believed it to be insur-mountable, and that there was no way round it.

**Patient** It depends on how I was feeling. If I was feeling very depressed, I think I would still see it like that. But I feel alright.

**Therapist** So you're saying that when you're O.K., when you're not depressed, it's not a problem. But if . . .

**Patient** If I became depressed, it wouldn't bother me, not going to college, it wouldn't be worth getting up then.

**Therapist** So there's always the chance, that if you become depressed, it all might shatter again.

**Patient** It might.

**Therapist** And you might be back at square one?

**Patient** Possibly.

**Therapist** What could you do to stop that happening?

**Patient** I don't know.

**Therapist** How have you stopped it happening in the past?

**Patient** You can ignore it.

**Therapist** So you just put up with it and carried on.

**Patient** I tried to for a while.

**Therapist** And then what makes it change?

**Patient**  I start doing more.

**Therapist**  And what makes it change when you start becoming better and start being more active, like you have done in the last 6 weeks?

**Patient**  I start feeling better and I start wanting to do more.

**Therapist**  So your mood improves.

**Patient**  Yes and that makes me feel like I want to get up and do something.

**Therapist**  Does it ever work the other way round? That you do something and that makes your mood improve?

**Patient**  Don't think so. Maybe a little bit. Not to a great extent. It certainly feels like I don't have any control. I mean, I can sort of manipulate it — if I feel a little bit depressed I can ignore it or do something I like, things like that. But if I'm going to get *really* depressed, I don't think there's anything I can do.

**Therapist**  How did you feel when we set the first target of getting up, in the mornings at 9 o'clock? Do you remember when we set that first target five weeks ago and beforehand you were having the problem of staying in bed indefinitely throughout the morning and rising fairly late morning or early afternoon?

**Patient**  Uh-huh.

**Therapist**  You had quite a lot of negative thoughts about that.

**Patient**  Uh-huh.

**Therapist**  But you did try and do the target, and you succeeded, didn't you?

**Patient**  Mostly.

**Therapist**  In the majority.

**Patient**  Yes.

**Therapist**  So how does that make you feel about how much control you have over what happens to you?

**Patient**  But it still wasn't a very big target. And, I wasn't all that depressed at the time.

> [The session continues with discussion of the extent to which the decision to go to college has helped his motivation to do other activities. The therapist then reviewed another area the patient had found difficult. . .]

**Therapist**  Yes — how do you find your decision making is generally, because that was something that used to worry you, wasn't it?

**Patient**  Yes, it's O.K.

**Therapist** It's improved?

**Patient** Yeah.

**Therapist** In what sorts of ways? What sort of things are easier to decide about?

**Patient** Well, I can't think of anything that's not improved, but I mean I haven't had any major decisions to make.

**Therapist** No, but it was small decisions that were . . .

**Patient** Everyday things are alright.

**Therapist** Yes, it was the everyday decisions that were difficult, weren't they?

**Patient** Yes.

**Therapist** What do you put that down to? What do you see as being . . .

**Patient** Feeling better, not feeling depressed.


**Part III: Strategies for Between-session Thought-catching**

In this section, samples from patients' thought-diaries are presented. Look particularly at the differential effectiveness of the 'rational response' category in alleviating the original emotional disturbance. Why do these responses sometimes work and sometimes not? [A possible reason may be that the 'rational response' represents a 'vain hope'. If there is no evidence for the rational response the optimism is empty and may not effectively challenge the validity of the negative thought (e.g. 1, 3). A second possible reason is that the rational response represents a 'must' or 'ought' or 'got to' statement which merely increases pressure on the patient (e.g. 8, 9). A third important variable is degree of belief in the response (e.g. 7).] In each case the intensity of emotion and degree of belief are rated on a 1-100 scale where high scores represent greater disturbance and greater belief, respectively.

(1) Situation: Watching holiday advertisements on television.
   Emotion: Hopeless (80)
   Negative Thought: I've been in this mess for a year — I'll never travel again (95)
   Rational Response: I managed to cope before. I could do it again (20)
   Emotion: Sad (50)
(2) Situation: Watching group of students talking
   Emotion: Sad (100)

Negative Thought: I don't think things will ever be the same again (60)

Rational Response: Things are gradually getting back to normal. Just wait a little longer (80)

Emotion: Sad (50)

(3) Situation: Trying to plan day, one morning

Emotion: Frustration (80)

Negative Thought: My friends are all living their own lives and I can't break out of this prison (80)

Rational Response: This time next year my life will be moving again (20)

Emotion: Frustration (80)

(4) Situation: Just returned from evening with friend

Emotion: Sadness (100)

Negative Thought: I hate being myself, I wish I could escape (50)

Rational Response: This is just reaction against knowing I must change (70)

Emotion: Sadness (50)

(5) Situation: Waking up (in dressing gown)

Emotion: Despair (80)

Negative Thought: This is going to go on forever. I wish I were dead (40)

Rational Response: I recognise this early morning feeling. It will go on for the next hour at most (80)

Emotion: Anxiety (50)

(6) Situation: Thinking about old friends

Emotion: Loneliness (80)

Negative Thought: I've made a terrible mess of my life (90)

Rational Response: I've made a mess of the last year, perhaps (10)

Emotion: Loneliness (70)

(7) Situation: Drinking with friends

Emotion: Rejection (80)

Negative Thought: I feel distant from those around me. People can't like me (40)

Rational Response: I'm expecting too much attention (unrated)

Emotion: Rejection (80)

(8) Situation: Thinking about my situation

Emotion: Hopelessness, despair, feeling of failure (90)

Negative Thought: There's no way out. There's no reason for continuing. I'm tired of struggling to keep up appearances. I'd like to just drive away (95)

Rational Response: I've got to keep trying to overcome this (60)
Emotion: Hopelessness — worse because I can't think of a rational
   response (95) (I know what to do but seem unable to do it)
(9) Situation: In office, sitting looking busy but not working
   Emotion: Despair (100)
   Negative Thought: I am a burden to my husband, children and
      everyone (100)
   Rational Response: I must attempt to get back the fight — the will
      to survive (unrated)
   Emotion: Continuing desperation (100)

Now you have read them through, how useful do you think the technique was with these patients? What do you think accounted for the
difference in effectiveness of rational responses? To what extent are the
rational responses only helpful when they represent attempts to modify
the factual basis of the negative thought (e.g. 5, 6)?
   Finally, consider the following sequence:

Situation: At home, sitting thinking.
Emotion: Nervy, anxious (70)
Negative Thought: I'm getting hooked on my pills. Joan (friend) said
last night 'once you're on pills, you're lost'. I always used to think
like that (70)
Rational Response: [I hate doing this bit; it makes me feel worse]
(1) I've mown the lawn today and talked to three interesting
people
(2) I've made dinner, and done some reading — the normal things of
life (20)
Emotion: [unrated]
[I find it difficult to think of rational responses. When I do, I don't
believe them. It's very demanding.]

Why might this patient be finding it so difficult to generate rational
responses? How representative of your own clients is this patient? At
what point would you want to give up this approach and try an alternative strategy? What alternatives would you consider? [For a discussion
of some aspects of this problem, see p. 125-6.]

**Part IV:  Techniques for Role Induction for Training Workshops**

As in the course of cognitive-behaviour therapy, so in training in therapeutic skills, the use of role-play is often beneficial. On many occasions
it will be sufficient for a group to assign roles to two of its members to
be 'therapist' and 'client' using pen portraits for cases (you could use
those in Part I, above) or based on actual case histories from their own
clients. Occasionally, however, the group may wish to concentrate more
attention on getting into the role of the client – to attempt to experience something of the feelings that depressed patients feel. There is
now an extensive research literature on Mood Induction Procedures (see
Goodwin and Williams, 1982; Clark, in press), and in this section I want
to describe two such procedures in enough detail to be usable in the
role induction context. Specifically, I suggest that half the members of
a group use the mood induction procedures to induce the role, which,
together with some pre-prepared biographical outline, will form the
basis of their roleplay of the client. The other group members, the
therapists, have access to the biographical information, but are not
present at the mood induction. Therapists have prepared instructions
to conduct, for example, an 'initial session' (in which part of their
agenda will be to explain the principles on which therapy will be based),
or to focus on explaining and using a particular technique. Roleplays
are then conducted in pairs, with the group coming together again after
a predefined interval to discuss their sessions. At other training sessions,
the roles may be reversed.

*Mood Induction I:  Negative Self-statements*

The following is a list of negative self-statements of the type used in
mood induction research. They are divided into self-devaluative statements and statements reflecting somatic concern or fatigability. You
may select some from each list or use each separately. Select 20 to 30
items and type each on a card. The procedure for mood induction has
varied from study to study, but a powerful procedure is for the
'subject' to study the cards, one by one, spending longer on the statements (s)he feels are particularly meaningful and less on those which
are not felt to be disturbing or appropriate. Continue this for 7-8
minutes, if necessary looking through the statements for a second time.
The individual is encouraged to identify with the mood associated with
the statement. (S)he will need some biographical detail supplied before
or after the role induction procedure. For example: 'You are a 33-year-
old mother of three children. Your husband works shifts in a factory.

The money is adequate but the shift-times are inconvenient, and leave you having to look after the house and children without much support. (Coming off shift-work would mean less money.) Recently you have lost contact with several friends, and lost interest in hobbies inside and outside the home. Things look very hopeless.'

Here, now, is the list of self-statements:

*Somatic Statements*
I'd really love to have an absolutely lazy day
Other people seem so much more lively than I am
I really can't be bothered to do anything
I don't feel very energetic
My whole body feels worn out
I do feel ready for a good rest
I do seem to get tired very easily
I feel heavy and sluggish
It seems such an effort to do anything
The mere thought of exercise is appalling to me
I feel as if it would take me twice as long to do anything
I feel so tired that I would rather just sit than do anything
I haven't even the energy to keep a conversation going
I just can't make the effort to liven myself up
I just feel drained of energy, worn out
I feel as if my whole body has been slowed down
I feel as if I haven't had a proper sleep for a week
I don't think I could exert myself even if I wanted to
I'm so tired I don't want to do anything at all
I just want to curl up and go to sleep
I feel absolutely exhausted
Sometimes it's just too much effort even to move
I'd like to go to sleep for a very long time
I'm so tired, my thoughts keep drifting away
I have to really concentrate to keep my eyes open
I'm having difficulty stopping myself from just falling asleep
I feel absolutely shattered

*Self-devaluative Statements*
I have too many bad things in my life
I often wish that I were somebody else
I have very little to look forward to
I am less successful than other people

I feel disappointed the way things have turned out
I don't get much pleasure about being with my friends
I am annoyed at myself for being bad at making decisions
I don't think I make a good impression on other people
I'm not too hopeful about the future
I don't get the same satisfaction out of things these days
There are things about me that I don't like
Everything I do seems to turn out badly
I regret some of the things I've done in the past
I know I've made mistakes in my life
I'm very aware of my faults
I often feel ashamed of things I've done
There are things about me that aren't very attractive
Some people don't have a very high opinion of me
Life seems boring and uninteresting
I feel lonely and isolated
The future seems just one string of problems
I'm miserable, and there's no way for things to get better

*Mood Induction II: Taped Depression Story*

The following story, developed by D. Rosenhan and his colleagues at Stanford in their studies on affective determinants of altruism, is also a powerful mood induction procedure (Williams, 1980). It is taperecorded, and played to the 'subject' who is asked to identify with the story. As with the self-statement role induction, the person role-playing the patient will need to be given some biographical detail, following the mood induction, onto which the disturbed affect may be 'attached'. For example: 'It is now 3 months after your friend's death. You have become tired and listless, and lost interest in your work. You don't go out much now, and your former hobbies are of no interest to you whatever, even the thought of them makes you feel drained of energy. You are thinking of giving up college, but on the advice of your tutor, have come to see a psychotherapist, though you doubt it will make any difference.'

Here is the mood induction story[1]:
Sit back, and close your eyes.
Relax. Let yourself sink into the chair. Focus all your attention on my voice. Let yourself relax and become absorbed completely in the things I am telling you. What I would like you to do is use your

imagination. Put yourself into the situation I will describe. Feel the same feelings. Think the same things. Experience the situation as if you were in it. Let yourself relax and react to your feelings. Picture the events happening to you. See yourself going through them. Try to create in yourself the emotions and thoughts that I describe to you. Imagine that you have a very good friend who is attending college with you. Imagine that you and your friend are very close – and that you like and respect her a great deal. When things go well in your friend's life you are happy for her, and when things go badly, you suffer nearly as much as she does. You and your friend have been through a lot together, and that has helped you to get to know each other very well.

Lately, you've become aware that your friend has not been feeling well. She's been dragging around – not doing much of anything. She seems to have lost her enthusiasm for course-work, and has become grumpy and irritable. She's really annoying, and you're upset because you don't know what's wrong.

One day she confides in you that she's been having a chronic series of headaches and has not felt well for almost two weeks. You are afraid that she might really be sick. At your urging, she goes to the Student Health Centre, but the doctors there find nothing wrong with her, and suggest she might just be overworked. Taking the doctors' advice, your friend drops two of her courses, and cuts back on all of her extra-curricular activities. But this does not help. As several days go by, you notice that your friend seems to have less and less energy and her headaches become increasingly severe and frequent. She looks terrible, and she's always irritated with you. Finally you convince her to return to the Health Centre and this time the doctors take her complaints more seriously. When your friend doesn't come back from the Health Centre after three hours you call the Centre to see if she's still there, and learn that your friend has been taken to the hospital where the doctors want to perform a series of tests immediately.

The next evening you go to visit your friend at the hospital during visiting hours and to your surprise find your friend's parents in the waiting room outside her ward. They've driven up from their home that morning. They look keyed up and anxious. You realise that there must be something really wrong with your friend. They don't know what the problem is yet, but the doctors' tests have eliminated all but the most serious possibilities.

You think back, and remember all the good times you and she have had together. They all seem so far away. It hurts you to see her so ill, but it hurts even more to think that those good times may never come again.

As the next few days pass, you live with constant depression, trying to be near a phone, spending all your spare time at the hospital and hoping for some change.

You think of all the worst things that could happen. She could die and you would lose her, never be able to talk to her again. Or worse, she could die slowly. Every minute with her could be your last time together. For months you would have to be cheerful for her while you were sad. You would have to watch her die in pieces, until the last piece finally went and you would be alone.

You know the tests are getting more painful. The spinal tap. The bone marrow extraction. The test in which she has to swallow a radio-active solution that leaves her ill for days. No-one has said it yet, but as every other possibility gets eliminated, you come to suspect cancer. That's a thought you don't want to have. It would hurt too much to lose her. Only old people get cancer – not people you know. It's often a long and painful disease with no cure. So you think; and worry; and try and keep it out of your mind as the tests continue.

Finally, the uncertainty ends. The doctors determine that your friend has lymphoma, an incurable cancer of the lymph nodes.

Your worst imaginings are now real. You are despondent and shocked. She has a year or two to live at most, and her death will be slow and painful.

You feel that it's so senseless and so unfair to end this way – she will be gone so fast. All the time you spent with her – all the crazy plans you made together are over. She will leave you alone; and constantly asking yourself what went wrong? You can feel some empty space inside you that will take a long time to fill. But the thought is too much to bear. You are hurt, and helpless, and upset that you will lose someone close to you to a disease that is so arbitrary and cruel.

### Notes

1. When the story is taped, the sex of the friend may be chosen to be male or female. The 'female' version is reproduced here.

# 8 THE COGNITIVE THEORY OF DEPRESSION REVISITED[1]

Although it was not until the late 1960s and 1970s that experimental clinical psychologists started seriously to develop theories about the onset and maintenance of depression, even from these early theoretical writings there emerged a controversy about the necessity to postulate cognitive mediators. There are two forms of this debate, the first, with which we shall not be concerned here, is the philosophico-theoretical issue about the status of 'private events' and their explanatory power.

The other debate is that between those who believe that cognitive events precede and cause the emotional disturbance, and those who believe that the emotional disturbance can be explained on other grounds (biological or behavioural) and see cognitive distortions and negative self-talk as a product or correlate of the emotional disturbance. Now this debate is crucial. If cognitive events are an epiphenomenon, accompanying though not playing a causal role in affective disorders, it would make less sense to devote years of research on how best to change cognitive styles or habitual self-talk strategies. Like ointment on a chickenpox rash, such treatment may soothe but have little prospect of treating the underlying disorder. Of course cognitive therapies do work (see Chapter 2) but it may be that they are inadvertently affecting other more significant subsystems. Let us then examine the status of the aetiological cognitive thesis.

Just to complicate matters further there are also two forms of the aetiological thesis. Let us call them the Precipitation Theory and the Vulnerability Theory. The first is a 'state' theory and argues that moment to moment fluctuations in mood may in part be accounted for by the thoughts, images, and memories that occur to the individual. Controlling the nature, frequency or intensity of these thoughts and images will thereby affect the mood that is consequent upon them. The Vulnerability Theory argues that long-lasting styles of thinking (e.g. attributional style, tendency to selectively abstract or think dichotomously) occur prior to and render a person vulnerable to depressive breakdown in the face of stress. Although often confused under the general title of cognitive theory of depression, these theories are quite distinct and ought to be discussed separately. We shall consider the evidence for each in turn.

171

## The Precipitation Theory

One of the best strands of evidence in favour of the theory that thoughts and images may precipitate moment to moment fluctuations in mood comes from studies of experimentally induced mood. These studies provide particularly useful evidence because, using experimental manipulation of mood, they can eliminate other variables which might otherwise be important contributory factors to disturbed mood (e.g. individual differences). Six forms of mood induction procedures (MIP's) have been used.[2]

*Self-referent mood statements* are the most widely used MIP. First described by Velten (1968), the method involves reading aloud 60 negative self-referent statements, e.g. 'I'm discouraged and unhappy about myself' or 'I feel worn out, my health might not be as good as it's supposed to be'. The statements progress from relative mood neutrality to dysphoria, the overall tone being that of indecisiveness, tiredness, unhappiness, inefficiency and pessimism. Investigators agree that this general procedure is a potent manipulator of mood, as assessed by visual analogue scales (e.g. Teasdale and Fogarty, 1979), the Depressive Multiple Adjective Checklists (e.g. Hale and Strickland, 1976; Brewer *et al.* 1980), the Personal Feeling Scale (e.g. Frost *et al.* 1979), and the Wessman and Ricks' Elation vs. Depression Scale (Coleman, 1975). Furthermore, independent ratings of general demeanour and 'mirth' outside the experimental situation (just having completed the experiment) have been found to differentiate between MIP and control groups (Coleman, 1975).

The *Autobiographical Recollections Method* was used by Brewer *et al.* (1980) in a comparison with Velten's MIP and various control conditions. Subjects were asked to close their eyes and recall three autobiographical mood-evoking events that made them feel lonely, rejected, defeated or hurt. The entire MIP lasted eleven minutes, the three events being spaced in time according to prerecorded instructions. Subjects had to try and recall three events which were progressively sadder and more unpleasant. The results showed that this method strongly affected mood, giving more affective disturbance on the DACL and Beck Depression Inventory than the Velten MIP. Spielberger State Anxiety Scores were also affected by this MIP.

*A taped depressive story* has been developed as an MIP by D. Rosenhan and colleagues at Stanford, and subsequently modified for use with a British population by myself (Williams, 1980) (Chapter 7). The taped story, with which subjects are asked to get involved, lasts approximately ten minutes. It asks the subject to imagine a friend becoming ill and eventually being diagnosed as having incurable lymphoma. The tape focuses on the subject's own feelings of helplessness and loneliness. I found that this MIP significantly raised anxiety, despondency, irritation and frustration levels, and significantly lower relaxation and happiness levels, when compared to a control condition.

*Failure feedback* has been used in a large amount of research on the learned helplessness and test anxiety phenomena. These have been comprehensively reviewed elsewhere (e.g. Abramson *et al.*, 1978; Weiner and Heckhausen, 1972). Although most studies have not aimed solely at manipulating depressed affect many of the studies reviewed by these authors report affective changes following failure experience, or exposure to noncontingency.

*Hypnosis* has been used by Gordon Bower in his studies of state-dependent mood-memory effects. He asks subjects under hypnosis to induce a sad mood by imagining an episode in which they had been grievously sad. If they could call up no such scene from their life, the experiment helped them construct an imaginary one that 'would have the intended emotional impact'. Subjects were told to adjust the emotion until it was intense but not unbearable. Bower *et al.* (1978) report that their sad subjects were long-faced, morose, slow to respond, and often on the verge of tears. No objective measure of mood intensity was taken, nor any subjective ratings by the subject used, so it is difficult to establish just how effective the procedure was. Bower *et al.* used only subjects who had demonstrated good hypnotic facility, which, although suggesting that the mood induced would have been subjectively intense, is also a drawback in interpreting how generalisable these results are.

Finally, Sutherland, Newman and Rachman (1982) have used *music* as a mood induction procedure. Subjects have a choice of music selected as having sad associations. They find the MIP more successful than that of Velten in changing subjective ratings of anxious, sad and happy moods, though ratings of 'apprehension', 'despondent' and 'tired' were not affected. This procedure is reviewed by Clark (in press).

All these procedures provide strong evidence that asking subjects to voluntarily create images, thoughts or memories which are unpleasant or unhappy affects mood. Nor can it be argued that subjects are only pretending to be depressed. Coleman (1975) asked observers to rate subjects after they had left the experimental situation. Reliable differences were found in the blind ratings of these observations of 'mirth' between the subjects who had and those who had not undergone the experimental induction of mood. Coleman also found, as

Velten (1968) had done before, that subjects differing on the Harvard Scale of Suggestibility did not differ in intensity of mood disturbance reported following mood induction. Finally, Polivy and Doyle (1980) actually told subjects that they would feel the mood opposite to the depressive statements by a 'comparison' effect (the more they read, the more they would feel happy they did not feel like this). Despite this very heavy counter-instruction, half the subjects still felt the mood suggested by the statements. Taken together with other investigators' use of a control group who are told to try and behave throughout as if they were depressed (which find that the quality and intensity of mood disturbance induced thus cannot match that obtained when a mood induction is carried out), the evidence in favour of the Precipitation Theory is very strong.

## Problems in Interpreting the Precipitation Theory

Despite the strong evidence for the theory, the value of having demonstrated these effects is rather doubtful. For what have we established? – that unhappy thoughts and images produce unhappy mood. But in what way is this anything specifically to do with depression? For mood is a rather unreliable indicator of clinical depression, since extreme mood disturbance can be found in other psychiatric states (anxiety neuroses, schizophrenia etc.) and in normal reactions to stress which one would not want to call a psychiatric state (e.g. grief reactions). Depue and Monroe (1978) give a very clear account of the inadequacies of using mood or self-esteem levels as the sole marker of depression and their lucid argument should be read by any would-be student of the subject. Some of these arguments have been touched on in Chapter 3, but are worth repeating. A high score on a self-rating mood scale – even if the scale is well designed (e.g. Beck Depression Inventory) cannot be used to identify the underlying state as depressive. For example, Hamilton (1960) insists that his scale (completed by the observer, but reliant for some items on the subject's self-report) should *not* be used as a diagnostic tool, but only as a measure of severity in patients already diagnosed as having a primary depressive disorder. A high score could result from a number of independent factors. Clinical diagnosis takes into account a wider range of factors than self-report or observations of dysphoria, e.g. onset characteristics, psychosocial factors, previous clinical history, presence of other psychiatric symptoms. In addition, a high score may be obtained on self-rating versions of scales because a person inadvertently inflates his score for a number of reasons (see discussion of the Anchoring Heuristic in Chapter 9). Now a self-rating form may include opportunities to report on objective signs and symptoms (e.g. weight loss, sleep disturbance etc.), but they are still weighted in favour of the self-report of subjective feelings. Interestingly, the more a scale is oriented away from the report of subjective feelings, the better it seems to discriminate between groups of patients who would, on other grounds, normally be considered to differ in severity of depression. Thus, for example, Carroll *et al*. (1973) compared the relative sensitivity of observer rated (Hamilton) and self-rated (Zung) depression in 'primary depressives' who were either G.P. patients, day patients or inpatients. It was found that the Hamilton discriminated successfully between all three groups, whereas the Zung only discriminated the day and G.P. patients. Thus, studies of mood do not necessarily tell us about clinical depression.

So are the findings that bad thoughts induce moods completely redundant in the understanding of clinical depression? I don't myself believe so. It is not only that experimental investigations of the Precipitation Theory offer us methods of studying how different types of thought and image affect mood. It is also that *clinical* observation suggests that *patients* suffer thought-induced fluctuations in mood. Although experimental demonstrations might not tell us anything that is unique to clinical depression, it is important for therapists to know that the depressed mood they are observing may not best be analysed in biological terms, but may have cognitive antecedents. If it can happen in the laboratory, it can certainly happen in real life; and it probably happens in the life of depressives more than most.

### The Vulnerability Theory

The notion that clinical depression of at least some subtypes is preceded by personality traits, self esteem deficits or cognitive distortions which render the person vulnerable to emotional breakdown is certainly not new in clinical psychiatry and psychology. Just three current exponents of the view will be mentioned; Beck, Seligman and Brown.

The vulnerability of the depression-prone person, according to Beck (1967, p. 227) is

'attributable to the constellation of enduring negative attitudes about himself, about the world, and about his future. Even though these attitudes (or concepts) may not be prominent or even discernible at a given time, they persist in a latent state like an explosive charge ready to be detonated by an appropriate set of conditions. Once activated, these concepts dominate the person's thinking and lead to the typical depressive symptomatology.'

The idea that these may be 'latent' should sound a note of caution for the experimentalist. A model which includes such variables is often hard to refute. We shall see that this caution is justified at the present time.

In stating the reformulated hypothesis Abramson, Seligman and Teasdale (1978) state that a persisting tendency to attribute negative events to internal, stable and global factors renders a person prone to depression, should he or she be exposed to noncontingent negative outcomes. Seligman (1981) has further argued that the maladaptive cognitive style detailed by Beck is reducible to the central tenets of the reformulated learned helplessness theory.

Brown and Harris (1978) argue that the factors which render women vulnerable to the effects of life events (loss of own mother before eleven years, no job, three or more children under fourteen at home, no confidante) are associated with low self-esteem. Self-esteem has a 'transitional position' in their account of the social origins of depression:

'as a background factor, low self-esteem can both predispose a person to a depressive reaction . . . (and can) . . . therefore become a prominent feature of the depressive disorder itself' (Brown and Harris, 1978, p. 265)

Before considering the status of the Vulnerability Model itself, there are two issues which first require discussion. The first is whether the cognitive distortions actually are found in the depressed person when depressed. The second is whether these theories require that an actual event occur in order to turn 'depression proneness' into a depressive reaction.

It may be thought odd that the first of these questions needs asking at all. Is it not an essential prerequisite of a diagnosis of depression that such distorted thinking is shown? The answer is that it is not. If a person has dysphoric mood, early morning wakening, diurnal mood variation, retardation or agitation, weight loss or anorexia and inability to concentrate, in the absence of prior diagnosis of alternative disorders the person will almost certainly be diagnosed as depressed. They may not show clear evidence of distorted thinking styles or malattribution. Research on mildly depressed students bears out possible dissociations between depressed mood and distorted thinking. Hammen (1978) found that among high Beck scorers, there was an inverse relationship between cognitive distortion and number of recent life events. Depressed subjects with low levels of life stress were more distorted; those with high levels of life stress were less distorted. Gong-Guy and Hammen (1980) reported that a depressive attributional style was associated with depression only when attribution for the more stressful life events were taken into account and more trivial events excluded. So maladaptive style of thinking is not a general and universal accompaniment of depression. More recent work in Newcastle bears out this conclusion at least for attributional style. In one study Cleaver (1981) found that although there was some evidence that attributions covaried with mood within individuals, there was little suggestion that these depressed patients showed a depressive attributional style in general. In the second study Davies (1982) found no evidence of a depressive attributional style in a group of 8 endogenous and 12 neurotic depressives (Spitzer criteria). A more extensive study by Hargreaves (1982) comparing 50 depressed patients with 50 matched controls found no evidence that the groups differed in attributional style. By contrast Raps *et al.* (1982) have found the predicted attributional style in depressives, but not in hospitalised schizophrenics. They have concluded that such a style was specific to depression and was not associated with psychopathology in general. That is a fair conclusion, but only up to a point, for current depression levels of the patient groups were not given although the schizophrenics were referred to as 'non-depressed'. If we suppose then that the depressed subjects were indeed more depressed, then the groups differ on two variables; diagnosis and mood level. So if the schizophrenics had also been dysphoric, they may have shown a depressive attributional style as well. Although this result then helps to establish that maladaptive attributional style is not a correlate of schizophrenia; it does not establish that it is uniquely associated with the diagnosis of depression, only with depressed mood.[3]

The second question is concerned with whether, given vulnerability, a life event is necessary to produce depression. It is interesting that out of one of Brown and Harris' samples of 114, 28 developed depression without a provoking agent. They call these patients 'susceptible to depression' (p. 267) to distinguish them from those who are 'vulnerable', but who seem to require the life event to provoke the depression. Interestingly, they found evidence to suggest that past loss, previous episode, and age of 40 years or over was strongly related to absence of a provoking agent. The presence of all three (but not less than three) was found to be associated with susceptibility to depression.

In Seligman's research there is some confusion as to whether an actual exposure to non-contingency is necessary for depression to occur or not. Seligman (1981) certainly accepts a correlation (in a sample of 143 undergraduates) between Beck scores and attribution of bad outcome internally, stably and globally as evidence to support the reformulated model.[4] But, this is too great a claim. The result is consistent with the model, but could equally well have been due to increased depression levels themselves causing the depressive attributional style and not the other way around. The result establishes neither a precipitation theory nor a vulnerability theory.

So does Seligman think an event is necessary or not?

The actual statement of the reformulated model seems clear enough (Abramson *et al.*, 1978). It contains four specific elements (p. 70); (a) an uncontrollable event, (b) attributional style which determines attribution for that particular event, (c) prediction of future occurrence of uncontrollable events, and (d) events in question to represent highly probable aversive outcome and/or very improbable positive outcomes. That is, the model implies that if no uncontrollable event occurred in the first instance, this causal sequence would break down, and attributional style, though producing 'depression proneness' would not precipitate depression.

In fact, in a more recent paper (1982), Metalsky, Abramson, Seligman, Semmel and Peterson seem to have cleared up any ambiguity in this matter by describing Abramson *et al's* reformulation as a *diathesis-stress* model. They write: 'the logic of the reformulation suggests that in the presence of positive life events or in the absence of negative life events, people exhibiting the hypothesised depressogenic attributional styles should be no more likely to develop depressive reactions than people not displaying these attributional styles' (p. 613).

Evidence consistent with this statement was found in a recent study on job redundancy by Neil Rothwell and myself. We examined whether men who had undergone a life event (closure of a large steel works in Consett, Co. Durham) would show a different pattern from that of control subjects in the relationship between attributional style and measures of depression (Beck) and self-esteem (Rosenberg). The reformulated model (Abramson *et al.*, p. 70; Metalsky *et al.*, p. 613) would predict that attributional style would only be correlated with depression in subjects who had experienced the uncontrollable event of redundancy. If the occurrence of the event is unnecessary there should

be the same level of correlation between the two irrespective of inter-
vening events. Interestingly, depression, self-esteem and attributional
style did not differ in overall levels or variance between the groups.

But the results showed that internality (the tendency to make internal
attributions) was correlated within the redundancy group both with
depression $(r(18) = 0.46, p < 0.05)$ and low self-esteem $(r(17) = 0.63,$
$p < 0.01)$. The control group showed neither relationship $(r(18) = 0.13$
and $-0.03$ for depression and self-esteem respectively). The differences
between the groups for the internality-self-esteem correlations was
statistically significant $(t(37) = 2.12; p < 0.05)$. This finding provides
tentative evidence for the view that the life event was necessary in
establishing the link between attributional style and depression. Taken
together with Gong-Guy and Hammen's (1980) report that depressive
attributional style was associated with depression only when attribution
for the more stressful life events were taken into account, it suggests
that the trauma of the life event is an important factor in making the
attributional dimension more salient (Rothwell and Williams, 1983).

Despite this, the picture remains confused. Some investigators have
found no evidence of malattributions in depressed patients, others have
done so. Some have found correlations irrespective of a life event,
others have pointed out that, on the reformulated model, a life event
is necessary to turn depression proneness into helplessness depression.
Still others have found that the salience of the life event is an important
factor. What, then, is the evidence for and against the Vulnerability
Theory itself?

## Evidence Consistent with the Vulnerability Theory

Few clinicians would disagree with the contention that some people are
vulnerable to depression, but the thesis to be discussed here concerns
the nature of that vulnerability. For at least Beck and Seligman and
their co-workers suggest that this vulnerability involves maladaptive
thinking styles, and these 'styles' are not far from Brown and Harris's
concept of low self-esteem. We have already noted how reported correlations between current depression and current attributions (Seligman
*et al.*, 1979) establishes neither that one variable preceded the other in
time nor the direction of cause when both occur together.

O'Hara *et al.* (1982) go further than reporting correlations between
depression and cognitive style measured at the same time. In their
study, 170 women were assessed in the second trimester of pregnancy
on the Beck Depression Inventory and measures of attributional and
cognitive vulnerability. They were followed up between 5½ and

20 weeks (mean 12 weeks) after the birth of their babies, and depression level assessed. Results showed that all scales correlated with each other and with post-partum Beck score. However most of the variance of the post-partum depression was accounted for by initial depression level, the cognitive style measures only accounting together for a further 4 per cent of the variance. Since there was no control group of women who had not had a child, or any life event, it is impossible to say to what extent even this result was due to the stress of childbirth acting upon vulnerable personalities.

A similar problem arises in the interpretations of an interesting study by Golin *et al.* (1981). They used a cross-lagged panel correlational analysis to examine 'the causality of causal attributions in depression'. They found that the level of correlation of attributional vulnerability at Time 1 with depression level at Time 2 (one month later) significantly exceeded the level of correlation of depression at Time 1 with attributional vulnerability at Time 2. That is, people who were more depressed at Time 2 had shown greater attributional vulnerability (e.g. tended to attribute failure to stable and global factors, and success to unstable factors) one month before, but people who showed this vulnerability on second testing had not been more depressed one month before. They claimed that these results showed that such attributions 'may act as causes of depressive symptoms', although they admit that the statistical method used acts as an indicator of temporal precedence rather than positive proof of causation: their caution in this regard is entirely justified. The overall level of depression over the time interval remained constant, and no record was made of whether individuals suffered a life event during that month. Analogous results to these from a medical setting may clarify why a causal conclusion is not justified. In a measles attack, the rash is often preceded by some symptoms of a common cold. A cross-lagged correlational analysis might show cold symptoms at Time 1 correlating with severity of rash at Time 2, but no correlation between severity of rash at Time 1 with cold symptoms at Time 2. However, it would be wrong to conclude that the cold symptoms *caused* rash. It *would* be fair, however, to say that something interesting had been documented about the temporal sequence of a measles episode. And it is this aspect of Golin *et al's* result which is important. For they have shown that, in some depressions at least, there is evidence of attributional distortion prior to the manifest depression.[5] Their results tell us something about the time course of depression at its early stages. Earlier on in this book mention is made of McLean's view that a common course for depression to follow is for cognitive symptoms to precede behavioural disturbance which is followed in turn by somatic symptoms as the depression becomes severe. Golin *et al's* results expand on knowledge about this temporal sequence. They do not establish the causal status of the Vulnerability Thesis.

Metalsky *et al*. have, however, claimed to test the causal thesis directly by carrying out a prospective study. They gave a measure of attributional vulnerability to 227 undergraduate students prior to taking their mid-term examination. They studied the correlation between this measure and how upset the students became following receipt of their results. Success and failure were defined by the students themselves who had declared beforehand what result they would be unhappy with, and what result they would be happy with (this level of aspiration, was, incidentally, not correlated with attributional style). Fifty-three students fell at or below a grade with which they were unhappy. Their subsequent mood disturbance correlated significantly with greater tendency to make internal and global attributions for bad outcomes. Twenty-eight students fell at or above a grade with which they were happy. Their subsequent mood disturbance was not significantly correlated with attributional style, though attributing bad outcomes to stable causes tended to correlate with upset mood even in these 'successful' students. The actual correlations are shown in Table 8.1.

Table 8.1: Correlations of Attributional Style Subscales for Negative Outcomes with Degree of Mood Disturbance (MAACL) Following Mid-term Exam Results (ns = not significant)

| | 'Successful' students (N = 28) | | 'Unsuccessful' students (N = 35) | |
|---|---|---|---|---|
| Attributional subscale | r | p | r | p |
| Internality | 0.12 | ns | 0.34 | 0.01 |
| Stability | 0.36 | 0.06 | 0.04 | ns |
| Globality | 0.22 | ns | 0.32 | 0.05 |

Like the results of Golin *et al*., this study provides evidence of a correlation between cognitive vulnerability at Time 1 and mood disturbance at Time 2. But have they shown what they claim to have shown – that is, that 'in the absence of negative life-events people exhibiting . . . depressogenic attributional styles . . . be no more likely to develop depressive reactions than people not displaying these attributional styles'? Note that the crucial test of their hypothesis is not the correlation within the 'unsuccessful' group, but the *difference* in correlations between this group (who had suffered the stress of failure) and the other group of 28 who had not. The authors do not test the significance of the difference in correlations. Table 8.2 shows the results of such a comparison, using $Z$ transformation of the $r$-values. None of the differences is significant. This implies that mood disturbance is no more related to attributional vulnerability when students have suffered the stress of exam disappointment than when they have suffered no such stress.

Table 8.2: Comparison of Correlations Between Attributions and Subsequent Mood Disturbances With or Without Exam Disappointment (ns = not significant)

| Attributional subscale | 'Successful' students N = 28 $Z_1$ | 'Unsuccessful' students N = 53 $Z_2$ | $Z_1 - Z_2$ | Critical* ratio | p |
|---|---|---|---|---|---|
| Internality | 0.121 | 0.354 | −0.233 | −0.95 | ns |
| Stability | 0.377 | 0.040 | 0.337 | 1.38 | ns |
| Globality | 0.224 | 0.332 | −0.108 | −0.44 | ns |

$$* \ CR = \frac{Z_1 - Z_2}{\sqrt{\dfrac{1}{n_1 - 3} + \dfrac{1}{n_2 - 3}}}$$

So although there is accumulating evidence for the correlation of depressed mood and cognitive style, and for the fact that this cognitive style might be assessable some time before the depression is manifest, the evidence for the causal Vulnerability Theory from the studies is weak.

An alternative to the correlational approach has been taken by Wittenborn and co-workers (Altman and Wittenborn, 1980; Cofer and Wittenborn, 1980). They have studied women who have recovered from a depressive episode and compared their personality characteristics with a control sample of 'never depressed' women. Because it is known that people who have been depressed, though recovered, remain vulnerable to further episodes, such a study may yield data on the correlates of this vulnerability. They found that a large number of individual self-report items distinguished the recovered group from the controls. These items, when factor analysed, yield such factors as low self-esteem, preoccupation with failure, pessimistic outlook, narcissistic vulnerability and general sense of competence. Unfortunately it is unclear from these studies how the initial diagnosis of depression was made during the prior episode, but we are told that the mean age of the women studied was 37 years. Paykel's (1971) analysis of 165 depressed patients suggests the existence of a moderately severe cluster who were middle aged, had a greater number of previous 'illnesses', and in whom there was a strong mixture of anxiety and additional neurotic manifestations (e.g. obsessional symptoms, depersonalisation, etc.). If the vulnerability factors found by Wittenborn's group are attributable to associated neurotic traits, then although this may explain this particular group's vulnerability, it may not be generalisable to other subgroups of depression. As will be seen below, when Wilkinson and Blackburn's similar study is mentioned, such caution is entirely justified at this time.

We now turn from studies which have purported to support the Vulnerability Theory, to those which have purported to weaken it.

## Evidence against the Vulnerability Theory

Lewinson *et al.* (1981) carried out a large scale prospective study in the community. They gave 998 individuals various cognitive measures one year apart. These measures included a locus of control measure, a measure of expectation for positive and negative outcomes, an Irrational Beliefs Questionnaire, a measure of Perception of Control and a measure of self-esteem. They hoped to identify those who became depressed during the year, then check back to see if these showed any differences on the cognitive measures. Of the 998, 85 became depressed during the follow-up period who had not been depressed at pre-test. So these investigators were able to compare the relationship between current depression and current cognitive style, as well as the relationship between cognitive style and future depression. Their results were clear cut. Currently depressed subjects differed on all measures except the attributional assessment. They expected less positive and more negative outcomes, were more irrational, perceived themselves to have less control and had lower self-esteem than people who were not currently depressed. However the 'to-be-depressed' group did not differ from controls on any measure. Indeed the only evidence for the effect of antecedent cognitions on future depression was that depressed subjects with the worst cognitions as assessed by the 'expectation of positive outcomes', and 'perception of control' questionnaire showed poorer subsequent rates of improvement. In the light of these results showing no prospective effect for cognitions, Lewinsohn *et al.* concluded that depressive cognitions are consequents of depression, rather than antecedents.

These results must be treated with caution, however, because we don't know why the 85 individuals became depressed during the interval of the study. It is reasonable to assume that the entire range of causes were implicated — biological, environmental and psychological precipitants. Cognitive theorists do not claim that their theories exhaust the aetiological possibilities for how depression comes about. Seligman (1975) is quite specific on this point. And we have already seen how Abramson *et al.* (1978) require exposure to noncontingent outcomes as part of the causal sequence, and how Brown and Harris (1978) require a 'provoking agent' to turn vulnerability (though not susceptibility, see p. 177, above) into clinical depression. But in Lewinsohn's study we do not know how many of the 85 subjects had a provoking agent prior to becoming depressed — for it is these that would be predicted to have antecedent maladaptive cognitive styles. Nor do we know how many of the people who remained well actually did or did not suffer a life event. There may have been many who were depression-prone (thus clouding the statistical comparison), but who never suffered a life event so did not become depressed. Still more interesting are those control subjects who did suffer a life event but remained well, for this is the group who should have most clearly not had a maladaptive thinking style — the true control group. In summary, some of the individuals who did not become depressed may have been depression-prone, but did not suffer a life event, and some of the individuals who did become depressed may have become so for reasons other than 'cognitive'. Without the data on 'provoking agents' Lewinsohn's data is suggestive, but not conclusive.

An alternative approach to the same problem is not to identify those who became depressed, but those who on other grounds would be considered vulnerable to depression. Two studies which have taken this approach will be discussed: Campbell, working in Oxford, and Wilkinson and Blackburn, working in Edinburgh.

Campbell (1982) identified a 'vulnerable' group by selecting from a community sample of women, those who had Brown and Harris's vulnerability factors (lack of confidante, 3 or more children under 14 years at home, no job, loss of own mother before the age of 11). Women were interviewed one year apart using the Present State Examination,

Brown and Harris's Life Event Inventory, the Rosenberg Self-esteem Scale, and a number of measures of cognitive distortion. She found that Brown's vulnerability factors were associated with increased levels of nonspecific neurotic symptoms and impoverished material resources, but not associated with low self-esteem (as Brown and Harris would surely have strongly predicted) nor with a negative cognitive style. Campbell concludes that the cognitive style results suggest a need for the modification of Beck's model of cognitive predisposition to depression. She could go further and suggest that her carefully computed data cast doubt on the sort of cognitive Vulnerability Theory proposed in general by such writers as Beck, Seligman and Brown. There is, however, evidence which may undermine to some extent Campbell's conclusion. She examined 'vulnerability' as defined by Brown and Harris. But what if Brown and Harris's vulnerability factors were not universally applicable? Costello (1982) has recently conducted a procedural replication study of Brown and Harris in Calgary, Canada, and has found that neither social class, nor loss of mother, nor 3 children (of any age) nor lack of employment were vulnerability factors. Only 'lack of intimate relationship with a confidante' emerged as rendering women more vulnerable to depression following a life event − and this item is, of course, not independent of the individual's 'premorbid' personality nor of her current depression. Costello concludes 'the role of social factors is community specific and the causal roles of events and difficulties in relation to depression remain uncertain'.

So a doubt is raised about Campbell's data. Were the women she studied truly vulnerable? On the other hand, one might still have expected an association between cognitive style measures and some of the vulnerability factors (e.g. lack of confidante), so her evidence remains damaging to the Vulnerability Theory.

Wilkinson and Blackburn (1981) approached the same issue by studying recovered depressives. They argued that 'patients who have recovered from a depressive illness can be defined as depression-prone individuals and . . . should still exhibit the typical thinking which made them vulnerable to depression', that is they should still show negative bias, typical logical errors in the interpretation of events and in their basic assumptions about the world. Fifteen patients (Beck score $< 8$) who had undergone routine psychiatric (drug) treatment for unipolar major depression and had recovered at least 3 months (mean 40 months) prior to the study, were compared with ten currently depressed (unipolar major) patients under inpatient or outpatient treatment. In addition there were two control groups: 'recovered other patient' (N = 10) and Normals (N = 15) recruited through newspaper advertising and matched with the recovered depressed group for age, sex, social class and educational level. All subjects completed the Beck, the Middlesex Hospital Questionnaire, Beck *et al's* (1974) Hopelessness Scale, a Cognitive Response Test (CRT-36) (Watkins and Rush, 1978) and a new Cognitive Style Test developed by the authors (see p. 73). It was found that the currently depressed group differed from the other group in having more distorted cognitions. These individuals were more hopeless, had more negative interpretations and non-self-attributions for positive events, more negative interpretations and self-attributions for negative events and more irrational negative responses. However, the recovered depressives showed none of these cognitive distortions, obtaining scores comparable to those of a normal sample who had never been clinically depressed. These results are contrary to the Vulnerability Theory.[6] The authors conclude: 'cognitive distortions would appear to be specific to the illness phase of depression and not to depression-prone individuals . . . a state not a trait'.

Taken together, the Lewinsohn *et al.*, Campbell, and Wilkinson and Blackburn studies constitute impressive evidence against the Vulnerability Theory. Although there may be some question marks against each study (we have already discussed the shortcomings of the first two, and Wilkinson and Blackburn admit their numbers are small – and because of this there could be no attempt to divide the groups into those whose depression had been preceded by a provoking agent and those which had not), the studies gain strength because each was conducted in very different ways and yet converged onto a similar conclusion.

Two let-out clauses remain for the Vulnerability Theory. Both are mentioned by Wilkinson and Blackburn though not developed in their paper. The first is that a depression-prone individual may be prone to show such cognitive distortions when under some sort of stress, but the distortions themselves are latent and/or inactive during nondepressed periods. At first sight this seems far too lenient a theory. If something is latent, how is it to be assessed at all, and if nothing emerges on closer examination, is that because it is *too* latent. Does 'latent' imply literally 'hidden' (but existing all the time) or nonexistent between depression phases? And does this theory say any more than that there are certain individuals who are prone to get depressed, and who, when depressed, will show this pattern of distorted thinking? It may be helpful to look at an analogy from biochemical phenomena in depression. Although it has long been suspected that the adrenocorticotrophic hormone system is at fault in some depressive states, in general, measuring *levels* of cortisol in the blood has not proved conclusive. Yet Carroll has over the years developed the Dexamethasone Suppression Test as a way of probing the efficiency of the Hypothalamo-Pituitary-Adrenal (HPA) axis (Carroll, 1982). The test introduces a dose of dexamethasone, which mimics the biochemical effect of cortisol. If the HPA axis is working efficiently it should, in order to restore equilibrium, suppress output of cortisol from the adrenal medulla. The body thinks it has too much cortisol, it therefore 'shuts down the system'. At least, that is the normal response shown by 96-100 per cent of normals and nonendogenous depressives. By contrast, about 60 per cent of endo-genomorphic depressives fail to suppress cortisol levels when assessed 17 and 24 hours later (Carroll, 1982). Note here how measurement of levels of a substance failed to be sensitive to a demonstrable disorder in a major biochemical subsystem. Is there a sense in which, then, the measure of 'levels' of logical distortion in individuals fails to demonstrate a real disorder of 'thinking under stress'? If so, what would the appropriate 'stress test' be, and would it even be ethically justifiable to use it? One obvious manipulation is the mood induction procedure, another is the use of speed tests (e.g. Nufferno) with 'IQ' type instructions. Researchers using these techniques have found marked individual differences in nondepressed student volunteers in the extent to which they respond to these procedures, but it is not at all clear what these individual differences reflect. The speculation could be made that had Campbell given a mood induction procedure or stress test to her sample of women, the most 'vulnerable' identified on other grounds (e.g. Brown and Harris) would have evidenced the greatest degree of cognitive distortion. This is perhaps the sort of question for which analogue research is most suitable. Metalsky *et al's* (1982) prospective study with students prior to taking a mid-term exam offers one paradigm. More recently, Chris Brewin and I studied individuals' reaction following driving test failure. Our pre-test measures, expectancy to succeed and incentive to succeed, did relate to post-test attribution for failure in some respects and also predicted reapplication delay in female subjects (Williams and Brewin, 1983). Again this is the sort of paradigm that lends itself to more thorough probing (using an MIP?) at a pre-test stage.

Perhaps then, the Vulnerability Theory may be prevented from disappearing down an inaccessibility 'black hole'. If a person differs from another in 'proneness', and this difference is something to do with a tendency to react illogically under stress, it should be a demonstrable tendency. If it is not, we had better settle for the idea that cognitive distortions are only shown during or just prior to a depressive episode, and admit that it may be difficult or impossible to finally establish the causal primacy of either.

I mentioned that there was a second let-out clause for the Vulnerability Theory, and before we close this discussion of cognitive aetiology, we ought to discuss it. It concerns the sensitivity of measuring instruments used to assess cognitive distortions. Wilkinson and Blackburn (1981, p. 290) go part way to making the point:

> 'it may be that the recovered depressed patient did have some specific cognitive dysfunction which was not identifiable on the measures used because they lacked sensitivity ... It had been hoped that by having a four-point scale on all items of the cognitive style questionnaire and by including pleasant and unpleasant events, a sensitive instrument could be developed to tap this proneness to depressive cognitive style, but the results clearly indicate that this was not the case.'[7]

This is an important point, for if Wilkinson and Blackburn's tests were insensitive, perhaps those of Lewinsohn *et al*. and Campbell were equally insensitive, and the evidence against the cognitive vulnerability theory would be considerably weakened. Wilkinson and Blackburn imply that adding more items or increasing the number of points on the scale of each item could be the sort of amendments that would need to be made to increase the sensitivity of their scale. Perhaps so, but there may be a more basic fault in questionnaire measures of cognitive distortion, that is, their confounding of distortion (errors of induction or deduction) with hedonic tone (the positive or negative valence of the item)[8]. The Cognitive Style Test (CST) illustrates the problem. Consider this item:

'You are involved in a minor car accident which is only partially your fault

(A) I shall be more careful from now on
(B) These things are bound to happen occasionally
(C) I'm really just glad I'm not hurt
(D) I think I must have been really stupid.'

In this case, endorsement of item D would fall into Wilkinson and Blackburn's most extreme category, 'strong negative emotional attribution to self'. Note that the item which represents most distortion is also the most negative.

The problem is not that this is a bad scale for assessing distortion in currently depressed individuals. We have already commented for example, on the great usefulness of Wilkinson and Blackburn's Scale. The problem is that when people are no longer depressed (or not yet depressed) they may *fail* to endorse the extreme items because they are too negative in tone for their current mood. These people may show logical errors and distortions, yet these may be masked by making a prior decision on the basis of the hedonic tone of the item. A very similar problem arose in relation to Rotter's Locus of Control Scale. Abramowitz (1969) found that this scale correlated with depression, a finding which has been taken by some to suggest that depressives are by nature more 'external' (believing that they have no control in their environment). However it has since pointed out that these typically weak correlations $(0.25 - 0.30)$ may be due to the fact that the external items are themselves (independently) rated as more 'dysphoric' in tone than the internal items. Depressed subjects may be responding to the tone of the item rather than to its logic.

How can one separate an item's logic from its tone? Maybe instead it will be necessary to turn to an information processing view of cognitive distortion. After all, 'distortion' consists of biases in selection of certain material, due perhaps to the differential salience for the patient of that stimulus material in the environment. It may then represent biases in how the selected material is encoded, how much weight is given to various items in the stimulus complex, and what categorisations are made. Perhaps, then, these errors in processing are too subtle to be assessed by questionnaire.

Chapter 9 (pp. 206-215) describes some more subtle tests of information processing, the development of which may make useful advances in this field.

Finally the options of looking for evidence of 'neutral' distortions associated with depression (and possibly depression proneness as well) must not be overlooked. For example, in a discussion of a reformulated 'self control' model for treatment of depression, Kanfer and Hagerman (1981) point out how self-regulation requires (a) the monitoring of one's own behaviour, and (b) the evaluation of that behaviour according to salient current concerns. These current concerns may be short- or long-term. Short-term criteria usually centre around performance or behaviour which is relevant only to the immediate situation of specific limited goals (e.g. stumbling when running to catch a bus may mean nothing more than a grazed knee and a 10-minute delay in getting to the office that morning). Long-term criteria, however, often relate to maintenance of enduring personal goals (e.g. stumbling when running in the athletic trials to determine who represents your country in the Olympics). In these examples, the situation clearly predefines the criteria which can be used to judge the significance of the same event (stumbling), but most situations are not so clear-cut. Failing to quickly see what you require in a supermarket is a common event, which, if thought about at all, may cause a nondepressed person to conclude that they are not 'on form' that day. A depressed person may conclude that they are dementing, because they will see it in the context of other similar events over a long time period. So it may be extremely important whether long-term or short-term standards are accessed in response to ambiguous situations. Note how similar these concepts are to Abramson *et al's* stability and globality dimensions. This does not matter so long as in either case we can assess such tendencies to access LT rather than ST criteria (or to make stable/global attributions) independently of the hedonic tone of the material being rated. We are not seeking new theories about cognitive precursors to affective disturbance, but rather new ways of making plain these variables (and amenable to test).

## Concluding Remarks

The cognitive model of the aetiology of affective disorders involves two models which we have chosen to call a Precipitation Theory (to describe the phasic changes in mood and response to negative thoughts imagery or memories) and a Vulnerability Theory (to describe the cognitive distortions and logical errors which occur prior and render a person vulnerable to depressive breakdown). The evidence for the first theory was overwhelming but the implications limited. The evidence for the second theory was patchy, and the model itself suffered attack from three sources, each having its own problems in drawing firm conclusions from data, but gaining strength from the way the same conclusion emerged from three divergent pieces of research. All however used only questionnaire measures of cognitive distortion which may mask genuine processing errors beneath the hedonic valence of the questionnaire items. Methods of assessing basic information processing variables in depression-prone individuals offers a way forward in this respect. We await the results of such enquiries with interest.

# Notes

1. Portions of this chapter were presented as a paper to the Zangwill Club, Department of Experimental Psychology, University of Cambridge, February 1983.

2. The first four MIP's mentioned have been reviewed recently by Goodwin and Williams (1982).

3. This research illustrates a more general problem throughout clinical research — that of grouping subjects according to an organismic variable (e.g. mood, intelligence, race, diagnosis) and then interpreting differences between groups in some dependent variable as being due to the organismic variable in question. The problem is that there are usually many other differences between groups allocated in this way than just the variable being studied. Depressed vs. nondepressed subjects may also differ in anxiety levels, so any differences may be attributable to the anxiety not the depression. Edwards (1968, p. 258) has a very good discussion of this problem, and ways around it by use of mixed factorial designs.

4. Note Seligman has never claimed that any aspect of his models are necessary for producing depression, merely that they are sufficient. He concedes that there are many ways a person may become depressed (e.g. biological). Here, however, I am asking whether Seligman considers an event is necessary within his own theory, to predict depressive breakdown.

5. A recent study by Peterson *et al.* (1983) addresses the same issue of causality over a time interval, but is equally liable to be explained in terms of time-dependent changes.

6. The apparent difference between this result and those of Wittenborn (p. 182) should be noted. The fact that Wilkinson's group included some men, and the average age was 55 years, may indicate that these studies are looking at different subgroups of depression.

7. There is a logical problem here. If the usefulness of the MIP would be to provide a real (if mild) stress, then one is suggesting that the reason cognitive distortion questionnaires do not pick up 'depression prone' responses is because the items do not probe genuine reactions to stressful events. And yet they *do* ask about stressful events. One therefore can challenge the validity of the questionnaire. If these people would react badly to this stress in *fact*, but say that they would not, then they cannot be answering the question correctly; the scale is invalid. And if it is invalid, why should it be considered valid when a currently depressed person actually shows the cognitive distortion. The currently depressed may merely be responding to the negative hedonic tone of the items in some quite global way. The exact nature of the logical errors are then specified by the experimenter who may be reading more into a respondent's answer than there is to read.

8. Krantz and Hammen's (1979) cognitive distortion questionnaire attempts to distinguish rational from irrational depressed thoughts, but the 'irrational' remains a more extreme response and the scale is still not well-researched with depressed patients.

# 9 COGNITIVE THERAPY AND EXPERIMENTAL COGNITIVE PSYCHOLOGY

Whatever psychological model of depression one considers — reduced reinforcer effectiveness or availability, learned helplessness, 'cognitive' theory, etc., in the end each has to deal with certain core aspects of the symptomatology of the depressive state: the reduced attention to positive aspects of the self and environment. It seems as though the entire information processing system of the depressed patient is biased to select and/or respond only to certain aspects of the environment. The branch of psychology most concerned with those processes by which individuals normally process information about the world is cognitive psychology. Experimental cognitive psychologists have studied individual's deployment of attention, encoding, categorisation, storage and retrieval of information as well as the reconstructive process involved in memory. Although there have been extensions of this experimental work to pathological states in neuropsychology — amnesias, dyslexias, dysphasias, etc., to the schizophrenics, and more recently to elderly populations, there has been surprisingly little research on information processing in depression (Huesmann, 1978; Kihlstrom and Nasby, 1981). There exists the need then to look for ways in which the cognitive psychologist's experiments and concepts can aid the clinician in this field.

The area of experimental cognitive psychology which is potentially most relevant to clinical depression is the research in factors affecting the errors made by nonclinical subjects when they are asked to make judgements about the world. Such judgements, about future probabilities, about the past, about explanations for events, are rarely error-free in the normal individual, since the information on which to base them is incomplete. This means that the normal subject must make inferences when remembering the past, perceiving the present, or generating expectancies about the future; inferences which may often be more due to factors internal or external to the individual of which the individual is not aware and which misrepresents 'reality'. Four areas of study will be mentioned: (a) heuristics used in making judgements under uncertainty; (b) hindsight judgements; (c) biases in eyewitness testimony; and (d) memory for non-occurrences. Detailed accounts of these areas is beyond the scope of this chapter, but each area is briefly mentioned together with possible clinical parallels. At this early stage in research these suggested analogies with the clinical field can only be speculative; some will prove to be wrong. The hope is that by elucidating the factors affecting biases in nondepressed individuals, we may discover variables which we can investigate in the depressed patient. With this in mind, the chapter finishes with some suggestions for experimental techniques which could be adapted for use with a depressed clinical population. Let us start, however, by considering the ways in which normal individuals have been found to bias their judgements.

## Normal 'Biases' and their Possible Clinical Counterparts

### Errors in Judgements Under Uncertainty

Tversky and Kahneman (1974) outlined several heuristics (rules of thumb) which people use when making judgements under uncertainty. One of these, the *availability heuristic* leads to a type of bias when people attempt to assess the likelihood of an event. It refers to the rule by which the frequency of an event or probability of an event is assessed by the ease with which relevant instances may be recalled. It is a useful rule in many instances, and may lead to correct conclusions: if you want to judge how likely it is that the traffic will be bad on a particular day at a particular time, it will be helpful to recall previous instances — and since instances of a large class of events are normally recalled better and faster than less frequent instances, assessing the probability of traffic hold ups by judging the ease with which relevant instances are recalled may be accurate. But biases occur when there is differential retrievability for reasons other than increased frequency of instances. For example, if a friend has a heart attack, the fact that one single instance of heart attack is important to you (a 'salient feature') would make it easy to retrieve and lead you to overestimate the probability that you yourself are vulnerable. In this respect such biases, though leading to incorrect conclusions, may also be useful. People take greater precautions against being vulnerable to heart disease if a friend has had a recent attack. We take more safeguards against fire if there is fire down our *own* street (more salient) than if we read about a more remote fire in a newspaper. Nor is this excess caution merely a 'rational' process. I found myself carefully unplugging a tape recorder in my office the other day (a caution I don't usually exercise) after I had been listening to a tape of a thunder storm in preparation to see a thunder-phobic client.

Despite the potential usefulness of such a heuristic, there can be little doubt that differential memorability may be a burden on the depressed patient, for the salient aspects of the depressed patient's past are often those times they have failed in the interpersonal, academic or occupational sphere. Lloyd and Lishman (1975) found that the more depressed the patient is, the latency to retrieve unpleasant memories becomes shorter relative to the latency to relieve positive memories. Thus in making judgements on the future probability of successful outcomes, the 'availability heuristic' will, in implying that the incidents which are easier to retrieve from the past are the more probable in the future, dictate a pessimistic view.

Tversky and Kahneman also outlined an *anchoring heuristic* – this rule reflects the finding that different starting points yield different estimates which are biased towards (or 'anchored by') the initial values. The most striking demonstration of this bias is that if a roulette wheel is spun and the number observed just before a person is asked to estimate something (e.g. number of countries in the United Nations), the estimate varies considerably depending on the value of the roulette number observed beforehand. Tversky and Kahneman reported mean estimates of 25 countries and 45 countries for a wheel of fortune outcome of 10 and 64 respectively.

What is so striking about this bias is the fact that the distracting values are so obviously irrelevant to the number being estimated. It is therefore not difficult to see how much more a subject may be biased by a relevant estimate of the same or similar variable. For example, in research of biased recall in depressives, investigators have given depressed or nondepressed subjects a series of tasks which they have either succeeded or failed (e.g. Nelson and Craighead, 1977). After completion of the series, subjects are asked how many they recall having succeeded. The typical finding that depressed subjects give a lower success estimate has often been taken as evidence of a failure to *recall* the success experience. However, no independent evidence has been produced to support the hypothesis that these subjects actually cannot remember those tasks on which they succeeded. An equally likely explanation is that depressed subjects would have given a lower estimate of success rate before starting the series, and in giving their 'recall' values, are merely reflecting this general estimate. The ease with which normal subjects' estimates of neutral variables such as numbers of UN countries may be affected by irrelevant distracting numerical values makes unsurprising the extent to which depressed subjects bias their own estimates of self-referent variables.

*Hindsight Judgements*

In the case of the 'anchoring heuristic' people were affected by a suggestion (the initial value) without being aware that they were so affected. The fact that the initial value could be determined at random showed how hard normal individuals find it to discard even uninformative information. The inability for normal individuals to ignore information is seen again in hindsight judgements. When confronted with an unfortunate accident, people tend to overestimate the probability that it would have occurred given only the prior information. People cannot, it seems, ignore the additional information that the event occurred, finding it difficult to reconstruct the uncertainties which would have faced people prior to the event (Fischhoff, 1977). Fischhoff points out how this bias makes people exaggerate the predictability of the past, and as a result systematically underestimate what can be learned from it. This bias has two implications for work with depressed patients. First, a constant source of frustration for the therapist working with depressed clients is how one bad event during the course of recovery may wipe out the positive progress by the client in previous weeks. No matter how much one has tried to gear the patient up for such bad experiences, e.g. by talking about them as an opportunity to use the technique, etc., Fischhoff's point suggests that following such a bad event, the previous positive events may not simply be being ignored by the patient, but may be being reinterpreted in the light of the subsequent event. A patient of mine had a good experience going swimming with friends and a few days later had a bad experience meeting other acquaintances at a party. It was not that being upset about the second event made her ignore the swimming event, rather she 'remembered' that it had been a struggle to get to the pool in fear of making herself look ridiculous, that it had been embarrassing to see herself in a swimsuit because of her weight problem, etc. and that on the basis of the swimming experience (thus recoded) bad experiences in the future should have been entirely predictable. Second, the hindsight bias implies that attributional theory accounts of depressed patients' dismissal of success as 'too easy' may be oversimple. This suggests that a depressed patient may claim that his successes were 'predictable' rather than 'easy' (because of hindsight reinterpretations) and thereby does not learn from these success experiences, i.e. success has little effect on future prediction.

*Biases in Testimony*

Eye-witness testimony has been an extensively researched area because of the evident importance of determining sources of error in people's eye-witness statements. The particular type of error that concerns us is that found by Loftus and Palmer (1974) because it shows how the very language used in asking a question can bias the response. Loftus and Palmer found that following a road traffic accident, eye witnesses gave a higher estimate of the speed of the car when asked 'how fast was the car going when it *smashed* the other car', as against 'how fast was the car going when it *hit* the other car'. This has been explained as the influence of the questioner on the respondent, i.e. the question-ner's belief that the car was going fast influencing the witness. Note how such influence affects actual objective speed estimates — to all intents and purposes the data base of the observer is being changed. To what extent then does the same bias apply to self-talk? Depressive's self-talk is often characterised by catastrophisation (or magnification). It is often assumed that such catastrophisation is the outcome (product) of the biased selection of data on which to base interpreta-tions. Loftus and Palmer's experiment raises the possibility that cata-strophisation itself affects a subject's estimates of the data to be inter-preted. For example, telling oneself one is 'shattered' at the end of the day may lead to overestimates of the number of hours worked and underestimates of the number of rest pauses taken.

*Errors in 'Remembering' Non-occurrences*

A favourite question of investigators of memory for nonoccurrences is: 'Have you met Harold Wilson?' (Brown *et al.*, 1977). If the answer is 'No', how can you be so sure? Indeed, how can one ever be sure that you can successfully discriminate those things in your past which have happened from those which have not. Apparently, it is not always easy. What makes it more easy to say you haven't met Harold Wilson is that (according to these researchers) it would have been a memorable event! Similarly, if a subject is shown a list of names, and then given a long list of names amongst which the previous names are embedded, he can say with greater confidence that some names were *not* there (e.g. unusual names such as Laetitia or Aloysius or their own name — because both would have been noticed if they had been there). Research on memory for things which haven't happened is clearly as important as the far more researched remembering and forgetting of actual occurrences. And although clinical researchers have more often been concerned with biases in actual events remembered in depressed patients, memory for nonoccurrent events may be important too.

As part of her research on cognitive distortions associated with experimentally induced mood, Anne Goodwin asked subjects to read ambiguous stories describing students in various familiar situations such as 'being alone on a Friday night'. Afterwards, she gave subjects a recognition test of items from the story embedded in a distractor list composed of some positive and some negative items, some of which had not actually been in the story and varied in how consistent they were with the original. She found that subjects varied considerably in their ability to adequately discriminate actual story items from negative filler items which had not been there. Subjects in whom depressed mood had been experimentally induced were also less confident about positive items which had been in the story. There are many possible explanations for these results. For example, current mood may bias the memory for events by causing a breakdown of the normal process by which real memories are discriminated from events which might have occurred but did not. If this were so, depressed patients would not only have their genuine negative memories of the past to deal with, but also an unspecified number of inferred negative episodes.

**Possible Remediation Strategies**

Experimental cognitive psychology has not addressed itself extensively to the methods by which these normal biases may be removed, but it is possible to speculate on the most likely measures. In the case of the *availability heuristic*, the aim is to make a person distrust the retrievability cue or salience of an event, when judging the likelihood that the event would recur. Reducing the salience by rehearsing the event until it becomes 'distanced', generating little affect, is perhaps the most likely clinical parallel. In Teasdale's studies of experimentally induced mood and clinical depression (p. 172), he and his co-workers have found differential retrievability correlating with depressed mood. Their work might suggest that any strategy which improves mood will make negative memories less retrievable, thus affecting judgements of future likelihood.

In the case of the *anchoring heuristic*, too, the aim is to make an individual distrust a cue. The cue on this occasion is a numerical estimate of doubtful relevance to the genuine estimation task being asked of the subject. In the case of the success/failure series, the interpretation of that result in terms of prior estimates biasing the final estimates, rather than as a recall bias, suggests that the remedial strategy warranted is one in which subjects are taught to suspend judgement while doing the series of tasks in hand, so that the extent to which they genuinely succeed or fail modifies their estimate. This is parallel to teaching a depressed patient to start the day with an open mind (despite the tendency to be pessimistic) in the hope that his/her end of day ratings will reflect the actual day, rather than merely reflecting the morning's anticipated day.

It is clear from the above that an assumption of many of these remedial measures is that it is possible to teach subjects a rule to make them aware of the danger of overemphasising some cues at the expense of others. This assumption is even more true of the other three biases, for it is difficult to see how hindsight biases, testimony biases or memory for nonoccurrences may be helped without the verbal strategy of warning the subject of the tendency and hoping they will self-correct. Training procedures, in which many similar instances of biases could be shown to the subject, may be employed. How optimistic can we be that such teaching of new rules would be successful in combating errors and biases?

## Problems in Correcting Errors and Biases

Just two possible problems in correcting problems will be considered at this point. First, the problem of teaching rules; second, the fact that wrong information has often been incorporated into an integrated 'schema'.

### The Problem of Teaching Rules

This is seen more clearly if errors are separated into two; errors of application and errors of comprehension (Kahneman and Tversky, 1982a). Take, for example, a typical error made in the following example. 'Linda was a student who was active in the various left wing political movements while at college' — which of these two propositions about Linda's current position is more likely to be true?

(a) Linda is a bank clerk.
(b) Linda is a bank clerk and is active in the feminist movement.

Many subjects would say that (b) was more probable because it seems to represent a more accurate picture on the basis of known (past) information. In fact, (a) is more likely on the statistical principle that a 'conjunction' (A + B) can never be more likely than either A or B alone (the 'conjunction rule'). Kahneman and Tversky (1982a) use an argument endorsement procedure to probe subjects' awareness of the rule. They give the two possible arguments '(a) is more likely because ... (see above) ...', '(b) is more likely because ... (see above) ...' and ask the subjects to endorse one or the other. Some subjects correct their mistake when they see the conjunction rule spelt out (they made an error of application). Others fail to see the rule at all (an error of comprehension).

The distinction between errors of comprehension and application is an interesting one. Some depressed patients can easily be made to see (in the safety of the clinic) how their judgements about the future are dependent on a biased view of the past. They can comprehend the rule. But applying that 'intellectual' knowledge when they next feel depressed is much more difficult. So how can cognitive therapy work at all? Why is it still important to discuss with the patient the biases which creep into their subjective judgements? Cognitive psychologists have pointed out that error-free principles of thinking are not learned from everyday experience because relevant instances are not coded appropriately. For example, we do not keep a tally of how many of our predictions turn out to be true, so we do not have the means to disconfirm our belief that an event is 90 per cent likely (when in fact it only occurs half the time). One technique in cognitive therapy is to ask patients to compute actual probabilities. When they say 'I'll never find another friend', the therapist asks them how likely it really is — one chance in a million, one in a hundred, or 10 per cent likely. The therapist gives the patient opportunity to become aware that some of his probability judgements are, on his own scrutiny, likely to be overpessimistic. The therapist attempts to emphasise realism, not necessarily optimism. It is interesting then to speculate that the therapist may be training a depressed patient to do something that even non-depressed people find difficult — to assess probability in an unbiased way. In this respect, cognitive therapy may not be a restorative therapy (simply re-establishing normal patterns of thought), but teaching a novel way of processing information — a new tool to help overcome the biases which in their case allow a depressive perspective.

Fischhoff *et al.* (1979) have done parallel work in attempting to correct normal biases. They have found that subjects do become sensitive to base rates and to reliability of evidence when they encounter successive problems that vary only in these critical variables. This is reminiscent of Beck's insistence that many instances of thought, feeling and behavioural links and biases will have to be discussed in successive therapy sessions before the patients themselves begin automatically to take a detached view of their negative thoughts. The possibility remains, then, that at the end of successful therapy, the client has been taught skills which most nondepressed individuals do not normally possess. These skills help the recovered depressive from processing information about the world and the self and the future in a less biased way because they make the person less prone to the biases which all individuals tend to make.

*Integrating Erroneous Information into Schemata* is a constant theme of Beck's cognitive theory of depression. According to the theory, patients have a 'depressive schema' operating which increases the probability of perceiving the world from a depressing point of view and remembering things selectively. Let us look at the concept of the schema, before discussing the way in which it affects biases in processing.

An illustration of Beck's use of the concept in a clinical context is given in the course of an interview with a depressed suicidal client (Beck *et al.*, 1979, p. 235). Here, a patient is having difficulty accepting that a period of past unhappiness ought to make herself doubt her current feeling that she 'always has and always will be depressed'. Beck tells her

> '. . . it's human nature, unfortunately, to negate experiences that are not consistent with the prevailing attitude, and that is what attitude therapy is all about. You have a very strong attitude, and anything that is inconsistent with that attitude stirs up cognitive dissonance . . . You have a prevailing belief. It just happens, fortunately, that the prevailing belief is wrong.'

(It may be relevant to point out that the client was a psychologist, who would therefore be likely to understand a term such as 'cognitive dissonance'.) Beck was saying that she had reinterpreted the facts in terms of her depressive schema.

The term 'schema' is not a new one. Many workers have used the concept of a 'schema' in their attempt to understand how people process information about events. Kihlstrom and Nasby (1981) give a very full account of the use of the term, and examine critically its usefulness in clinical contexts. They indicate that 'the adoption of the concept of schema by clinicians is likely to be fraught with difficulty . . . there has been much controversy among experimentalists concerning how the construct is to be defined, how its structure is to be conceptualised and how the structure actually operates to influence perception, memory and behaviour.' These ambiguities can be easily seen in just three definitions of schema:

(1) Bartlett (1932) defined a schema as an 'active organisation of past reactions, or of experiences'.
(2) Neisser (1976); 'the schema accepts information as it becomes available at the sensory surfaces, and is changed by that information; it directs movement and exploratory activities that make more information available, by which it is further modified' (p. 54).
(3) Beck's (1964) definition is 'a structure for screening, coding and evaluating impinging stimuli'. Beck goes further than this to suggest that 'in terms of the individual's adaptation to external reality, it is regarded as the mode by which the environment is broken down and organised into its many psychologically relevant facets; on the basis of the matrix of schemas, the individual is able to orient himself in relation to time and space and to categorise and interpret his experiences in a meaningful way.'

It is clear from Kihlstrom and Nasby's review that cognitive psychology's view of the 'schema' is confused. Nevertheless it is clear that individuals do organise stimulus material in certain ways which then determine how subsequent material is processed, and that these tendencies may obstruct progress in eliminating particular thinking errors. This may be more understandable within an associative theory of memory. According to Bower (1981) an event is represented in memory by a cluster of descriptive propositions. It is recorded in memory by establishing new associative connections among instances of the concept used in describing the event. Thus the basic unit of thought is the 'proposition', and the basic process of thought is the activation of a proposition and its concepts. But how does this help our understanding of how the schema operates? Let us look at the example of one type of error — the hindsight bias — to see how interpretation of that bias is affected by an associative explanation. In Fischhoff's research on hindsight it was seen how the additional information (the occurrence of an event) could not be ignored by subjects in attempting to evaluate the prior probability of the event through hindsight. An explanation for this effect commonly given is that the additional information has been 'assimilated' to form a new 'schema' in the context of which the events prior to the target event are recalled. Because associations between events and not only the events themselves are stored in memory, this would suggest that knowledge of the subsequent events actually changes the elaborative network of the previous memories — they can take on a new meaning in which case they could not be recalled in any other form.

If nondepressed people find it difficult to reconstruct previous uncertainties once new information is assimilated because the meaning (associative network) of prior memories changes, it is not difficult to see the relevance for depressed patients. It is not that positive events, when they occur, are ignored, rather that they are reinterpreted or assimilated into an associative network of predominantly negatively toned elaborations. How to disengage the perception of positive events from this network ought to be a major focus of clinical research, but hopefully this endeavour will be helped by an integrated model of the processes that are underlying the distortion. Here the schema is seen as a context processed prior to other stimuli and determining their meaning by determining their associative links. It is this way of conceiving perception and expectations in terms of an associative network of semantic concepts which may prove the most profitable way of understanding 'schemata' in depression research. A deficiency of this way of looking at 'schemata' is that it does not capture the 'hierarchical' nature of perception that seems to exist. For example, some theorists have interpreted perception as a 'bet' on reality (Kilpatrick, 1961). The most striking demonstration of a situation in which a person is induced to bet wrongly is the Ames Room (Ittelson and Kilpatrick, 1961) in which an objectively distorted room seen from a certain angle is perceived as nondistorted, but the people in it are perceived as too large or too small. What is seen is not a compromise between a half distorted room and half distorted people. Rather the contextual cues (room) are given priority in perception and the stimuli (people) are processed secondarily. Thus the schema concept needs to include this aspect of perception which can be seen as a hierarchical process in which certain features are given greater contextual weight in setting the conditions for perception of other stimuli. Notice that in the Ames Room demonstration we have an example of where the perceivers 'know' one thing (that the person does not get smaller as they walk across a room), but 'perceive' another. It is to another similar distinction — between the 'intellect' and 'emotions' that we now turn.

## Intellectual vs. Emotional Knowledge

The above discussion has assumed that all depressed clients showed depressive biases to some extent, and that they tend to believe their distorted conclusions to an equal extent. This is not the case. Nor would it be true to imply that all errors in processing information are of the same sort. Some patients are quite well aware of the way in which, when they get a downswing in mood, they see the world in a distorted way. Other patients are never so lucid in describing their style of thinking. In this section, I should like to discuss the problem of the patient who knows intellectually that the world is not as bad as they paint it, but finds it difficult to accept emotionally.

Consider this statement by a patient: 'I understand with my *mind* that I am *not* that bad but I still feel bad', or 'I know intellectually that I may feel better eventually, but I don't feel it emotionally', 'I know what I ought to do, but I can't get the energy to do it'. Each statement represents for the patient a dichotomy between what they 'think' and what they 'feel'. A similar distinction is discussed by Watts (1977) in his discussion of what kinds of cognitive processes cognitive-behaviour therapy for anxiety is involved in changing. Watts considers the case of the spider phobic. The spider phobic 'knows' there is no reason to be frightened and yet shows extreme fear. The fact that these phobics notice spiders in the environment where the nonphobic would not, would be taken by Watts to show an underlying, unconscious process (stimulus differentiation) at work which may need direct modification. Modification only of explicit self-talk of the patient may be insufficient to effect the change in the cognitive processes necessary for therapeutic benefit. This message of caution is important. Modifying self-talk responses in depressed patients, but leaving underlying susceptibility to errors in processing unchanged may be a waste of time. This raises questions of how changes in the unconscious dimension may be assessed, and we shall be returning to this question later on. But first I want to discuss the problem where it manifests itself most clearly in the clinic.

Consider a patient of mine who lacked the energy to do a do-it-yourself job he had been meaning to do for some time. He said 'Although I know I could do it, it all seems so difficult.' Interestingly he did not believe he had lost the skill, but that it would take too much effort — he kept saying 'it would be difficult'. We agreed to cognitively rehearse all the stages of making the particular fitment — getting out tools, measuring up, writing down measurements, getting in car, driving to DIY shop, asking for timber, bringing it home, sawing timber, etc. When the list was complete we went over it carefully analysing how difficult each component seemed. In fact it was shopping for the wood which was the major roadblock, and further breakdown of this one activity into its component parts was necessary. From this breakdown the hypothesis emerged that it was the interpersonal situation which was causing the block — and other elements in the patient's history suggested a similar conclusion that assertiveness had been a problem.

This case illustrates the dissociation between the thought 'it ought to be easy' and the bodily feeling of sluggishness every time he even thought about doing the job. But can this phenomenon be brought under experimental control? Although research is a long way from explaining such effects satisfactorily, an analogous dissociation between cognitive and physiological variables has been investigated by Kahneman and Tversky (1982b). They made use of the P300 component of the evoked potential (the positive deflection in the EEG occurring approximately 300 msec after an event). If the event is repeated, habituation of the P300 deflection results, indeed many studies have shown a close correlation between the prior probability of an event and the magnitude of P300 deflections they elicit. Now in a random series of events, a subject 'consciously' expects less repetitions (showing the gambler's fallacy that a number that hasn't come up for some time must appear soon and that a number which has come up often won't come up for some time, i.e. he thinks that the series will self correct). But, at the same time, if the P300 is measured, it shows evidence of attenuation as any one event becomes more frequent. That is, physiologically the person is showing evidence of expecting an event which 'consciously' the person believes will not occur. Conversely, a subject shows physiological evidence of surprise at the occurrence of an event that was consciously predicted. An individual may have conflicting probabilities for the same event at the same time. This demonstration is reminiscent of Watt's spider phobic who consciously expects that the spider will do them no harm but feels intense orienting reactions physiologically. In the case of my patient, his judgement seems to have been inadvertently influenced by his disposition to feel fear and frustration in interpersonal situations. It may be that some situations or activities for other depressed patients have become associated with fatigue and exhaustion, so that even contemplating an activity induces such feelings, despite the person 'knowing' that it won't really take very much effort (e.g. to go to work, make the beds etc.). But that is not the only issue raised by this case, for this

patient reported similar senses of fatigue, sluggishness or fear and apprehension at other times of day, 'out of the blue', when he seemed not to
be thinking of anything. It could be that these moments were caused
by endogenous changes in activation level that were little to do with
cognitive processing at all. On the other hand the cognitive therapist
would wish to assess the thought pattern of the patient in some depth
to check that there weren't momentary images flashing through his
mind that were causing the problem. Indeed, careful assessment did
reveal that vague images were detectable prior to these depressive
feelings, but when consciously explored in discussion, the images and
thoughts themselves seemed to create no such affective disturbance.
Indeed it seemed that the passive, uncontrollable way in which the
thoughts occurred contributed in whole or for the most part to their
disruptive effect. The same image if actively brought to mind was
innocuous. Interestingly, there is a similar distinction made in the
experimental cognitive psychology laboratory.

Investigators have distinguished between 'active expectancy' which
is conscious and occupies attention and 'passive expectancy' which is
automatic and effortless. Passive expectancy may be relatively long-
lasting or relatively temporary. It is the temporary passive expectancy
which is interesting because the difference between it and active
expectancy can be demonstrated experimentally. For example, passive
expectancy can be demonstrated in the effect of context on recognition: if a certain letter is included in a warning signal it facilitates recognition of that letter in the subsequent task. Note the subject is not aware
of this facilitative priming effect and recognition speed of other letters
is not affected. However, if the subject is told to expect a certain letter
(active expectation) this actually inhibits perception of the other letters
in the recognition task.

The implications of this distinction for clinical depressives must
remain pure speculation at the moment. Nevertheless, it may be that
there exists a subgroup of depressed patients, my patient included, in
whom the active bringing to mind of depressive events (e.g. during the
therapy session) actually inhibits the process of scanning for other
unpleasant material and thus precludes associated emotional reaction.
Perhaps, though, when the same image occurs passively it does not
inhibit associated images, and the emotional consequences of the entire
train of thought, conscious or unconscious, are felt. Can this speculation
be tested? It may be possible using tests of lexical priming to be
described below. It implies that for such depressed subjects, active
consideration of depressive material will inhibit the recognition of
associated material (which for others would be facilitated) whereas

passive (masked) concepts will facilitate recognition to a greater than normal extent?

It is to the assessment of these and other such variables that we now turn.


## Techniques for Investigating Cognitive Processes in Depression

In this final section, I want to discuss techniques of investigating cognitive processes. Earlier on, I mentioned the problem of modifying self-talk responses in depressed patients, but leaving underlying susceptibility to errors in processing unchanged. But how can we assess susceptibility to and changes in cognitive biases of which a subject may not be consciously aware?

The reader will find a good description of the issues raised by problems of measurement in Kihlstrom and Nasby's chapter in Rehm's (1981) book, and also in Merluzzi *et al's* chapter in their 1976 book. Kihlstrom and Nasby, for example, illustrate the use of both category judgements (to investigate aspects of an individual's self-schemata) and release from pro-active inhibition (to investigate the extent to which an individual encodes information with respect to a certain category attribute). Merluzzi *et al.* include reference to the work of Davis, and Derry and Kuiper, who have used incidental recall of material learned under different orienting instructions to investigate the degree to which depressives use a self-schema to process information.

I should like to mention three other techniques which, although not yet used in research investigations, offer hope as sensitive procedures: the first is a method of investigating attentional salience; the second is a method of investigating what individual's use as active encoding dimensions, the third is a method of investigating biases in the memory for (recognition of) ambiguous material.

### *Attentional Salience and Semantic Priming*

The aim of these techniques is to assess the degree to which depressive concepts are 'primed' in an individuals consciousness, irrespective of whether they are able to report having depressing thoughts. Two related techniques may be used – pattern masking and a lexical guessing task.

In the pattern masking paradigm a word is presented in a tachisto-scope shortly followed by a jumble of letters. If the word is shown briefly enough, the subject fails to detect it, but if asked to guess what the word was, he or she often guesses a word which is semantically related to the correct word ('yellow' for 'red', 'king' for 'queen'). Note how the guess need not resemble the true word in syllable length, letters used, etc., suggesting that the perception is not of merely one or two letters from which the subject guesses the word. If this were the case then 'reed' or 'rebel' might be a more frequent response to the masked word 'red' or 'queue' and 'queer', a more frequent response to the masked word 'queen'. Clearly, the meaning of the word has been processed even though the subject is not aware he has even seen a word at all except by the experimenter's suggestion. One problem with this technique is that some subjects, of course, will not guess any word, since they are not aware of having seen a word at all. But there is a way around this problem devised by Marcel (1978). As mentioned when discussing the difference between active and passive expectancy, above, a warning signal which contains the letter which is to be recognised on the subsequent trial produces a reduced latency to respond to the target letter. Similarly, if strings of letters are presented and the subject asked to say if it is word (e.g. d-a-k-e would elicit a 'no' response whereas d-a-t-e would elicit a 'yes' response) subjects respond faster with a 'yes' if the preceding word is semantically associated with the target word (e.g. bread – butter). Marcel used this effect to see if associative priming occurred when the primer word was pattern masked. He found that even though subjects were quite unaware of the existence of the primer word, associative priming occurred as strongly as if the first word was not masked. This demonstration confirms that information may be analysed at the semantic level without requiring conscious awareness. It must be stressed however, that these effects are of very short duration. The 'meaning' of the word is not held in the system for more than a few seconds.

However the importance for depression is that such priming may be a *constant* source of selective bias in perception. For instance Bower maintains that mood 'acts like a constant cognitive element in short-term memory, automatically influencing the direction of memory search from current focus.' The suggestion is that the depressed mood of patients may be constantly providing the sort of semantic priming which Marcel demonstrates for discrete words. That such phasic changes in subjective state can have longer lasting priming effects has been demonstrated by Geller and Shaver (1976) who were interested in the priming of self-referent words by a self-awareness manipulation (having subjects do a test in front of a mirror). They examined a version of the Stroop colour-word naming test, asking subjects to name the colours in which either a neutral word (table, chair) or self-referent word (stupid, capable) was printed. They found that as predicted, in the mirror condition subjects were slower to name the colours of the self-referent word, leaving the other colour-naming latencies largely unaffected. They suggested that the mirror acts to increase a subject's self-awareness level, one component of which is to prime self-referent concepts. Under these conditions, the fact that subjects could not so easily ignore the meaning of the self-referent words produced a longer colour naming latency. There are difficulties here in the exact interpretation of the Stroop Test results, arising out of difficulties in knowing what level of processing the Stroop interference represents. However, it at least provides evidence that some sort of priming occurred over a time interval — the mirror acting as a 'constant cognitive element' in Bower's sense. This implies that pattern masking, though a discrete technique, may nevertheless be able to detect effects which may have longer lasting implications for the subject, and suggests that the technique may thus be valid for looking at which concepts are 'primed' and acting as sources of bias for depressed patients. If a neutral word is masked, a depressive should show facilitation at guessing its associate as for a nondepressive, but a depressive should show facilitated guessing at negatively toned words without the necessity for semantic priming.

## Depressives' Encoding Strategies

Kihlstrom and Nasby's review mentions using the release from proactive inhibition to study an individual's encoding strategies. An alternative to this procedure which has not so far been explored is use of the Cue Overload Paradigm. The 'cue overload principle' was outlined by Watkins and Watkins (1975, 1976) in order to account for forgetting in various verbal learning situations. It stated that 'the recall probability of a target declines as more targets come to share the same retrieval cue'. For example, if a subject has to remember six animal names, but is then given an interpolated task involving more animal names, recall of the six original names suffers (retroactive inhibition). This is thought to be because the subject uses the category 'animal name' as an encoding dimension. The addition of the same category in the interpolated task means that the retrieval cue has more associations, becomes overloaded and is less efficient as a result.

Two aspects of this task may be varied: (a) the category of the interpolated material (e.g. vegetables rather than animals), and (b) the level at which the subject is asked to process the material (e.g. count the syllables — phonemic coding, rather than say which animals are domesticated — semantic coding). In both cases, making these changes in the interpolated task decreases the retroactive inhibition. The material stops interfering because the semantic category 'animal' is no longer overloaded by the different category or nonsemantic nature of the interpolated material (Parkin, 1980). Since the conditions governing cue overload must depend on the *level* at which interpolated activity is processed it offers an additional way of studying the salience of certain features of stimulus material. Thus, if a subject was asked to remember a number of self-referent negative adjectives, and the interpolated material were more such adjectives, which the subject was asked to process non-semantically, a depressed or depression-prone person should nonetheless not be able to ignore the semantic aspect of the interpolated material and equivalent retroactive inhibition should be noted to a situation in which semantic processing of the interpolated material was explicitly encouraged. In this respect, the task offers a way of validating the lexical guessing measure of attentional salience referred to above. The important aspect of this paradigm is that it allows the assessment of what represents an active encoding dimension. If there is no difference in retroactive inhibition given 'same' or 'different' conditions (between to-be-recalled and interpolated material) that particular organisational feature being manipulated has not acted as a retrieval cue. By varying the category of the interpolated material and observing the extent to which the original category cue becomes overloaded, one may gain information about the cues being used to encode the stimulus material. Interpolated material could be varied in hedonic tone (pleasant, unpleasant or neutral) and/or self-reference. The relationship between the cue overload phenomenon and subjects' incidental recall of self-referenced material (Davis and Unruh, 1981) will be interesting to note.

## Memory for Ambiguous Material

In an appendix to this chapter is reproduced one of the stories derived from Hammen and Krantz's (1976) Cognitive Distortion Questionnaire and modified for mood induction research by Goodwin (1982). Read it through once and answer the questions about it. Research has found that depressives and mood-induction depressed students answer the questions in a more depressive and distorted way (more overgeneralisations, selective abstraction, magnification or minimisation and so on). As such, stories such as these may be used to assess the distortions in thinking to which depressed patients are prone. The results ought to correlate highly with Wilkinson and Blackburn's Cognitive Style

Measure (p. 72), but what about the assessment of the underlying distortion in memory for the stimulus material?

Goodwin has devised methods of examining variables which may contribute to cognitive distortion. She asks subjects not only the questions laid out in the Appendix, but also uses a recall and recognition task. Do more distorted individuals show a recall bias? Not in her researches so far, but they do show biases in recognition (see Appendix). For example some subjects underestimate the probability that certain positive items appeared in the story, thus possibly revealing an element of the decision strategy of the individual which the individual surely could not have spontaneously reported. Further research may reveal that clinically depressed patients have a similar difficulty in confidently rejecting memories for negative items which did not actually occur. If so, the burden of the past must be even heavier for the depressed patient to bear than had been previously thought from a simple analysis of selective bias in genuine memories or facilitated recall of unpleasant material. Furthermore, outcome measures following cognitive-behavioural therapies may need to ensure that such biases in the underlying cognitive processes are corrected in addition to the more conscious self-talk responses. Goodwin's strategies may be very useful in these respects.

Taken together with the techniques mentioned by Kihlstrom and Nasby (1981) and by Merluzzi *et al.*, (1976) the development of these procedures offers new sources of information about biases in cognitive processing in depression. Several questions may be helped to be answered by this research: Are such biases removed following cognitive or behaviour therapy or physical treatment? If so, which techniques are more effective? Do such cognitive processes co-vary with mood and/or any other variables in depression (e.g. sleep disturbances, retardation or agitation, suicidal ideation, appetite). Do some subtypes of depression evidence such processes more than others? Does it change over time? What is the extent of correlation with cognitive distortion of the more explicit kind?

## Concluding Remarks

This essay began by expressing the hope that by examining examples of biases in nonpathological information processing we may be better placed to understand depressive biases. Has this greater understanding been achieved, or is the situation now even more confused? Perhaps a little of each. What has become clear is that in making judgements under uncertainty, in making hindsight judgements, in eye-witness testimony and in distinguishing real memories from plausible non-occurrences, normal individuals are prone to make a great deal of errors. Taking just one example, that of hindsight, it can be seen how an individual's view of the past changes markedly in the light of knowledge of subsequent events. In this light, the depressive's habit of reinterpreting positive or neutral episodes in the light of subsequent upsetting events can be seen as instances of common information processing errors, rather than as anything distinctively pathological in itself. As such, then, knowledge of normal biases demystifies some depressive biases. One might even go further to suggest that clinicians must avoid falling into the trap of attributing the biases they see in their depressed patients to the depression, when in fact they are evidencing normal processing errors. Studying the literature on normal subjects' methods of probability estimation should remind the clinician how wide of the mark is the nondepressive's estimate (often overly optimistic – see Lewinsohn *et al.*, 1980), so that the relative pessimism of the depressive does not necessarily imply that he or she is more 'wrong' in absolute terms than the nondepressed individual.

It is this which leaves the situation a little more confused than it was at the outset. For it seems now unreasonable to make the assumption that cognitive therapy is a restorative therapy. Rather, it must aim to teach clients procedures which are not routinely used by nondepressed individuals. These procedures include, for example, how to compute genuine probability estimates, and how to record frequencies of occurrences and nonoccurrences in order to test our hypotheses about the self or the world or how the future will turn out. It is likely that it is not only depressive schemata which are challenged by these procedures, but schematic thinking in general; not only connections between cognitive expectancies and depressive physiological reactions, but connections between cognitive and somatic variables in general. With the development of the more sophisticated investigative techniques we may discover whether psychological treatment for depression can really claim to do all of these things.

# APPENDIX

**Instructions**

This is a story about some ordinary events whi⁻h might happen to someone who is on a course away from home. You are asked to read the story and to imagine that these events were happening to you. Imagine that you are on a training course for your job or for some organisation that you are involved in and are living away from home for a while. Read the story at your own pace. It is not necessary to take in all the details, but just to get an impression of what it would feel like if you were in that situation.

*Story*

You go to see the course supervisor about your progress. He seems surprised to see you. You go into his room and sit down. He tells you that your work is about average. You chat generally about the course and how you are coping. He goes over some of the more difficult parts with you. He also gives you some tips on study techniques.

After a while, he looks at his watch and says he didn't realise how much time had passed. He asks you to excuse him as he is quite busy. He says he hopes you'll have no more problems with the course.

Later on, you go back to your digs. Your room is right up in the attics of an old house. The other lodgers are already out. You haven't anything planned for the evening. You decide to do some background reading for the course. You take your books over to the café nearby. As you're sitting there alone, you see two people from your course come in. You call them and wave. They take their trays to another empty table on the far side of the room. A group of people you don't know come in then, chatting and laughing, and join the pair from your course. They mention going to a night club later on.

*Questions*

How would you feel in the situation described in the story? Listed below are various possible reactions and feelings. Which ones would be most likely to apply to you? Circle the appropriate number alongside each statement to represent how well it describes what your feelings would probably be in this situation. For example, if a statement

212

describes definitely what you feel, circle 4; if it describes something you would definitely *not* feel, circle 0. Use the numbers in between to reflect increasing agreement, i.e. 1 = possibly how I would feel, 2 = probably how I would feel, 3 = very likely how I would feel.

(1) Are you satisfied with your meeting with the supervisor?

Definitely — Definitely Not

   (a) Yes, because he was quite pleased with my visit and will probably give me a good grade in the course.    0 1 2 3 4

   (b) No, because he obviously thought it was wrong of me to bother him.    0 1 2 3 4

   (c) Although it's upsetting for me to realize it, I probably needed tips on studying.    0 1 2 3 4

   (d) Yes, he answered all my questions and I made a good contact.    0 1 2 3 4

   (e) No, he probably thinks I'm stupid, which is why he gave me tips on study habits.    0 1 2 3 4

(2) You thought the supervisor was rather nice in walking you to the door. Your reaction to his gesture was:

   (a) Embarrassment. He was trying to hurry me out.    0 1 2 3 4

   (b) Appreciation that he realized that it was worth his time to help me.    0 1 2 3 4

   (c) Appreciation. He seemed interested and concerned.    0 1 2 3 4

   (d) Annoyance: he obviously thinks I'm stupid and feels sorry for me.    0 1 2 3 4

   (e) Sort of sad and let down that the meeting had to end.    0 1 2 3 4

(3) When you see the others sit down in the café you think:

   (a) They must really dislike me to snub me like that.    0 1 2 3 4

   (b) They must be in a dreamworld and didn't see me.    0 1 2 3 4

   (c) I'm disappointed that they prefer to eat on the other side of the café.    0 1 2 3 4

|  | Definitely | | | | Definitely Not |
|---|---|---|---|---|---|

(d)  I'm sad that they don't want to sit
with me.                                      0   1   2   3   4

(e)  They probably think that I'm too
busy to chat to them today.        0   1   2   3   4

(4)  What is your first reaction when you
overhear the group planning to go
to the night club?

(a)  Unhappiness. They probably would
have asked me to come if they
liked me more.                           0   1   2   3   4

(b)  Unhappiness. Sounds like I'll be
practically alone here.               0   1   2   3   4

(c)  I could ask if they'd mind if I
came along.                              0   1   2   3   4

(d)  Unhappiness. No-one ever invites me
to come out with them.             0   1   2   3   4

(e)  Relief. They seem unfriendly, so
I'm glad that I'm not going with them.   0   1   2   3   4

(5)  Thinking about making friends while
you're on the course:

(a)  I'm sad that it's not easy to make
friends, but I'll keep trying.        0   1   2   3   4

(b)  I feel as if I'll never find any
true friends here.                       0   1   2   3   4

(c)  Since I can't make friends, I must
be a really horrible person.       0   1   2   3   4

(d)  It just takes time and patience to
make new friends.                     0   1   2   3   4

(e)  People in this town just aren't
worth knowing.                         0   1   2   3   4

(6)  Being alone that evening:

(a)  Doesn't bother me because I'm sure
to have a hectic social life soon.   0   1   2   3   4

(b)  Upsets me and makes me feel lonely.   0   1   2   3   4

(c)  Upsets me and makes me start to
imagine endless days and nights by
myself.                                      0   1   2   3   4

(d)  Isn't that important because I can
find things to do.                      0   1   2   3   4

(e)  Is so depressing I don't think I can
cope with it.                            0   1   2   3   4

*Construction of the Recognition Test*

The story was divided into 20 discrete idea units, omitting connecting phrases such as 'after a while'. For 16 of these idea units, three alternative versions were constructed, one being a possible inference from the idea unit that would be construed as positive, one a negative inference and the third a neutral inference or paraphrase of the original. Thus, together with the original format, there were four different versions of each of the 16 idea units as follows:

(A) positive inference
(B) negative inference
(C) original version
(D) neutral inference/paraphrase

The recognition test consisted of a list of some version of all 20 idea units, presented in their logical order, and the task of the subject was to decide which items were from the story and which were not, and to give a confidence rating.

*Examples of Recognition Items*

(A) He is pleased that you have come
(B) He is annoyed that you have come
(C) He seems surprised to see you
(D) He was not expecting you
(A) He offers you a comfortable chair to sit on
(B) You feel uneasy about where you should sit
(C) You go into his room and sit down
(D) You go in and take a seat
(A) Your work is good on average
(B) Your work is only average
(C) Your work is about average
(D) Your work is of a medium standard
(A) You get into an interesting conversation
(B) You find it difficult to make general conversation
(C) You chat generally about the course
(D) You discuss your impressions of the course
(A) He gives you some help with the difficult parts of the course
(B) He thinks you are having more difficulty than others
(C) He goes over some of the more difficult parts
(D) He explains some of the harder parts of the course

# REFERENCES

Abramowitz, S. I. (1969) 'Locus of control and self-reported depression among college students.' *Psychol. Reports*, *25*, 149-50

Abramson, L. T., Seligman, M. E. P. and Teasdale, J. D. (1978) 'Learned helplessness in humans: Critique and reformulation.' *J. Abnorm. Psychol. 87*, 49-74

Alloy, C. B. and Abramson, L. Y. (1979) 'Judgement of contingency in depressed and nondepressed students: sadder but wiser?' *J. Exp. Psychol: Gen. 108*, 441-85

Altman, J. H. and Wittenborn, J. R. (1980) 'Depression-prone personality in women.' *J. Abnorm. Psychol. 89*, 303-308

Antaki, C. and Brewin, C. (1982) *Attributions and Psychological change*, Academic Press, New York

Anton, J. L., Dunbar, J. and Friedman, L. (1976) 'Anticipation training in the treatment of depression' in J. D. Krumbolz and C. E. Thoresen (eds.) *Counselling Methods*, Holt Rinehart and Winston, New York

Ayllon, T. and Azrin, N. H. (1968) *The Token Economy: A Motivational System for Therapy and Rehabilitation* , Appleton-Century-Crofts, New York

Bartlett, F. C. (1932) *Remembering: A study in experimental and social psychology*, University Press, Cambridge

Beck, A. T. (1963) 'Thinking and depression: 1. Idiosyncratic content and cognitive distortions.' *Arch. Gen. Psychiat. 9*, 324-33

Beck, A. T. (1964) 'Thinking and depression: 2. Theory and therapy.' *Arch, Gen. Psychiat. 10*, 561-71

Beck, A. T. (1967) *Depression: Clinical, Experimental and Theoretical Aspects*, Hoeber, New York (Republished as *Depression Causes and Treatment*, University of Pennsylvania Press, Philadelphia, 1972)

Beck, A. T. (1976) *Cognitive Therapy and the Emotional Disorders*, International Universities Press, New York

Beck, A. T., Kovacs, M. and Weissman, A. (1975) 'Hopelessness and suicidal behaviour: An overview.' *J. Am. Medical Assoc. 234*, 1146-9

Beck, A. T., Shaw, A. J., Rush, B. F. and Emery, G. (1979) *Cognitive Therapy of Depression*, J. Wiley & Sons, New York

Beck, A. T., Ward, C. H., Mendelson, M., Mock, J. E. and Erbaugh, J. K. (1961) 'An inventory for measuring depression.' *Arch. Gen. Psychiat. 4*, 561-71

Beck, A. T., Weissman, A. W., Lester, D. and Trexler, L. (1974) 'The assessment of pessimism: The Hopelessness Scale?' *J. Consult. Clin. Psychol. 42*, 861-5

Bellack, A. S. and Schwartz, J. S. (1976) 'Assessment for self-control programs' in M. Hersen and A. S. Bellack (Eds.) *Behavioural Assessment: A Practical Handbook*, Pergamon, Oxford

Benatov, R. (1981) *Evening Therapy: Psychotherapy of short-term memory*. Paper presented at First SPR European Conference on Psychotherapy Research, Trier FRG, Sept. 1981

Blackburn, I. M., Bishop, S., Glen, I. M., Whalley, L. J. and Christie, J. E. (1981) 'The efficacy of cognitive therapy in depression: a treatment trial using cognitive therapy and pharmacotherapy, each alone and in combination.' *Brit. J. Psychiat. 139*, 181-9

Blaney, P. H. (1977) 'Contemporary theories of depression: critique and comparison.' *J. Abnorm. Psychol. 86*, 203-23

Blaney, P. H. (1981) 'The effectiveness of cognitive and behavioural therapies' in Rehm, L. P. (ed.) *Behaviour Therapy for Depression*, Academic Press, New York

Bootzin, R. (1973) *Stimulus Control of Insomnia*. Paper presented at annual meeting of APA Montreal, Sept. 1973.

Borkovec, T. D. and Boudewyns, P. A. (1976) 'Treatment of insomnia with stimulus control and progressive relaxation procedures' in J. D. Krumbolz and C. E. Thoresen (eds.) *Counselling Methods*, Holt, Rinehart and Winston, New York

Bower, G. (1981) 'Mood and Memory.' *Amer. Psychologist, 36*, 129-48

Bower, G. H., Monteiro, K. P. and Gilligan, S. G. (1978) 'Emotional mood as a context for learning and recall.' *J. Verb. Learning Verb. Behav. 17*, 573-85

Brewer, D., Doughtie, E. B. and Lubin, B. (1980) 'Induction of mood and mood shift.' *J. Clin. Psychol. 36*, 215-26

Brown, G. and Harris, T. (1978) *Social Origins of Depression – a Study of Psychiatric Disorder in Women*, Tavistock, London

Brown, J., Lewis, V. J., Monk, A. F. (1977) 'Memorability, word frequency, and negative recognition.' *Q. J. Exp. Psychol., 29*, 461-73

Burgess, E. P. (1969) 'The modification of depressive behaviours' in R. D. Rubin and C. M. Franks (eds.) *Advances in Behaviour Therapy*, Academic Press, New York

Campbell, E. A. (1982) *Vulnerability to depression and cognitive predisposition: Psychosocial correlates of Brown and Harris' Vulnerability factors.* Paper presented at British Psychological Society Conference, York, April 1982.

Carroll, B. J. (1982) 'The Dexamethasone Suppression Test for Melancholia.' *Br. J. Psychiat. 140*, 292-304

Carroll, B. J., Fielding, J. M. and Blashki, T. G. (1973) 'Depression rating scales: a critical review.' *Arch. Gen. Psychiat. 28*, 361-6

Clark, D. M. 'On the induction of depressed mood in the laboratory: evaluation and comparison of the Velten and musical procedures.' *Adv. Behav. Res. Therapy*, (in press).

Cleaver, S. (1981) *'Atributional modifications in the treatment of depression.'* Unpublished MSc Dissertation, Department of Psychiatry, University of Newcastle upon Tyne.

Cofer, D. H. and Wittenborn, J. R. (1980) 'Personality characteristics of formerly depressed women.' *J. Abnorm. Psychol., 89*, 309-14

Coleman, R. E. (1975) 'Manipulation of self-esteem as a determinant of mood of elated and depressed women.' *J. Abnorm. Psychol., 84*, 693-700

Costello, C. G. (1972a) 'Depression: Loss of reinforcement or loss of reinforcer effectiveness.' *Behav. Ther., 3*, 240-7

Costello, C. G. (1972b) 'Reply to Lazarus.' *Behav. Ther., 3*, 251-3

Costello, C. G. (1982) 'Social factors associated with depression: A retrospective community study.' *Psychol. Med., 12*, 329-39

Coyne, J. C., Metalsky, G. I. and Lavelle, T. L. (1980) 'Learned helplessness as experimenter induced failure and its alleviation with attentional redeployment.' *J. Abnorm. Psychol., 89*, 350-7

Davies, E. (1982) *'An investigation into the effect of internally and externally focussed tasks on depressed mood.'* Unpublished MSc Thesis, Department of Psychiatry, University of Newcastle upon Tyne.

Davis, H. and Unruh, W. R. (1981) 'The development of the self-schema in adult depression.' *J. Abnorm. Psychol., 90*, 125-33

Depue, R. A. and Monroe, S. M. (1978) 'Learned helplessness in the perspective of the depressive disorders: conceptual and definitional issues.' *J. Abnorm. Psychol., 87*, 3-20

Derry, P. A. and Kuiper, N. A. (1981) 'Schematic processing and self-reference in clinical depression.' *J. Abnorm. Psychol., 90*, 286-97

Eastman, C. (1976) 'Behavioural formulations of depression.' *Psychol. Rev., 83*, 277-91

Edwards, A. L. (1968) *Experimental design in psychological research*, 3rd Edition, Holt Rinehart and Winston, New York

Eysenck, H. J. and Eysenck, S. B. G. (1975) *Manual of the Eysenck Personality Questionnaire*, Hodder & Stoughton, Sevenoaks, Kent

Feighner, J. P., Robins, E., Guze, S. B., Woodruff, R. A., Winokur, G. and Minoz, R. (1972) 'Diagnostic criteria for use in psychiatric research.' *Arch. Gen. Psychiat., 26*, 57-63

Ferster, C. B. (1966) 'Animal behaviour and mental illness.' *Psychol. Record, 16*, 345-56

Ferster, C. B. (1973) 'A functional analysis of depression.' *Am. Psychol. 28*, 857-70

Fischhoff, B. (1977) 'Perceived informativeness of facts.' *J. Exp. Psychol: Hum. Percept. Perf., 3*, 349-58

Fischhoff, B., Slovic, P. and Lichtenstein, S. (1979) 'Subjective sensitivity analysis.' *Organiz. Behav. Hum. Perf., 23*, 339-59

Frost, R. O., Graf, M. and Becker, J. (1979) 'Self-devaluation and depressed mood.' *J. Consult. Clin. Psychol., 47*, 958-62

Fuchs, C. and Rehm, L. F. (1977) 'A self-control behaviour therapy program for depression.' *J. Consult. Clin. Psychol., 45*, 206-15

Garber, J. and Hollon, S. D. (1980) 'Universal vs. Personal helplessness in depression belief in uncontrollability or incompetence?' *J. Abnorm. Psychol., 89*, 56-66

Geer, J. H. and Katkin, E. S. (1966) 'Treatment of insomnia using a variant of systematic desensitisation – A case report.' *J. Abnorm. Psychol., 71*, 161-4

Geller, V. and Shaver, P. (1976) 'Cognitive consequences of self awareness.' *J. Exp. Soc. Psychol., 12*, 99-108

Goldberg, D. (1982) 'Cognitive therapy for depression.' *Bri. Med. J., 284*, 143-4

Golin, S., Jarrett, S., Stewart, M. and Drayton, W. (1980) 'Cognitive theory and the generality of pessimism among depressed persons.' *J. Abnorm. Psychol., 89*, 101-104

Golin, S., Sweeney, P. D. and Shaeffer, D. E. (1981) 'The causality of causal attributions in depression. A cross-lagged panel correlational analysis.' *J. Abnorm. Psychol., 90*, 14-22

Gong-Guy, E. and Hammen, C. (1980) 'Causal perceptions of stressful events in depressed and nondepressed outpatients.' *J. Abnorm. Psychol., 89*, 662-9

Goodwin, A. M. (1982) *'Factors mediating cognitive distortion in depression.'* Unpublished paper: University of Newcastle-upon-Tyne.

Goodwin, A. M. and Williams, J. M. G. (1982) 'Mood-induction research – its implications for clinical depression.' *Behav. Res. Ther., 20*, 373-82

Gotlib, I. H. (1981) 'Self reinforcement and recall: differential deficits in depressed and nondepressed psychiatric in-patients.' *J. Abnorm. Psychol., 90*, 521-30

Gray, J. A. (1978) 'The neuropsychology of anxiety.' *Br. J. Psychol., 69*, 417-34

Greene, S. (1981) 'Levels of measured hopelessness in the general population.' *Br. J. Clin. Psychol., 20*, 11-14

Hale, W. D. and Strickland, B. R. (1976) 'Induction of mood states and their effect on cognitive and social behaviours.' *J. Consult. Clin. Psychol., 44*, 155

Hamilton, M. (1960) 'A rating scale for depression.' *J. Neurol. Neurosurg. Psychiat., 23*, 56-61

Hamilton, M. (1967) 'Development of a rating scale for primary depressive illness.' *Br. J. Soc. Clin. Psychol., 6*, 278-96

Hammen, C. L. (1978) 'Depression, distortion and life stress in college students.' *Cog. Ther. Res., 2*, 189-92

Hammen, C. L. and Glass, D. R. (1975) 'Depression activity and evaluation of reinforcement.' *J. Abnorm. Psychol., 84*, 718-21

Hammen, C. L. and Krantz, S. (1976) 'Effects of success and failure on depressive cognitions.' *J. Abnorm. Psychol., 85*, 577-86

Hargreaves, I. R. (1982) *'A test of the reformulated learned helplessness model of depression.'* Unpublished MSc Dissertation, University of Aberdeen, Scotland, UK.

Herson, M., Eisler, R. M., Alford, G. S. and Agras, W. S. (1973) 'Effects of token economy on neurotic depression: An experimental analysis.' *Behav. Ther., 4*, 392-7

Hersen, M., Eisler, R. M., Smith, B. S. and Agras, W. S. (1972) 'A token reinforcement ward for young psychiatric patients.' *Am. J. Psychiat., 129*, 228-32

Hiroto, D. S. and Seligman, M. E. P. (1975) 'Generality of learned helplessness in man.' *J. Pers. Social Psychol., 31*, 311-27

Hockanson, J. E., DeGood, D. E., Forrest, M. G. and Brittain, T. M. (1971) 'Availability of avoidance behaviours in modulating vascular stress responses.' *J. Res. Social Psychol., 19*, 60-8

Hollon, S. D. (1981) 'Comparisons and combinations with alternative approaches' in L. P. Rehm (ed.) *Behaviour Therapy for Depression*, Academic Press, New York

Hollon, S. D., Bedrosian, R. C. and Beck, A. T. (1979) *Combined cognitive-pharmacotherapy vs cognitive therapy in the treatment of depression*. Paper presented at the Annual Meeting of the Society for Psychotherapy Research, Oxford, England.

Huesmann, L. R. (1978) 'Cognitive processes and models of depression.' *J. Abnorm. Psychol., 87*, 194-8

Ittelson, W. H. and Kilpatrick, F. P. (1951) 'Experiments in perception.' *Sci. Am., 185*, 50-5

Jackson, B. (1972) 'Treatment of depression by self-reinforcement.' *Behav. Ther., 3*, 298-307

Kahneman, D. and Tversky, A. (1982a) 'On the study of statistical intuitions.' *Cognition, 11*, 123-41

Kahneman, D. and Tversky, A. (1982b) 'Variants of uncertainty.' *Cognition, 11*, 143-57

Kanfer, F. H. (1970) 'Self-regulation: Research, issues and speculations' in C. Neuringer and J. L. Michael (eds.) *Behaviour Modification in Clinical Psychology*, Appleton-Century-Crofts, New York

Kanfer, F. H. and Hagerman, S. (1981) 'The role of self-regulation' in Rehm, L. P. (ed.) *Behaviour Therapy for Depression*, Academic Press, New York

Kendall, P. C. and Korgeski, G. P. (1979) 'Assessment and cognitive-behavioural interventions.' *Cog. Ther. Res., 3*, 1-21

Kihlstrom, J. E. and Nasby, W. (1981) 'Cognitive tasks in clinical assessment: an exercise in applied psychology' in Kendall, P. C. and Hollon, S. D. (eds.), *Assessment Strategies for Cognitive-Behavioural Interventions*, Academic Press, New York

Kilpatrick, F. P. (1961) *Explorations in Transactional Psychology*, N.Y. University Press, New York

Kovacs, M., Rush, A. J., Beck, A. T. and Hollon, S. D. (1981) 'Depressed outpatients treated with cognitive therapy or pharmacotherapy: a one-year follow up.' *Arch. Gen. Psychiat., 38*, 33-9

Krantz, S. and Hammen, C. (1979) 'Assessment of cognitive bias in depression.' *J. Abnorm. Psychol., 88*, 611-19

Lang, P. J. (1971) 'The application of psychophysiological methods to the study of psychotherapy and behaviour modification' in A. E. Bergin and S. L. Garfield (eds.) *Handbook of Psychotherapy and Behaviour Change: An Empirical Analysis*, J. Wiley, New York

Lazarus, A. A. (1968) 'Learning theory and the treatment of depression.' *Behav. Res. Ther., 6*, 83-9

Lewinsohn, P. M. (1975) 'Engagement in pleasant activities and depression level.' *J. Abnorm. Psychol., 84*, 729-31

Lewinsohn, P. M. (1976) 'Activity schedules in treatment of depression' in J. D. Krumbolz and C. E. Thoresen (eds.) *Counselling Method*, Holt Rinehart and Winston, New York

Lewinsohn, P. M. and Graf, M. (1973) 'Pleasant activities and depression.' *J. Consult. Clin. Psychol., 41*, 261-8

Lewinsohn, P. M., Mischel, W., Chaplin, W. and Barton, R. (1980) 'Social competence and depression: the role of illusory self-perceptions.' *J. Abnorm. Psychol., 89*, 203-12

Lewinsohn, P. M. and Shaw, D. A. (1969) 'Feedback about interpersonal behaviour as an agent of behaviour change.' *Psychother. Psychosom., 17*, 82-8

Lewinsohn, P. M., Steinmetz, J. L., Larson, D. W. and Franklin, J. (1981) 'Depression related cognitions: antecedents or consequences?' *J. Abnorm. Psychol., 90*, 213-19

Lewinsohn, P. M., Weinstein, M. S. and Alper, T. A. (1970) 'A behavioural approach to the group treatment of depressed persons: A methodological contribution.' *J. Clin. Psychol., 26*, 525-32

Lewinsohn, P. M., Weinstein, M. S., and Shaw, D. (1969) 'Depression: A clinical research approach' in R. D. Rubin and C. M. Franks (eds.) *Advances in Behaviour Therapy*, Academic Press, New York

Liberman, R. P. (1981) 'A model for individualising treatment' in L. P. Rehm (ed.), *Behaviour Therapy for Depression*, Academic Press, New York

Liberman, R. P. and Roberts, J. (1976) 'Contingency Management of Neurotic Depression and Marital Disharmony' in Eysenck H. J. (ed.), *Case Studies in Behaviour Therapy*, Routledge & Kegan Paul, London

Lloyd, G. G. and Lishman, W. A. (1975) 'Effect of depression on the speed of recall of pleasant and unpleasant experiences.' *Psychol. Med., 5*, 173-80

Lobitz, W. C. and Post, R. D. (1979) 'Parameters of self-reinforcement and depression.' *J. Abnorm. Psychol., 88*, 33-41

Loftus, E. F. and Palmer, J. C. (1974) 'Reconstruction of automobile destruction: An example of the interaction between language and memory.' *J. Verb. Learn. Verb. Behav., 16*, 585-9

Lubin, D. (1965) 'Adjective check lists for the measurement of depression.' *Arch. Gen. Psychiat., 12*, 57-62

McLean, P. D. (1976) 'Therapeutic decision-making in the treatment of depression' in P. O. Davidson (ed.), *The behavioural management of anxiety depression and pain*, Brunner/Mazel, New York

McLean, P. D. and Hakstian, A. R. (1979) 'Clinical depression: comparative efficacy of outpatient treatments.' *J. Consult. Clin. Psychol., 47*, 818-36

McLean, P. D., Ogston, K. and Grauer, L. (1973) 'A behavioural approach to the treatment of depression.' *J. Behav. Therapy and Exper. Psychiat., 4*, 323 ∠0

MacPhillamy, D. J. and Lewinsohn, P. M. (1971) *Pleasant events schedule*, University of Oregon, mimeograph

Maier, S. F. and Seligman, M. E. P. (1976) 'Learned helplessness: Theory and evidence.' *J. Exp. Psychol. (General), 105*, 3-46

Malan, D. H. (1979) *Individual psychotherapy and the science of psychotherapy*, Butterworth, London

Marcel, A. J. (1978) 'Unconscious reading: experience on people who do not know that they are reading.' *Visible Lang., 12*, 391-404

Marzillier, J. S. (1980) 'Cognitive therapy and behavioural practice.' *Behav. Res. Ther., 18*, 249-58

Meichenbaum, D. (1974) *Cognitive Behaviour Modification*, General Learning Press, Morristown, New Jersey

Meichenbaum, D. (1977) *Cognitive Behaviour Modification. An integrative approach*, Plenum, New York

Merluzzi, T. V., Rudy, T. E. and Glass, C. R. (1976) 'The Information processing paradigm implications for clinical science' in Merluzzi, T. V., Glass, C. R. and Genest, M. (eds.), *Cognitive Assessment*, Guildford Press, New York

Metalsky, G. I., Abramson, L. Y., Seligman, M. E. P., Semmel, A. and Peterson, C. (1982) 'Attributional styles and life events in the classroom: vulnerability and invulnerability to depressive mood reactions.' *J. Person. Soc. Psychol., 43*, 612-17

Miller, W. and Seligman, M. E. P. (1975) 'Depression in humans.' *J. Abnorm. Psychol., 84*, 228-38

Neisser, U. (1976) *Cognition and reality: Principles and implications of cognitive psychology*, Freeman, San Francisco

Nekanda-Trepka, C. J. S., Bishop, S. and Blackburn, I. M. (1983) 'Hopelessness and depression.' *Br. J. Clin. Psychol., 22*, 49-60

Nelson, R. E. and Craighead, W. E. (1977) 'Selective recall of positive and negative feedback, self-control behaviours, and depression.' *J. Abnorm. Psychol., 86*, 379-88

O'Hara, M. W., Rehm, L. P. and Campbell, S. B. (1982) 'Predicting depressive symptomatology: cognitive-behavioural models and post-partum depression.' *J. Abnorm. Psychol., 91*, 457-61

Overmier, J. B. L. and Seligman, M. E. P. (1967) 'Effect of inescapable shock upon subsequent escape and avoidance learning.' *J. Comp. Physiol. Psychol., 63*, 28-33

Padfield, M. (1976) 'The comparative effects of two counselling approaches on the intensity of depression among rural women of low socioeconomic status.' *Counselling Psychol., 23*, 209-14

Parkin, A. J. (1980) 'Levels of processing and the cue overload principle.' *Quart. Journ. Exp. Psychol., 32*, 427-32

Patterson, G. R. and Hops, H. (1972) 'Coercion, a game for two: Intervention techniques for marital conflict' in Ulrick, R. E. and Mountjoy, P. (eds.), *The Experimental Analysis of Social Behaviour*, Appleton-Century-Crofts, New York

Paykel, E. S. (1971) 'Classification of depressed patients: a cluster analysis derived grouping.' *Br. J. Psychiat., 118*, 275-88

Peterson, C., Luborsky, L. and Seligman, M. E. P. (1983) 'Attributions and depressive mood shifts: a case study using the symptom-context method.' *J. Abnorm. Psychol., 92*, 96-103

Polivy, J. and Doyle, C. (1980) 'Laboratory induction of mood states through the reading of self-referent mood-statements: affective changes or demand characteristics?' *J. Abnorm. Psychol., 89*, 286-90

Premack, D. (1959) 'Towards empirical laws: I. Positive reinforcement.' *Psychol. Rev., 66*, 219-33

Prusoff, B. A., Weissman, M. M., Klerman, G. L. and Rounsaville, B. J. (1980) 'Research Diagnostic Criteria Subtypes of Depression: their role as predictors of differential response to psycho-therapy and drug treatment.' *Arch. Gen. Psychiat., 37*, 796-801

Rachman, S. (1976) 'The passing of the two-stage theory of fear and avoidance.' *Behav. Res. Ther., 14*, 125-31

Raps, C. S., Peterson, C., Reinhard, K. E. and Seligman, M. E. P. (1982) 'Attributional style among depressed patients.' *J. Abnorm. Psychol., 91*, 102-108

Rehm, L. P. (1977) 'A self-control model of depression.' *Behav. Ther., 8*, 787-804

Rehm, L. P. (ed.) (1981) *Behaviour Therapy for Depression*, Academic Press, New York

Rehm, L. P., Fuchs, C. Z., Roth, D. M., Kornblith, S. J. and Romano, J. M. (1979) 'A comparison of self-control and assertion skills treatment of depression.' *Behav. Ther., 10*, 429-42

Rehm, L. P. and Kornblith, S. J. (1979) 'Behaviour therapy for depression. A review of recent developments' in M. Hersen and P. M. Eisler (eds.), *Progress in behaviour modification (Vol. 7)*, Academic Press, New York

Rippere, V. and Adams, N. (1982) 'Clinical ecology and why clinical psychology needs it.' *Bull. Br. Psychol. Soc., 35*, 151-2

Rosenberg, M. (1965) *Society and the Adolescent Self-Image*, Princeton University Press, New Jersey

Rothwell, N. and Williams, J. M. G. (1983) 'Attributions and Life Events.' *Br. J. Clin.*

*Psychol. 22*, 139-140

Rotter, J. B. (1966) 'Generalised expectancies for internal-external locus of control of reinforcement.' *Psychol. Monogr., 80*, No. 1

Rotzer, F. T., Koch, H. and Pflug, B. (1981) 'A cognitive-behavioural treatment programme for depressed out-patients' in Minsel, W. R. and Herff, W. (eds.) *Research on Psycho-therapeutic Approaches*, Proceedings of the 1st European Conference on Psychotherapy Research, Trier 1981, Vol. II. Peter Lang, Frankfurt

Rozensky, R. H., Rehm, L. P., Pry, G. and Roth, D. (1977) 'Depression and self-reinforcement behaviour in hospitalised patients.' *J. Behav. Ther. Exp. Psychiat., 8*, 35-8

Rush, A. J., Beck, A. T., Kovacs, M. and Hollon, S. (1977) 'Comparative efficacy of cognitive therapy and pharmacotherapy in the treatment of depressed out-patients.' *Cog. Ther. Res., 1*, 17-37

Sammons, R. A. (1974) *Systematic resensitisation in the treatment of depression*. Paper presented at meeting of Association for Advancement of Behaviour Therapy, Chicago.

Seligman, M. E. P. (1974) 'Depression and learned helplessness' in R. J. Friedman and M. M. Katz (eds.), *The Psychology of Depression; Contemporary Theory and Research*, J. Wiley, New York

Seligman, M. E. P. (1975) *Helplessness: On depression, development and death*, W. H. Freeman, San Francisco

Seligman, M. E. P. (1978) 'Comment and integration.' *J. Abnorm. Psychol., 87*, 165-79

Seligman, M. E. P. (1981) 'A learned helplessness point of view' in L. P. Rehm (ed.), *Behaviour Therapy for Depression*, Academic Press, New York

Seligman, M. E. P., Abramson, L. Y., Semmel, A. and Von Baeyer, C. (1979) 'Depressive attributional style.' *J. Abnorm. Psychol., 88*, 242-7

Seligman, M. E. P. and Maier, S. F. (1967) 'Failure to escape traumatic shock.' *J. Exp. Psychol., 74*, 1-9

Snaith, R. P., Constantopoulos, A. A., Jardine, M. Y. and McGuffin, P. (1978) 'A clinical scale for the self-assessment of irritability.' *Br. J. Psychiat., 132*, 164-71

Spitzer, R. L., Endicott, J. and Robins, E. (1978) *Research Diagnostic Criteria (RDC) for a selected group of Functional Disorders*, 3rd Edition, N.Y. State Psychiatric Institute, Biometrics Research

Stuart, R. J. (1967) 'Casework treatment of depression viewed as an interpersonal disturbance.' *Social Work, 12*, 27-36

Sutherland, G., Newman, B. and Rachman, S. (1982) 'Experimental investigations of the relations between mood and intrusive unwanted cognitions.' *Br. J. Med. Psychol., 55*, 127-38

Taylor, F. G. and Marshall, W. L. (1977) 'Experimental analysis of a cognitive or behavioural therapy for depression.' *Cog. Ther. & Res., 1*, 59-72

Teasdale, J. D. and Fogarty, S. J. (1979) 'Differential effects of induced mood on retrieval of pleasant and unpleasant events from episodic memory.' *J. Abnorm. Psychol., 88*, 248-57

Tversky, A. and Kahneman, D. (1974) 'Judgement under uncertainty: Heuristics and biases.' *Science, 185*, 1124-31

Velten, E. (1968) 'A laboratory task for the induction of mood states.' *Behav.*

*Res. Ther., 6*, 473-82

Watkins, J. T. and Rush, A. J. (1978) *Measurement of cognitions, beliefs and thought patterns in depressed persons*, Presentation at Symposium 19, Twelfth Annual Association for Advancement of Behaviour Therapy Convention, Chicago, Illinois.

Watkins, D. C. and Watkins, M. J. (1975) 'Build-up of proactive inhibition as a cue overload effect.' *J. Exp. Psychol: Hum. Learn. Mem., 1*, 442-52

Watkins, M. J. and Watkins, D. C. (1976) 'Cue overload theory and the method of interpolated attributes.' *Bull. Psychon. Soc., 7*, 289-91

Watts, F. N. (1977) 'What sort of cognitive processes are involved in cognitive behaviour therapy? Beyond Mahoney.' *Br. Assoc. Behav. Psychoth. Bull., 5*, 21-26

Weiner, B. and Heckhausen, H. (1972) 'Cognitive theory and motivation' in Dodwell, P. C. (ed.), *New Horizons in Psychology*, Penguin, Harmondsworth

Weiss, J. M. (1971) 'Effects of coping behaviour with and without a feedback signal on stress pathology in rats.' *J. Comp. Physiol. Psychol., 77*, 22-30

Weissman, M. M. (1979) 'The psychological treatment of depression. Evidence for the efficacy of psychotherapy alone in comparison with and in combination with pharmacotherapy.' *Arch. Gen. Psychiat., 36*, 1261-9

Weissman, M. M., Klerman, G. L., Paykel, E. S., Prusoff, B. A. and Hanson, B. (1974) 'Treatment effects on the social adjustment of depressed patients.' *Arch. Gen. Psychiat., 30*, 771-8

Weissman, M. M., Klerman, G. L., Prusoff, B. A., Sholomskas, D. R. and Padian, N. (1981) 'Depressed out-patients: Results one year after treatment with drugs and/or interpersonal psychotherapy.' *Arch. Gen. Psychiat., 38*, 51-5

Weissman, M. M., Prusoff, B. A., DiMascio, A., Neu, C., Goklaney, M. and Klerman, G. L. (1979) 'The efficacy of drugs and psychotherapy in the treatment of acute depressive episodes.' *Am. J. Psychiat., 136*, 555-8

Whitehead, A. (1979) 'Psychological treatment of depression: a review.' *Behav. Res. & Ther., 17*, 495-509

Wilkinson, I. M. and Blackburn, I. M. (1981) 'Cognitive style in depressed and recovered depressed patients.' *Br. Clin. Psychol., 20*, 283-92

Williams, J. G., Barlow, D. H. and Agras, W. S. (1972) 'Behavioural measurement of severe depression.' *Arch. Gen. Psychiat., 27*, 330-3

Williams, J. M. G. (1980) 'Generalisation in the effects of a mood induction procedure.' *Behav. Res & Ther., 18*, 565-72

Williams, J. M. G. (1981) 'Internal vs. external focus of attention: paradoxes in factors mediating cognitive-behavioural psycho-therapy in depression' in Minsel, W. R. and Herff, W. (eds.), *Research on psychotherapeutic approaches, Proceedings of the 1st European Conference on Psychotherapy Research Trier.*, 1981, Vol. II.

Williams, J. M. G. (1982a) 'Cognitive therapy for depression.' *Br. Med. J., 284*, 506

Williams, J. M. G. (1982b) 'E x V: A model of how attributions affect educational attainment' in Antaki, C. and Brewin, C. (eds.), *Attributions and Psychological Change*, Academic Press, New York

Williams, J. M. G. and Brewin, C. R. 'Cognitive predictors of reactions to a minor life event: the British driving test.' *Br. J. Social Psychol.*, (in press)

Williams, J. M. G. and Teasdale, J. D. (1982) 'Facilitation and helplessness: the interaction of perceived difficulty and importance of task.' *Behav. Res. Ther.,* *20*, 161-71

Wilson, P. K. (1982) 'Combined pharmacological and behavioural treatment of depression.' *Behav. Res. Ther., 20*, 173-84

Wilson, P. H., Goldin, J. C. and Charbonneau-Powis, M. (1983) 'Comparative efficacy of behavioural and cognitive treatments of depression.' *Cog. Ther. and Res., 7*, 111-24

Wing, J. K., Cooper, J. E. and Sartorius, N. (1974) *The Description and Classification of Psychiatric Symptoms: An Instruction Manual for the PSE and Catego Programme*, University Press, Cambridge

Wolpe, J. (1972) 'Neurotic depression: experimental analog, clinical syndromes and treatment.' *Am. J. Psychother., 25*, 362-8

Youngren, M. A. and Lewinsohn, P. M. (1980) 'The functional relation between depression and problematic interpersonal behaviour.' *J. Abnorm. Psychol., 89*, 333-41

Zeiss, A. M., Lewinsohn, P. M. and Munoz, R. F. (1979) 'Nonspecific improvement effects in depression using interpersonal skills training, pleasant activity schedules, or cognitive training.' *J. Consult. Clin. Psychol., 47*, 427-39

# INDEX

## SUBJECT INDEX